This is one of the most important books to have been written in a time of what, for the church, is one of intense scrutiny and dark and disturbing exposure. It is an account of personal courage and gracious spirit, and a story of remarkable faith. It is a book full of invitation, of possibility and of hope.
Rev Dr David Ranson, Senior Lecturer, Sydney College of Divinity,

My journey from childhood to maturity, through being an altar boy, the shame of sexual abuse, to the seminary, then nursing with disabled children, marriage and fatherhood, to legal practice and finally my present life's work as an advocate for other survivors would not have been possible without my mentors: people who shared their wisdom distilled from the pain and joy of life and who showed me courage in the face of pain. I share a vision that no one should journey in sorrow without hope. 'Child, Arise!' offers hope: it lifts the shame of child sexual abuse from 'victims' and presents practical encouragement for ways to access light, vitality and insight in the darkest of times, when suffering seems unending.
John Ellis, lawyer and survivor

As a lawyer and psychotherapist advocating for sufferers of childhood sexual abuse, I was delighted with the reflectivity encouraged by this beautiful book. An emerging capacity for reflection is integral to trauma recovery. 'Child, Arise!' uses biblical language to anchor reflection and yet its genesis in lived experience renders this book potentially useful even to those whose faith has been devastated by abuse by clergy. In the telling of her own story, the author demonstrates so vividly that, despite an early history of sexual trauma, self-awareness, aliveness and creativity can emerge and flourish.
Nicola Ellis, lawyer, psychotherapist

This is a book by a victim of sexual abuse for other victims, a victim who has spent countless hours meditating on the scriptures and applying them to her situation. It is an abundant source of consolation and inspiration, not just for victims but for the whole community.
Bishop Geoffrey Robinson, author of For Christ's Sake: End Sexual Abuse in the Catholic Church ... for Good (2013)

This spiritual handbook is welcome, constructive and unique ... This is a gentle, informed, non-confronting resource for survivors to reconnect with their spiritual selves and their God, in a healing and transformative way, transcending their past and engaging their future.
Dr Jennifer Herrick, sexual abuse survivor and independent theological scholar

Dedication

To God,
My source of Life and Love
and my strength.

To my mother,
who first spoke to me of God.

To my brother,
who has stood by me, believed in me
and given me unending support and strength.

To all survivors
living with the long-term effects of sexual abuse
and also to those no longer with us – may they rest in peace.

CHILD, ARISE!

THE COURAGE TO STAND
A spiritual handbook for survivors of sexual abuse

JANE N. DOWLING

Foreword by Fr David Ranson

First edition published in 2015 by

David Lovell Publishing

Second edition published in 2019 by

Jane N. Dowling
Sydney Australia
jane@childarise.com

© Copyright 2015 Jane N. Dowling

This work is copyright. Apart from any fair dealing for the purposes of private study, research, criticism or review, as permitted under the Copyright Act, no part may be reproduced by any process without written permission. Enquiries should be addressed to Jane N. Dowling

Scripture quotations are from *The New Revised Standard Version Bible*, © 1989, Division of Christian Education of the National Council of Churches of Christ in the USA, and *The New American Bible*, © 1983, Thomas Nelson, Inc.

Cover design and illustration: Ride High Graphic
Typeset in 12/16 Perpetua
Printed by Lightning Source Australia

National Library of Australia Cataloguing-in-Publication data

Dowling, Jane N.
Child arise!: the courage to stand: a spiritual handbook for survivors of sexual abuse / Jane N. Dowling.

  9781863551533 (paperback)
  Sexually abused children – Counseling of.
  Sexual abuse victims – Counseling of.
  Spiritual healing – Biblical teaching.
  Healing – Religious aspects.

362.76

Foreword
Fr David Ranson

THIS IS, I BELIEVE, ONE OF THE MOST important books to have been written in a time of what, for the church, is one of intense scrutiny and dark and disturbing exposure. It is an account of personal courage and gracious spirit, and a story of remarkable faith. It is a book full of invitation, of possibility and of hope.

This book presents an unmistakable light in the experience of darkness; it effects the power of goodness against a contour of evil. Where one might have expected paralysis, here one finds awakening and continuing journey. Where one would expect bitterness, here one finds engagement. Where one would have expected to find self-enclosure, here one finds self-giving. It is an eloquent demonstration of that transformation of vulnerability into hospitality which lies at the very centre of the Gospel's dream for us.

It is, indeed, the voice that the entire Christian community has desperately needed since those days nearly thirty years ago when the extent of the pain suffered by people both abused and ignored by elements of the church —crucified by the church's self-interest — began to be shared. It is the required voice for this time because it has brought to the fore for the church its most genuine source of healing and transformation – the living Tradition of the Word of God itself. One person's remarkable, deeply personal journey presents in this work as a living template of healing for the whole church. We all stand in profound debt to what is shared here.

As a priest, a member of that caste which has brought such suffering to bear, I am deeply humbled to be invited to write this Foreword – a sign itself of the author's remarkable grace. As one who carries the shame of the church in his heart, I am all too conscious of the enormous wound we bear as a church. Under the banner of religion, people have been abused in the most horrific ways; people have had their lives destroyed.

From a range of perspectives institutional responses have not been adequate and they have compounded the hurt people experience. As a church we have tried to respond – largely in a misguided way to control the damage – but our attempts have not been adequate. Good intentions do not heal. Neither does a concern for the preservation of the church's reputation placed over the pain experienced by people who have been so deeply betrayed and hurt.

We cannot but accept that between ideal and reality there has, in many, many instances been an enormous gulf. This is the truth. It is a hard truth for us to accept with stark honesty, and no appeal to the good that the church has done, and does now, can shield us from that truth. People have been hurt, and they are hurting now, because of their experience of the church. This is the moment, therefore, in which we must learn to stand before our society and in complete humility say,

> We confess to Almighty God
> and to you our brothers and sisters
> that we have greatly sinned,
> in our thoughts and in our words,
> in what we have done and in what we have failed to do,
> through our fault, through our fault,
> through our most grievous fault.

In account after account we have now been forced to move beyond the delusion that such disclosures are about the criminal behaviour of a few. Sexual abuse in our church is not relegated to various incidents. It is cultural in character. The very volume of incidents demands we recognize this. My own conviction is that the experience of sexual abuse in the church occurs in the intersection of the dysfunctional elements of three matrices.[1] We are confronted with a trinity of dysfunctional matrices: a theological matrix; a psychological matrix; and a social matrix. Not one of them can be taken in isolation. To deal with one, to the exclusion of the other two, is unsatisfactory and comprises an inadequate and short-term response to the experience

---

[1] See David Ranson, 'The Climate of Sexual Abuse', *The Furrow* 53 (July/August 2002), pp. 387-397.

of sexual abuse within the church. Failure to adequately address the dysfunctions of all three matrices, and their intersection, simply perpetuates the climate out of which misconduct occurs in the church.

Further, it is clear to me as a pastoral theologian there can be no future in a living church without there being space for those who have been hurt so horrifically, and who have had their lives undermined, if not destroyed, to be heard in all their torment. Their stories not only expose the way in which people's hurt has not been well attended to by various persons and agencies in the church. They also teach us the lessons of what contributes to cultures of abuse. It is critical for us as a church to live in this moment with the greatest humility, ready to be radically self-reflective, ready to learn, open to conversion precisely through the conversation with those who have suffered the most.

Yes, the church stands in need to develop new instruments of transparency and accountability. We must better distinguish between the moral and the criminal, the legal and the pastoral. We must learn better those processes of transparent engagement when incidents of abuse might occur, so that when abusive incidents occur - and even in the future they invariably will, given human weakness – compassion, justice and compensation for both individuals and communities become more, not less, apparent. I am not one to consider naively that 'it's all in the past' or that 'it will never happen again'. Abuse in the church is far more complex than that. Certainly, protocols are a most necessary response to inadequacies within the church's social matrix, but they do not address the other two matrices. Therefore, the church will need to do more than establish better protocols and procedures. Protocols will not, in themselves, prevent abuse from occurring. No, the church stands in need of radical conversion of heart and mind.

As the late Sebastian Moore wrote, 'We need conversion not so much from sin as we need conversion from innocence.'[2] What did he mean by this but that any illusion to innocence needs to be shattered if we are to truly receive the call of the Spirit. As John V. Taylor wrote,

---

[2] Sebastian Moore, *Jesus, the Liberator of Desire*, (New York: Crossroad, 1989), p. 37.

The Spirit does not give itself where our encounters are glib, masked exchanges of second-hand thoughts. Our defences must be down, broken either by intense joy or despair. One way or the other we must come to the end of ourselves. So this shameful humiliation of Christians, not only in our generation but all times, is better than self-congratulation, for it is the pre-requisite for a renewal of the Holy Spirit. It is worth remembering that the root of the word humiliation and humility is humus. To be down in the straw and the dung and the refuse in Paul's words is to become the soil in which the seed of Christ's manhood falls and dies and brings forth the harvest.[3]

Bishop Geoffrey Robinson, former Auxiliary Bishop of Sydney, used to comment, 'There is nothing so beautiful, nor so ugly as the Catholic Church.' It is the truth of this paradox, and our full engagement with it, that alone offers us a future. The beauty we hold as a church does not negate the ugliness we have experienced; the ugliness does not negate the beauty. Both exist. And both must be engaged. If we only engage the celebration, the beauty, the light, we have no guarantee that we do not get caught up in a grand illusion of ourselves – something which is the opposite of Gospel humility and which defends us from the difficult pathway of sustained conversion to which the Gospel unquestionably always calls us. If we only engage the ugliness, then we can become overwhelmed by the darkness, and be left paralyzed and in despair. The ugliness we have to face ensures that the beauty has realism; the beauty that we celebrate ensures that the ugliness is not the whole, or the final, word. The pages of this book, so honestly and so beautifully crafted, give us unmistakable illustration of this engagement.

We are at a new point in this difficult journey. This is what this particular book invites us a church to consider. We must move beyond remorse, and, yes, beyond even questions of redress and compensation. What might happen if we were now truly prepared to 'sit with' and listen deeply to the pain of stories and to wonder in the midst of such pain, how such trauma acts as the catalyst for theology, and our self-understanding as church? How

---

[3] John V. Taylor, *The Go-Between God* (London: SCM Press, 1972), p. 128.

Foreword

does people's pain in this instance shape our sense of God, of Christ, of the church, of redemption? This is precisely what this work achieves through such a sustained and deep immersion with the author's own experience of anguish, on the one hand, and on the other hand her profound attentiveness to the very Word of God, the normative reference for the church's life.

Edward Schillebeeckx recognises that 'any theologian who claims history as the starting point for speech about God must grapple with the realities of senseless suffering and the multiple ways in which history is laced with the non-sense of evil.'[4] For Schillebeeckx, suffering and salvation are intrinsically related: 'Salvation cannot ... be found *outside* suffering.'[5] For another theologian, Johannes Metz, too, one can only theologize through a narrative identification with those who have suffered. As Downey summarizes, 'in narrative we remember and connect. By participating in a narrative we trade experiences with others. This keeps memory and solidarity alive.'[6] Keeping memory and solidarity alive means entering into a radical conversation with the one who suffers. It means allowing that conversation to unfold in new and unexpected ways.

> Christianity is not an unmediated identity, but a praxis of identification with the non-identical, the non-I, the other, identification especially with the injustice suffered by others. If man [sic] is the fundamental symbol of God then that place where he is shamed, wounded and enslaved, both in his own heart and in suppressive society, is at once the privileged place where religious experience becomes possible *in* a living praxis that intends to give shape to that symbol, to heal it, and to restore it to its own identity [Italics in the original].[7]

---

[4] Mary Hilkert, 'Edward Schillebeeckx OP (1914-): Encountering God in a secular and suffering world', *Theology Today* 62 (2005), p. 380.

[5] Edward Schillebeeckx, *Christ: The experience of Jesus as Lord*, translated by John Bowden (New York: The Seabury Press, 1980), pp. 769-770.

[6] John K Downey, ed., *Love's Strategy: The political theology of Johann Baptist Metz* (Harrisburg, Pennsylvania: Trinity Press International, 1999), p. 8.

[7] Edward Schillebeeckx, 'God, Society and Human Salvation', in *Faith and Society/Foi et Societé/Geloof En Maatschappij: Acta congressus internationalis theologici Lovaniensis 1976* (Paris: Éditions Duculot, 1978), 98, cited in Tillar, 'The Influence of Social Critical Theory', pp. 166-167.

In such a conversation, it is the 'church's living memory of Jesus … embod[ied] in scripture and encountered in concrete experiences of suffering' that remains the pivotal point of reference.[8] As Hilkert points out, for Schillebeeckx,

> … [in] the life story of Jesus, human suffering is not theoretically resolved, but practically resisted, and ultimately defeated by the power of God. The life-praxis of the followers of Jesus who stand in solidarity with the crucified of the contemporary world is an active remembrance and retelling of the story of Jesus.[9]

In our own present context, it is the voice of those who have suffered abuse within the church who thus bear the retelling of the story of Jesus for us. We read this re-telling in the pages that follow.

We can only hear that story of redemption again, for our own time and in our own circumstances, if we are first prepared to listen to another's struggle to make meaning in the midst of such pain. In the mid-twentieth century the Jewish mystic and feminist, Simone Weil, recounted in one of her insightful essays that in the first legend of the Holy Grail it is said that the Grail belongs to the first comer who asks the guardian of the vessel, a king three quarters paralyzed by the most painful wound, 'What are you going through?'[10] Only when Parsifal has learnt how to ask this question is he ready to receive the Grail, that the king once paralyzed retrieves his health, and vitality is restored to the land. In Weil's exposition, only when Parsifal has learnt how to attend to the other, not just as a unit in a collection, or a specimen from the social category labelled 'unfortunate' (or 'abused' as in our case today), but as a person … only when he has learnt how to gaze upon the other full of attention, emptying himself of his own agenda in order to receive the truth of the person he is encountering, does true healing occur for the kingdom.

---

[8] Elizabeth K. Tillar, 'Critical Remembrance and Eschatological Hope' in Edward Schillebeeckx's Theology of Suffering for Others', *Heythrop Journal* 44 (2003), p. 26.

[9] Mary Hilkert, 'Hermeneutics of History in the Theology of Edward Schillebeeckx', *The Thomist* 51 (January 1987), p. 134.

[10] Simone Weil, 'Reflections on the Right Use of School Studies', in *Waiting for God* (London: Collins Fontana Books, 1950), pp. 69-70.

Foreword

Simone Weil illustrates in her discussion that the capacity to give one's attention to a sufferer is a very rare and difficult thing: it is almost a miracle, it is a miracle. And yet it is the key to healing. Weil thus presents the church today with a metaphor for its own healing. It is only when the church learns to encounter persons full of attentiveness, asking, beyond mere warmth of heart, impulsiveness and pity, 'what are you going through?' that new horizons can possibly disclose themselves for it. The alternative is to remain paralyzed with a kingdom in deep decay and morbidity.

A simple question is a key that the church, however, is largely fearful of turning. The church is not used to listening; it is used to proclaiming. It is not used to asking questions; it is used to giving the answers. It is not used to serving another from their terms; it is used to giving on its own terms. It is not used to asking for forgiveness; it is used to dispensing forgiveness. And therefore, like Parsifal, it is destined to be ejected from the Grail Castle and to wander along the pathways of desolation for some time to come yet until on its own Good Friday morning it finally acknowledges that there is only one way forward: to listen and to learn. What is being asked of the church in this current experience is nothing other than a fundamental attitudinal shift — the hardest shift of all to make. 'But the heart of this people has grown coarse, their ears are dull of hearing and they have shut their eyes for fear that they should see with their eyes, understand with their heart, and be converted and healed by me' (Matthew 13:10-17).

The principal challenge to the church, I suggest, is therefore twofold: conversation and conversion. The two words of conversation and conversion are obviously akin: their very similarity implies that conversion occurs through conversation; conversation can become a means of deep conversion. The Christian community must risk a conversation in which it acknowledges a mutual vulnerability whilst it must allow this conversation to become a means of conversion, an avenue of change.

Conversation begins with a listening heart. Loughlin Sofield has commented that both the desire and the ability to listen are the foundation of genuine ministry. It reveals the leader's wanting to learn and to grow through understanding the wisdom others offer. Listening, he says, implies dialogue, the respectful exchange at the adult-to-adult level. It involves the suspension of one's own viewpoint to attempt to truly hear and understand another. He emphasizes that, because listening is a complex process, leaders need to develop their listening skills to be able to sort through all they might hear to get to the essential truth of a situation. And then, he most significantly concludes, listening gives the leader access to people and their needs, hopes, weaknesses and strength. It reveals the state of the community. In other words, the quality of listening will manifest the health of the community: where there is little to no listening, the community will simply spiral into dysfunction. The presence or absence of listening acts as the barometer of the church's health and vitality.

With a listening heart, the church is called to enter into conversation. The theologian David Tracy would claim that in this postmodern, pluralist environment conversation is our only hope. For Tracy conversation acts as a method for the theological enterprise itself. In the response to the disclosure of sexual abuse among its members, I am suggesting that it is the only effective pastoral response for the church. I am also suggesting that it is the demand of the situation. But I dare also to suggest that it manifests as opportunity for growth and change in the church, and as such that it presents as a very means by which theological and ecclesial reflection itself must take place from here on in.

This is the gift and the blessing that the voice of those who have suffered abuse in the church can be to the church. That voice is 'other' than the church's self-image. It is 'other' than the church's rhetoric about itself and its intentions. It is 'other' than the face of harmony and well-being. It thus confronts complacency and delusion; it opens up, and not without terror, new possibilities of being, as does all authentic conversation with that which is 'other'.

The 'otherness' of the voice of the one who has suffered 'disrupts' and 'transgresses'. Therein lies precisely its giftedness for the church, if only the church can be humble enough to welcome this. Unfortunately, it is not yet, and therefore the wandering Parsifal must remain its operative metaphor. However, if the church could welcome such 'disruption' and 'transgression',

Foreword

if it could enter into the conversation with the 'otherness' of the voice of its own abused, it might find itself blessed as does the desert nomad who welcomes with hospitality the stranger at first perceived as demon and only later recognized as angel.

Truth manifests itself through conversation and the truth revealed leads us to new praxis. In this particular conversation, engaged with such personal poignancy in these pages, those terms for God that might legitimate patriarchal structures of ministerial autonomy and self-sufficient authority are challenged. Such structures support, albeit subliminally, patterns of domination and control which constitute the climate out of which abuse occurs. The church is invited to a more radical evangelical language about God – one which invites attendance to vulnerability and process, participation and empowerment. This is the language that this book engages.

Further, the long, ambiguous tradition of the church's understanding of sexuality, in which matter and spirit suffer from a divorce which renders sexuality into shadowy patterns of fear and secrecy, is questioned. In those patterns we are taken into the dysfunctional elements of the psychological matrix in which we have detected such a pathological denial of eros with all its consequences: the confusion of simplicity with minimalism; the truncation of ascesis to physical discipline; the debasement of poverty into shame; the equation of obedience with conformity; and the identification of priestly celibacy with control and lovelessness and passionlessness.

We recognize that the distortion of eros builds into a celibate clerical caste built on suspicion and fear. We realize the dehumanizing character of clericalism, a hermetically sealed culture in which there is an overdeveloped masculine ethos. We are taught that where the feminine is denied there is a growing incapacity of genuine interior reflection, the loss of the ability to relate with intimacy, the dependency on role and work for self-identification. And it is revealed to us that not all vocational aspirations are as they seem, that so often such aspiration masquerades as unresolved emotional tension which, although spiritualized, remains the ground out of which abusive patterns sprout. Throughout the conversation I am calling for the dysfunctional elements of the church's social life are also highlighted: the absence of professional accountability, the appalling lack of adequate formation and ongoing vocational accompaniment of church workers, notably priests, the pathology of many residential situations of these people.

Thus the conversation becomes a most profound sacrament of conversion. Parsifal finally learnt the question which released vitality into the kingdom once again through a painful journey of suffering and confusion. Parsifal provides us with a metaphor of the crisis in which the church finds itself. Its transparency and relevancy for the people of our own generation will depend on our readiness to follow his example or otherwise.

And what provides us hope in this tumultuous period? The word of grace drawn from the church's living memory of the Word of God that we see exemplified in these pages. This is a word of invitation. It is not a moralizing word or a word which condemns but a 'poetic' word – a word which seizes people's imagination because it deeply respects them and evokes in them the desire for something more, something different – that 'new beginning' which is the mark of the Spirit. This is the word which nurtures, which nourishes and always invites.

> ... the wisdom that comes from heaven is first of all pure; then peace-loving, considerate, submissive, full of mercy and good fruit, impartial and sincere. Peacemakers who sow in peace reap a harvest of righteousness (James 3:17-18).

This is prophetic wisdom. Each of us as a minister is commissioned to speak with this wisdom a word offered, as Brueggemann implores, 'neither in rage or cheap grace, but with the candour born of anguish and passion.'[11] As evidenced in this Handbook, such a word can only come through intense listening and waiting. The author, as a prophetic minister who speaks out the 'poetic' word, listens to the story of pain, particularly her own, attending to how the presenting story represents the vaster, eternal story of slavery seeking freedom, of death giving way to life, of despair being transformed into possibility and confidence.

---

[11] Walter Brueggemann, *The Prophetic Imagination* (Philadelphia: Fortress Press, 1978), p. 50.

Foreword

When we approach life with this ear then, with the author, we recognize that the stories of Scripture are actually being lived out in front of us, before our own eyes. They are not simply the stories of 2000 years ago. They are the expressions of what the Spirit effects even now in our midst. We then speak, as the author does, with that same imagination as 'the young Galilean poet of the haunted spirit. He who was able to image the incarnation and inhabit it, and who thereby opened out one of the most amazing imaginative symbols and sources of all time: the Trinity as source of distance and intimacy, belonging and dislocation, selfhood and otherness.'[12]

In the swirl of all these considerations there is one further thing that will bring us forward to a new shore. And it is the most important means by which our exile might be transformed into that experience of coming home to ourselves once again.

Recently I had the fortune of being able to visit the island of Malta upon which Paul had been shipwrecked on his way to Rome. It was an extraordinary opportunity to enter into those accounts of Paul's story. I realized especially that the texts of Paul's time on Malta were not simply historical in character but were, in fact, highly elaborate commentaries, not simply on Paul, but on the church itself for which Paul is presented as a metaphor. The account of Paul's shipwreck detailed in the twenty-seventh chapter of the Acts of the Apostles teaches us it in a very particular way.

Taking the peculiarities of the chapter into account, this is not just a chapter about Paul's arrival on Malta. It is not just a story of Paul battling rough seas and seeking to reach the shore safely. Much more profoundly, it is the story of the early Church at sea and in the midst of storms threatening to shipwreck it, discovering that which is most essential to it – the very mystery of the Eucharist. What brings Paul to safety in the midst of his own storm is the mystery of the Eucharist. At the heart of the storm, as the text says, 'he took bread, gave thanks to God in everybody's presence, broke it and began to eat. All were encouraged and they ate too' (Acts 27:35-36).

This is a clear scriptural allusion to the Eucharist and demonstrates

---

[12] John O'Donohue, 'The Agenda for Theology in Ireland Today I', *The Furrow* 42 (1991), p. 698.

what is most central for us. In the midst of the storm of our own moment in history we too must not cease to take bread, give thanks, break it and share it. This means that in the midst of all that we face we must come back to the essential Christian act: the act of self-emptying become a self-giving, which is what the Eucharistic mystery is about. This is the mystery that is its true anchor and through which alone the church must find its harbour and safety at this time. As the story alludes, everything else can be jettisoned overboard. In the very midst of the storm the mystery of the Eucharist, that mystery of Jesus' self-emptying become a self-giving, is the one thing, however, we must remain true to, that gives meaning to all else, and that holds us together. Thus, the current experience of exile into which we have been led by circumstances is resolved only by a renewed witness of sacrificial love. We can say nothing in our defence. We have sinned, through our fault, in what we have done and in what we have failed to do. We can however act. And the way of action forward must exemplify a Eucharistic love. Such action alone will bring us forward to a new harbour.

Through the story of the Crucified One, retold through the narrative of those who are crucified and who suffer now, no words suffice. Redemption does not come to us in explanations. Redemption comes to us only in an event, the crucifixion of our status and the resurrection of a praxis which lives the salvific love of Christ himself. Both the call of God and our response to that call are only known 'through self-giving to [others] in a world [which we are] to humanize.'[13] Schillebeeckx terms this 'political love'. This is the love at the heart of the Eucharistic mystery. It is the love into which we are now being summoned as a church. It is the love that saturates these pages, a love which embodies that most poignant of prayers by the spiritual writer Carlo Carretto:

> How much I must criticize you, my church, and yet how much I love you.
> You have made me suffer more than anyone and yet I owe you more than I owe anyone.

---

[13] Edward Schillebeeckx, *Jesus: An experiment in Christology*, translated by Hubert Hoskins (New York: Seabury, 1979), p. 630.

Foreword

I should like to see you destroyed and yet I need your presence.
You have given me much scandal and yet you alone have made me understand holiness.
Never in the world have I seen anything more obscurantist, more compromised, more false, yet never have I touched anything more pure, more generous or more beautiful.
Countless times I have felt like slamming the door of my soul in your face – and, yet, every night I have prayed that I might die in your arms!
No, I cannot be free of you, for I am one with you, even if not completely you.
Then too – where should I go?
To build another church?
But I cannot build another church without the same defects, for they are my own defects.
And again, if I were to build another church, it would be my church, not Christ's church.
No, I am old enough. I know better.[14]

Fr David Ranson TheolM, PhD
Senior Lecturer, Sydney College of Divinity

---

[14] Carlo Carretto (1910-1988), 'Letter to the Church', in *I Sought and I Found: My Experience of God and of the Church* (Maryknoll, NY: Orbis Books, 1984).

Acknowledgements

With heart-felt thanks I wish to acknowledge each person who has contributed to helping this book become a reality. I am truly grateful for your enthusiasm, encouragement, effort, and the gift of yourselves.

I begin by giving thanks to God, who not only moved me in prayer to write this book but who then provided me with an abundance of Life and Love, and the inner resources to work through all the experiences that are contained within it. I thank my mother and my siblings for all your enduring love and support. I am very aware that the pain of my own journey has extended to each one of you but nevertheless you have each stood by me bravely. I thank my brother who encouraged me throughout the writing process and who always believed that I could bring this book to completion. I thank Richard White, writer and editor, who was the first to read a draft of my manuscript. Thanks to your interest, encouragement and enthusiasm, all of which I greatly valued, I found the courage to proceed towards publishing.

I am also enormously thankful to Nicola Ellis, John Ellis, Jennifer Herrick, Fr David Ranson and Bishop Geoffrey Robinson who gave so generously of their time to read and endorse this book. Particular thanks to Phillip Pavich, who was able to translate my ideas for the illustration of the book cover design with remarkable creativity. I hold each of you in high respect and it has truly been an honour to work with you and receive support from you for this project.

A special note of thanks to the other gifted people who have shown me their genuine care and constant support on my journey, and without which I would not have been able to accomplish this book: my psychologist, Dr Alison Smith who has worked tirelessly with me in trauma therapy, my spiritual director who has taught me to be attentive to Life, the counsellors at ASCA who have leant me a generous listening ear on many occasions, and all my health professionals who have attended to my physical well-being.

I thank my Community and each of the missionaries, who in the past were a genuine witness to the unconditional love of God and who nurtured my spirituality through the charism of Prayer and Ministry of the Word.

Finally, I would like to extend my tremendous and fervent gratitude to my publisher, David Lovell, who made it possible for you to hold this book in your hands. David's keenness and eagerness was present from the very beginning to the end of this project and I thank him for all the energy he has invested throughout the process and most especially for grasping the importance and urgency of making this book available for survivors of sexual abuse, particularly in Australia where the Royal Commission into Institutional Responses to Child Sexual Abuse is currently taking place.

Contents

Foreword by Fr David Ranson TheolM, PhD   vii
Introduction   1

Part I Listening to our personal story from a loving God

In the beginning	20
Then God said …	22
'Let there be light!'	26
'Let us make humankind'	29
'Everything … is very good!'	32
God has loved us first	35
Our true Father	39
God knows us deeply	45
God loves us	49
God suffers with us	53
God doesn't abandon us	57
God comforts us	61
God is with us always	64
God strengthens us	66
To the end of our life	69
Through the gift of Jesus	71

Part II Working through our issues with a loving God

Time out	78
Keeping faith as we process trauma	87

Stability in instability	94
Panic attacks – 'Quiet! Be still!'	99
Revealing what is concealed	103
Facing trouble with courage	110
Grieving and consolation	114
Hopelessness – the power to transcend it	121
A boost of confidence	126
Being gentle with self	131
Walking through fire	138
Difficult decision making	143
Running on empty …	148
Re-establishing healthy boundaries	153
The terror of the night (sleeplessness)	159
Valuing our contribution	165
Breaking old patterns	170
A clean touch – healing	174
Safety comes first	180
Anger: channelling it for good	184
Discovering power in vulnerability	190
Set free from paralysis	195
Stripped but not broken	201
Suffering for a purpose	216
It is finished	224
Plans to prosper	236
Appendix 1 – A blueprint for praying with the Bible	243
Appendix 2 – Support Services	245

Introduction

THROUGH THE GRACE OF GOD, I survived sexual abuse. Like others who have passed through the same trauma, I refer to myself as a 'survivor' rather than a victim. From my early childhood up until my mid-teens I was sexually abused by a family relation. When this finally stopped, I was sexually abused by a Catholic priest.

At the age of twenty-one, also through God's grace, I became a member of an international Catholic missionary community and I completed my Theology degree. The specific ministry of the community I belong to is Prayer and Ministry of the Word (the 'Word' refers to the Word of God, particularly as expressed in the Bible).

As a consecrated member of the community, I have practised this ministry for the past twenty-two years. During this time I have been involved mainly in giving spiritual retreats based on Scripture and facilitating prayer and formation groups that introduce people to a relationship with God through the Bible. An important and enriching part of my ministry has been accompanying people on their spiritual journey and offering them pastoral care. Currently, my plans are to complete a Masters Degree in Arts, leading to a specialization in clinical pastoral care and chaplaincy.

My journey of facing the trauma of childhood sexual abuse began four years after I entered the community. I had just returned to Australia from Spain where I had lived for four years to complete my initial missionary formation, when I began recalling the trauma of my childhood through nightmares, flashbacks, a variety of body language and memories triggered by geographical places associated with the abuse. As my body remembered the trauma, I began re-living the emotions, physical sensations and even the behaviours that I experienced as a child during that time. All survivors know how painful and despairing this part of the journey is! At that time,

I experienced that my whole life was suddenly interrupted by a turbulent chaos as I found myself trying to deal with two realities; the reality of me as the adult who was trying to attend to the responsibilities and commitments of my ministry and the reality of my terrified inner child who was living the trauma of sexual abuse and calling on my adult self to attend with kind attention.

Although this was the beginning of my journey to sanity, I experienced a great fear of insanity as I walked through it. The trauma I was re-living in my body was so strong that I could not deny it or separate it from my daily activity of personal prayer because at the time this was 'who I was' and the fruitfulness of my prayer and ministry depended on me being in God's presence in my truth, that is, being who I was.

Coming to prayer meant learning to sit with God in my reality, bringing to the encounter whatever trauma I was re-living (and this was not easy for a long period of time because of the constant temptation to avoid the pain). Sometimes I was the fearful five-year-old who was hiding from my perpetrator, at other times I was the muted eleven-year-old who could not speak or articulate what was happening to me, sometimes I was the isolated nine-year-old. As I connected to what my inner child was experiencing, I opened the Bible and slowly read a particular scripture reading or a single verse and, as I did this repeatedly, I began to experience that God was speaking to my inner child so gently and compassionately, yet so powerfully and soothingly.

Listening to God's words through Scripture became a lifeline for both my inner child and adult (and it still is). Every time I woke up with a nightmare, or went through the terror of a flashback[1], or was suddenly filled with fear because of a memory – even if it was the middle of the night – I would open up the Bible and let God speak to my inner child and calm me through the words of Scripture. I tried to keep these words in my heart during the day and I practised recalling them in relevant situations. Over time, I began to experience the immense potential that God's words from Scripture have

---

[1] 'Flashback': The re-emergence of a traumatic memory as a vivid recollection of sounds, images and sensations associated with the trauma. The person having the flashback typically feels as if they are re-living the event.

Introduction

to powerfully transform, integrate and heal the life of someone who has survived sexual abuse and is experiencing the serious effects and consequences of this particular trauma in their being. I also accompanied this spiritual processing of my trauma with ongoing professional support from psychologists who were trained in the area.

Meanwhile, I continued to fulfil the commitments of my ministry in the best way I could. Along the way, I was fortunate and privileged to meet other survivors of sexual abuse, some who were attending a spiritual retreat and disclosed their secret for the first time, and others because I believe it was God's will. Although I was walking my own journey, I felt blessed to support and accompany these survivors on their spiritual journey, because I could understand what they were going through from my own experience, and through my ministry I was able to offer them the gift of God's Word as a unique means for integrating and healing the effects of sexual abuse. It has also been an honour for me to see the courage of other survivors and how God's Word was powerfully transforming and healing their life.

After years of processing my own memories and trauma, I was diagnosed with a chronic auto-immune illness and this disrupted the stability of my life that had only been reached through the grace of God and such painstaking labour. Chronic illness brought with it a whole new set of challenges and it also unravelled some new and deeper layers of the trauma and effects of sexual abuse. All the skills I had previously developed through the means of praying with Scripture were extremely useful in learning to deal with all the issues that are part and parcel of chronic illness.

However, during the years 2010-2012, I began to experience more regular flares of my chronic illness and through some certainly unanticipated events, when further stress was added to my physical condition and my symptoms worsened, I acted on the advice of my medical professionals and sought leave of absence from my community and ministry for health reasons. This happened quite quickly and unpreparedly.

It was through the unfolding of events that took place while I was living away from the community that I began to experience a personal call and the drive to put this spiritual handbook together.

The drive behind this spiritual handbook

After twenty-two years of experiencing the powerful, transformative and healing love of God as a survivor of sexual abuse, I have always wanted to make this experience available to other survivors by putting together a handbook where I could speak 'survivor to survivor' and, in a written form, walk with survivors, accompanying each to have their own personal experience of God's healing love. However, with many pressing ministry commitments in the past, I did not have the time to dedicate myself to this task.

In November 2012, when Prime Minister Julia Gillard announced that a Royal Commission into Institutional Responses to Child Sexual Abuse was going to be established, and that victims/survivors would be invited to come forward and to tell their stories, I felt this call beginning to stir within me again. During the next couple of months, the establishment of the Royal Commission was given ample media coverage and many survivors were already lining up to tell their stories. I also joined the line to tell my story to the Royal Commission, believing that it was my contribution to this great moment in history. Survivors could finally have a voice and be heard so that measures could be sought to make our institutions a safer place for children and to prevent sexual abuse from happening in the future and, at the same time, survivors could achieve some form of justice.

I was very aware that for all survivors who would come forward to tell their stories there was a very high risk of being re-traumatized as terrifying events were re-visited, and that survivors would need of a lot of support both before and after telling their stories, be it from counsellors, psychologists, or advocacy and sexual abuse support groups. I began to wonder if any sort of spiritual support would be offered to survivors, especially being aware of the serious spiritual harm that is done to them when the perpetrator is or has been a priest or member of the clergy. It made sense to me that this spiritual support should be provided by and is appropriate to the Catholic Church as part of its mission and also its basic duty of care to survivors. At least, by providing spiritual support in the form of spiritual retreats or support groups for

Introduction

survivors the Catholic Church would be acknowledging the spiritual harm that has been done and taking responsibility to respond to their need for spiritual healing.

I searched for what spiritual support was available for survivors, particularly in the Catholic Church in Australia, but found very little. I did discover some books that had been written by members of the clergy identifying the scandal of sexual abuse in the church and challenging the church to a more just response to victims, and I also discovered other books written by survivors. However, there was very little offering spiritual support to survivors and this left me feeling very restless. Being a Catholic missionary dedicated to the ministry of prayer and evangelization through the Word of God, I experienced a profound call to respond to this spiritual need which was urgent, particularly in light of the establishment of the Royal Commission and the thousands of survivors who would be coming forward to tell their stories.

It seemed as if all the events unfolding before me were indicating that it was now the right time to act on this personal call – to provide survivors with spiritual support by writing a book that could be used as a practical spiritual biblical handbook.

At the time I began working on this book, I was also facing new layers of the effects of sexual abuse in my life triggered by a recent trauma, so I was dealing with what is referred to as 'complex trauma', one typically experienced by survivors of sexual abuse. At the time, I was also awaiting my private hearing session with the Royal Commission and I was preparing for this and what would follow spiritually, emotionally and psychologically, making sure I had my appropriate supports in place.

So, during the development of this handbook, what I was living, although it was enormously painful, prepared the perfect ground in me and provided me with the raw material (from my own life) that was also to become God's working field and the place where God would meet me and speak to me through the Scriptures, and the place from which I would then speak to you and communicate what is contained in this handbook. As I was going through this process, I experienced the constant gift of God's transforming and healing love at work in my life in the Scriptures. This has been a life-saving experience for me, and I know that it can be for other survivors too and this has been my greatest impetus to complete this book.

Our personal story from the perspective of God's love

Quite often, when we share our personal story, we share it from our own perspective, from what we have known, lived and experienced. If others were to tell our story for us, I have no doubt that they would tell it quite differently because the other person was not 'in our shoes', feeling what we felt, experiencing what we experienced, and living what we lived.

However, it was at the time of trying to overcome my own traumatic experiences of childhood sexual abuse that grace awakened and called me to listen to my own personal story from the perspective of God's love. Through this invitation, God was gently inviting me to spend time in prayer so that I could listen to God's narration of my story.

Initially, this was not easy. I had so many barriers, walls, resistances and blocks in my own relationship with God that stemmed from the trauma of being sexually abused. During my ministry and my encounters with other survivors, I began to see that this was a familiar experience especially for those who have been abused by a member of the clergy and left spiritually broken and wounded. Initially, I could not trust God. I felt that God had let me down in the past by failing to protect me from the perpetrators who caused me grave harm. And one of these was a Catholic priest, supposedly representing God – and look what happened! 'Where were you God? Why didn't you do anything to protect me? How could you say you love me and care for me and allow this to happen to me? How am I supposed to trust you again? ' These questions burned in my heart for a long time. I could not enter a church and I could not see a priest: both were strongly associated with the abuse and yet both were connected to God. I was spiritually wounded and these reactions were only a small reflection of the grave spiritual consequence that survivors of clergy abuse suffer.

Introduction

My turning point came at a time when I had hit rock bottom (this was more than once). I was in a very deep and very dark hole. Despair, desolation and hopelessness covered me completely and I could not see any light either in or at the end of the tunnel. It was an unbearable state to be in day in and day out. I was very suicidal as a result.

Then I did something that was life-changing for my personal journey of healing and overcoming the trauma of childhood sexual abuse (although I was not aware of the great impact that this would have on my journey at the time). I picked up the Bible, opened it up randomly and began to read very slowly.

The scripture passage I happened to open up at was from the Prophet Isaiah (43:1):

> But now, thus says the Lord, who created you, O Jacob, and formed you, O Israel. Fear not, for I have redeemed you. I have called you by your name: you are mine.

These words left me in absolute awe. It was as if they went to the very core of my heart beyond that very deep darkness and they found me and spoke to me personally. I felt that they were coming from someone who was very familiar with my life, who knew what I was experiencing. This someone was God and God was reminding me through these words that I am God's creation and not to be afraid.

God knew that I was full of fear as a consequence of the abuse. God was tuned in to my situation and knew exactly what I was experiencing. God knew how despairing and desperate I was but wanted to remind me through these words that he was close to me: in fact 'calling me by my name'. Like a parent calling out to a child in distress, God was calling to me in my distress. This really touched my heart and even more so did the discovery that I wasn't a 'nobody' for God but I was someone with a name.

I was not sure why God was calling me by name, and I wondered why. God wanted to tell me something. It was an overwhelming but life-giving experience. It was as though God had come in search of me that day and found me where I was, in that 'very deep and very dark tunnel', and there

God spoke to me a personal word that struck a chord with me. Previously I had never had this sort of faith experience.

This was the beginning of a relationship that God had wanted to establish with me from long ago and in this quite unexpected and surprising encounter: a door of hope and light opened up in my darkness and I welcomed it. Previously I had put God down to being like my human perpetrators, yet from this single encounter I experienced that there was something incomparably different about God. I realized that I might have made some wrong assumptions about God and it opened up my mind and heart to seeing God with new possibilities.

Through the prompting of God's grace working in my heart, I took the risk to give God another chance in my life so that God could prove to be different. It was very scary for me at the time because I thought at the back of my mind that this could backfire and I could come away feeling destroyed again – but it could also turn out to be the opposite! If so, I didn't want to lose the opportunity. So I made my choice: I chose to open the door of my heart to God.

'Opening the door' sounds simple, but it took me some time to do it because I had so many issues of trust and fear to overcome. In this process, God's presence remained constant. I knew from the day God entered my darkness that God's presence was there and throughout all my struggles God was waiting patiently for me with an unconditional love. There was nothing forceful about God: God left me free throughout the process. Eventually, through God's words in the Bible, I learned to let go of my barriers so that I could gradually open the door of my heart to God's presence there.

As I listened to God's Word with an open heart, the most amazing thing began to happen. I began to listen to the narration of my story spoken from God's heart: a heart full of tender compassion and authentic love. On many occasions, as I listened, I was moved to tears because of the immense warmth that came from God. How astoundingly different was it to listen to God in my personal story!

God enriched my personal story in so many ways. God added meaning and purpose to it and made me aware of some essential things I was not

Introduction

aware of during the time of the abuse – God's constant presence and unconditional love for me; how God felt my pain and suffered immensely with me; and how much God suffered because of the wrong my perpetrators had done to me. God also helped me see the good and positive things in myself that I had not recognized in the past, and, with great sensitivity and delicacy, brought out the best in me: hope, love, courage, resilience, life, perseverance, confidence, faith and renewed self-esteem.

Listening to God empowered me to begin integrating the painful experiences of my past and to rebuild my life again. I did not need to worry about where my inner spiritual resources would come from to achieve this because God was supplying them as I listened through the Scripture. It has been, and is, a truly wonderful process where I am constantly witnessing how God miraculously transforms the tragedy of my past into a well of new life and continually opens my eyes up to see my own life with new possibilities.

My hopes for this book

My first hope is that this will be a practical spiritual handbook for survivors of sexual abuse and that it will assist in the journey of integration and healing through Scripture. However, it is not meant to replace other psychological therapies or supports that survivors may already have in place. On the contrary, I would recommend that it be used in conjunction with these and in fact should complement them.

I also hope that this book can be a useful guide for those who are pastorally and spiritually accompanying survivors of sexual abuse and even serve as the basis for the formation of facilitated spiritual support groups for survivors.

I hope this handbook will also assist members of the clergy and religious, as well as families and friends of survivors, to gain a deeper understanding of and insight into the life-long effects of sexual abuse and the healing journey that survivors are invited to walk. You too may find yourself doing the walk as you work through the Scripture reflections offered in this handbook.

While some survivors taking up this handbook may not have had any faith exposure, there may be others, like me, who have been raised in a family of faith but then in later years abandoned it and are now coming back to it, perhaps with doubts and hesitations, perhaps with fear and trepidation, or, on the contrary, with openness and expectation. No matter what context each survivor is coming from, or where each one is on their healing journey, my hope is that the reflections in this handbook will resonate with you and that you will be able to engage with them in a positive and uplifting way.

It is very easy for survivors of sexual abuse to become isolated and disconnected, and often this is the case. Many choose never to reveal their long-kept secret or to reach out for professional help or support. Other survivors may be surrounded by people who care about them and support them, however, they too may tend to be isolated and experience a deep sense of loneliness. One of my hopes is that through this handbook survivors can discover that they are never alone because the loving God who created us and gave us life is with us in all the ups and downs of our healing journey. I hope that these reflections on God's Word in the Bible can connect us to the loving God who lives within each one of us.

A very real consequence for survivors, especially for those who have been abused by members of the clergy, is a distorted image of God. God is often described by survivors as being far away, distant, uncaring, tough, punishing and angry. God is therefore someone who survivors are afraid to trust. Such false images of God were developed as we suffered the traumatic experiences at the hands of our perpetrators.

My hope is that through the scriptural reflections in this handbook these false and distorted images we have attached to God and that rightfully belong to the perpetrator of the sexual abuse can be dismantled so that we can enter into listening to the narratives of our personal story from the perspective of God who relates to us as a close, familiar and, most of all, loving God – for 'God is love' (1 John 4:8).

As you do this, it is my hope that you will be able to experience both the healing and integrative power that comes from God's Word when it is believed and practised in life, and how, through it, God will do new things

Introduction

in your life that will become hope and light for many others who are also walking on this healing journey.

My final hope is that, by the time you come to the end of the reflections in this book, you will have unwrapped in your own life and story the greatest gift we could ever be given – the gift of God, who is the true image of Love and a faithful friend who will continue to 'make all things new' in us (Revelation 21:5) while leading us with unconditional tender kindness on our healing journey.

May we completely enjoy the gift of God in our life and constantly experience the new shades and colour that God's love adds to our story. May we find in God all the inner resources we need to walk our journey to the very end.

A guide to the reflections in this book

There are two parts to this book: Part I and Part II. The aim of the first part is that survivors can begin to listen to the narrative of their story from the perspective of a loving God.

On my introductory encounters with people during my years of ministry, I would say that only a handful would share their personal story from the narrative of God's love, for the simple reason that they themselves have not listened to it because they have not known how to. No one has ever taught them how to listen to the God of Love in their life.

To be able to tell our story from the narrative of God's love, we first need to listen to it and discover how God looks at us with love, how God feels for us because God loves us, and how God thinks about us with love. As we do, we will understand new and positive things that perhaps we have been deaf to in the past such as a deeper truth in our being that goes beyond the truth of being a survivor of sexual abuse, how we are unique, esteemed and profoundly loved. Then we will see what we have been unable to see in the past, particularly God's greatest desire to give us life from within, now and always.

CHILD, ARISE!

The reflections in the first part of this handbook refer to readings from the Old Testament (also referred to as the Hebrew Scriptures), beginning with the Book of Genesis. I have heard people often describing God in the Old Testament as an 'angry' and 'punishing' God they have not found very attractive. This is an image that is more accentuated in survivors of abuse because of our traumatic experiences. Hopefully, as you spend time with each one of the reflections in Part I, you too will discover that a God of Love is very evident in the Old Testament.

What makes this handbook special is that the biblical readings used in the reflections, in parts I and II alike, have been specifically applied to the context of survivors for the purpose of assisting survivors to experience the closeness and healing love of God.

It is important to say here that, out of sensitivity to those who have been wounded by men, and for greater inclusiveness, I have tried to refrain from using masculine terms to refer to God, even though God is mostly referred to in masculine terms throughout the Bible. There are times when I have used masculine terms, either because I am being faithful to the scriptural text I refer to or because it is important in the context of that sentence. While there are other biblical references to God using feminine images, particularly that of the mother, it is important to keep in mind that God is beyond human gender, whether male or female – God is God. To remember this may be helpful to the reader whenever 'he' or 'him' or 'his' is used.

The reflections in Part I of the handbook will introduce you into an 'amazing grace' experience and create in you great wonder, awe and astonishment. You may even find yourself searching for extra time and quiet space to be able to absorb and soak up the loving narrative you are listening to.

Becoming familiar with God's narration of our personal story prepares us for the second part of this handbook which is a series of reflections mainly from the New Testament/Christian Scriptures (although there are a few readings from the Old Testament). These reflections focus on a particular issue survivors are confronted with on their healing journey and the explanations help us discover how Jesus dealt with such issues in his own life: there-

Introduction

fore they give us clues how to integrate these issues in our own life. When Scripture is used in this manner, it becomes a powerful tool of integration for our life.

The idea of these reflections is not to approach them as reading material but as 'reflections of life', which means making time and creating the space to ponder over them and pray with them in our own life.

You may choose to do the reflections of Part II in the order they appear or you may choose a particular reflection that responds to an issue you are trying to deal with on a certain day. You can be as flexible as you like. There is no set time to spend on any given reflection. You can move on to the next one when you feel ready to. You may find that, down the track, certain issues re-surface (which is quite normal as we go deeper into the layers of our life) in which case you may choose to re-visit the reflection. The wonderful thing about reflecting on God's Word is that, although the words of a given scripture passage will be the same each time we read them, what we listen to from God each time may be very different because what we are experiencing and living every day is always different. We will not experience today exactly what we experienced yesterday; there will be something in our experience today that is new and different from our experience of yesterday.

Finally, it was impossible for me to address all the issues that survivors of abuse are faced with and invited to deal with along their journey – since sexual abuse affects us in so many ways and aspects of our life. The reflections contained in this handbook are some of the issues I was facing at a particular time on my journey. As most survivors of abuse would appreciate, while there may have been common traits in the process leading up to and during the sexual abuse, each survivor's story is unique! So, while there are effects and issues that are common to adult survivors, the prevalence of the issue in each survivor may vary greatly. What may be a debilitating issue in one survivor may be to a lesser degree in another. This does not mean that one survivor has suffered a lesser trauma than the other but it points out that there were possible differences in the personal circumstances and context of the sexual abuse, as well as the personal responses to it.

Of course, as we learn to identify and confront our issues in our daily lives, we begin to experience that the intensity of the issue diminishes significantly. I hope this spiritual handbook can assist us in this process.

How to get the most out of this handbook

This book is meant to be a practical spiritual handbook that survivors of sexual abuse can refer to and use time and time again as a tool for their own personal healing.

This book is not meant to be used as a study guide of the Bible – which is why the scriptural reflections contained in this book do not attempt to explain fully the historical, religious or cultural contexts behind the specific scripture readings. Instead, it is meant to be a practical tool that can be used for prayerful reflection on Scripture so that practical applications can be made and later practised. To achieve this, you will notice that the scriptural reflections in parts I and II highlight issues that are significant for survivors and provide an explanation of the theological relevance for survivors of sexual abuse. It is important to keep this aim in mind when you are reading these reflections.

I would suggest that you keep a Prayer Journal to accompany this book so that you can write your daily experiences, particularly for the 'Praying with Scripture' section in the reflections found in Part II. Keeping a written account of our encounters with God and our daily experiences is something that we will find valuable in the future. In my own personal journey, particularly those stages where I found myself immersed in darkness and despair, it was a very encouraging and life-giving activity to go back to my prayer journal and re-read previous dialogues and conversations with God where I could recall the work of grace that God was achieving in my personal story.

Part 1: Listening to our personal story narrated by a loving God

It is important to do each one of the scripture reflections in Part I in

Introduction

the order in which they appear, since each reflection is like a stepping stone to the one that follows it.

I would suggest doing one reflection per day or you may choose to spend several days on a single reflection.

As you do the reflections, keep in mind that it is quite normal to have a variety of questions and reactions as we ponder the biblical readings – questions like, Why didn't I understand or see this earlier? Why didn't I know that about my life? Why couldn't I experience what you are saying to me earlier God? – and to have all sorts of mixed reactions such as surprise, gladness, peace, disbelief, shock, fear, consolation, awe and so on. Each survivor's questions and reactions will be different because each one of us is unique.

The ideal is to give ourselves the appropriate time and space to ponder the truth that God is communicating to us through the particular scripture reading and, as we do, to bring to God all our deeper questions and reactions. Through this process we will find that we are able to delicately untangle our false images of God as God confirms and re-affirms who God is through Scripture. You may find it helpful to write down your questions and what you understand from the scripture reading in your prayer journal. Once you feel that you have sufficiently savoured the truth of faith that is presented in the reflection then the idea is to move on to the next reflection.

As you come to the end of the reflections in Part I, it is my hope that you would have begun to listen to the narration of your personal story from the perspective of a loving God and that this is already transforming the way you see your own story, the way you feel about it and the way you will tell it (to those you trust).

Part 2: Working through our issues with a loving God

Try to make a set time every day to do a reflection. Choose a time that works best for you, when you know you will not be interrupted or distracted by other responsibilities or needs.

I would suggest keeping a prayer journal for this section of each reflection.

Each reflection follows the same structure:

The issue is named

A specific issue that survivors are faced with is outlined and at times I allude to how I was experiencing this issue in my life at the given time.

Scripture reading

A scripture reading is referred to and explained, highlighting the specific issue that the reflection is addressing. The explanation given does not attempt to address the cultural, historical or religious context of the scripture reading but it attempts to explain the spiritual relevance, referring to the issue in a way that is practical and applicable for survivors. This introduces survivors to experience how God's Word can respond to their needs and the issues and effects of sexual abuse that are experienced on a daily basis.

Praying the scripture reading

Note here that I have used the word 'praying' instead of 'reflecting on'. Prayer and reflection are very different. 'Prayer' underlines a relationship with God that is developed through dialogue: God talks to us and we listen to God. Whereas 'reflecting on the scriptures' means applying our mind to think about God. Thinking about God and relating to God are very different. Relating to God implies using our whole being: body, mind, heart, spirit, and emotions. The aim of 'Praying with the scripture reading' is to learn to relate to God and to listen to the Word of God in the Bible.

These steps are a guide to facilitate your own personal time of praying with the scripture reading. By following these steps, you will gradually learn how to let the words of Scripture speak to your own life and the issues you are dealing with on your journey.

You will notice that the last step of this section invites you to make a practical resolution for your day. Practising what we listen to and understand in prayer keeps us moving on our healing journey. If we try to practise and fail, we do not need to despair and give up. Practising does not mean that we

Introduction

always will succeed. In fact, many times we will try to practise and probably get it wrong – but that's why we practise something, isn't it! The secret behind practising is knowing that we are not experts yet and this gives us reason to humbly try again every time we do fail. The more we do, the better we become at the task we are trying to accomplish. It is the same for us on our healing journey.

By the time you reach the end of this book, it is my hope that by following the steps in this section, you will be more familiar with this method of praying with Scripture which will enable you to continue praying on your own (using other scripture readings not mentioned in this book) using the steps in this section as a guide.

To facilitate this, I have annexed a blueprint for Praying with Scripture at the back of the book.

The scripture experienced in my life

Not only is it important to listen to Scripture but it is also important to believe and practise it in our life. The more we do this, the more we are able to experience the transformation and healing that God is bringing to our life and the more whole we become.

In this section of each reflection I give a brief and personal account of how God invited me to practise and live out the words of Scripture in my daily life.

The scripture experienced in your life

This is where you have the opportunity to write your own personal account of how God invites you to practise and live out the words of Scripture in your daily life.

I would recommend that you do this at the end of each day and write it down in your prayer journal. The beauty of this is that you will begin to have your own personal account of how God's love is working in and transforming your own personal story.

I am about to do a new thing;
now it springs forth,
do you not perceive it?
I will make a way in the wilderness
and rivers in the desert.

Isaiah 43:19

PART I

Listening to our personal story narrated by a loving God

In the beginning ...

In the beginning, when God created the heavens and the earth, the earth was a formless wasteland, and darkness covered the abyss, while a mighty wind swept over the waters ...

Genesis 1:1-2

GOD EXISTED FROM THE BEGINNING of time, even before the creation of the heavens and the earth, and, yes, before you and I were created. The earth in the beginning was not as you and I know it today. The book of Genesis describes the earth in the beginning to be 'a formless wasteland', where 'darkness covered the abyss'. This is not a pretty picture but an unattractive one that presents a seemingly bottomless chasm where chaos abounds.

However, in this despairing image we cannot fail to see that there is a visible sign of hope – the 'mighty wind' that swept over the waters. This mighty wind is the wind of God, the Spirit of God. It is the creative power of God that will bring universal order out of primordial chaos.

It is awesome to read the First Story of Creation in the book of Genesis and to realize how the creative Spirit of God from the beginning of time was at work in creation.

What is even more awesome to ponder is that the same mighty wind that existed in the original chaos of the earth is also in us. In the New Testament, St Paul sought to make the church of Corinth aware of this magnificent reality when he said to the community: 'Do you not know that you are the temple of God and the Spirit of God dwells in you?' (1 Corinthians 3:16).

This knowledge can give us great hope and comfort. In the midst of

In the beginning ...

the inner chaos and the abyss of darkness and emptiness we can experience at distinct times of our life, God's creative Spirit is present and, in the same way that it 'swept over the waters' and brought order to creation, God's Spirit too will sweep over our inner chaos, bringing about order and beauty in us. God will re-create us and form our life anew.

Today, try to spend time pondering on this great and wonderful reality – God's creative spirit is dwelling in you. Because the creative Spirit of God dwells in us, we can be hopeful and not despair. God's Spirit is in the midst of all the inner chaos caused by the trauma of sexual abuse, actively working there, giving us form, re-creating us and making us new.

This reinvigorates our belief that healing and change is possible. Let us be strengthened today as we ponder on the mighty Spirit of God in us.

Then God said …

Then God said …

Genesis 1:3a

IT IS AWE-INSPIRING TRYING to imagine how, from the earth originally being 'a formless wasteland' where 'darkness covered the abyss', a beautiful creation gradually came to be (Genesis 1:1-31).

Who or what was the powerful source instigating such unimaginable wonder? It was God's Word – 'Then God said …' God's Word is so mighty that God simply begins to speak and magnificent things begin to happen in creation. But, interestingly, creation is not completed by God speaking only once but it is a breathtaking process where God keeps speaking repeatedly over seven days (Genesis 2:3), each time saying, 'Let there be …' And each time God speaks there is something splendidly new that comes to be in creation until it is completed (Genesis 2:1). But what is certain is that God's Word was the beginning and the end of the creation process.

The creation story in the book of Genesis demonstrates so clearly that when God speaks it is never in vain. At no time in the creation story do we see that when God says 'Let there be …' creation remains unchanged. On the contrary, we see that each Word of God generates a creative power that brings about a superb change and transformation in creation. The more God speaks, the more glorious and abundantly fruitful creation comes to be.

So what does this say to us today? Is there a message in the Creation Story from the book of Genesis for survivors of abuse?

I believe that the creation story is one that can give survivors so much hope. In the same way that God's Word was the powerful source of initiating

Then God said ...

such unimaginable wonder in the creation story, it can be a powerful source generating the re-creation of our own life as adult survivors.

Today our life is the 'earth' that God wants to re-create. Yes, God wants to re-write the creation story in each of our lives, transforming them so that they too are just as glorious and abundantly fruitful as creation is! This is something to get excited about and, although we won't be totally re-created in one day, we will have the joy of experiencing that, as God speaks to us day by day, we will gradually be made new ('I make all things new' – Revelations 21:5). And, in the process, what is devastating, heart-breaking, grievous, destructive, sad and tragic will miraculously be transformed into consolation, comfort, happiness, peace, joy, enrichment, and fruitfulness.

A vital question is yet to be addressed. How does God speak to us today? Is it really possible to experience that God has said something to us?

It *is* possible and we can all experience it! God speaks to us today through the Sacred Scripture. St Paul tried to emphasize this in his second letter to Timothy when he said, 'All scripture is breathed out by God' (2 Timothy 3:16a). (Some other versions say 'All scripture is inspired by God.') In other words, every time we open the Bible and read the Scriptures, God is speaking to us. We are not simply reading words written down on paper as in any other book but we are listening to the Living God who is present in the Word and who speaks to us personally.

It makes a huge difference to be aware of this whenever we are reading anything from the Bible because, if we are, we no longer read the Bible as if we are reading stories that simply tell us about the history of our past ancestors in the faith which perhaps have no relevance to our life today.

Instead, when we read the Bible, even though it may be a story about another person – for example, the great prophet Moses in the Old Testament who led the people of Israel out of Egypt where they they had been slaves to the Egyptians (Exodus 3:10-11), or Blind Bartimaeus in the New Testament who was given his sight back by Jesus (Mark 10:46-52) – we can experience God speaking personally to us through these stories just as God spoke to Moses or Jesus spoke to Bartimaeus. The story is no longer just about God and Moses or Jesus and Bartimeaus but it also the story of God and Jesus and their unconditional love for us.

It is a story that God wants to continue telling us every time we open the Bible and read the Scriptures. I am sure that as we listen to God speaking in our stories through Scripture we will be surprised, captivated and intrigued by God's unstoppable love for us. What will be even more fascinating is to experience the creative power of God's Word at work in our story and how by spending time reflecting on God's Word our own stories and our very being are gradually being transformed, re-created and made new.

So, whenever you are using this handbook and reading the scripture references, try to keep in mind that it is God who is speaking to you. The Bible enables us to listen to the 'then God said' in our own life and story.

For me, this has been life-saving! Until I began to read the Scripture, my story was all 'then I said …' It was a story that I alone told, a story with a single narration, and, sadly, it was a tragic story that lacked a consoling and warm response. This all changed for me when God began to speak in my life. It was no longer just 'then I said …' but it became 'I said' and then 'God said' in response. Today I cannot say enough how grateful I am that someone made me aware that God speaks to us through the Scriptures.

So today let us try to initiate these three little words, 'then God said', in our own life. Today let us spend time pondering how awesome it is that the God of all creation wants to speak to us.

Let us then try to think about the mighty deeds that God's Word achieved at the beginning of creation and how all things came to be as God spoke – light, the sky, the sea, the creatures of both land and sea, birds and animals, trees of all kinds, and the creation of man and woman.

If God's Word could bring about this transformation at the beginning of creation, think of the transformation that God's powerful Word can bring about in your own life and story. (You may like to write it down in your prayer journal.)

Believe in your heart that this transformation in your life is possible, as the Prophet Isaiah reminds us: 'Just as from the heavens the rain and snow come down and do not return there till they have watered the earth making

Then God said ...

it fertile and fruitful, giving seed to those who sow and bread to those who eat, so shall my word be that which goes forth from my mouth; it shall not return to me void but shall do my will, achieving the end for which I sent it' (Isaiah 55:10-11).

Even though we may not instantly see or feel the results of God speaking in our life, God's word is always doing something and change is gradually taking place within us.

As you continue your daily journey, you may like to tell God how you feel about the thought of God speaking in your life.

'Let there be light'

Then God said, 'Let there be light', and there was light. God saw how good the light was.

Genesis 1:30

THE FIRST THING GOD BRINGS ABOUT in creation is light. This is quite thought-provoking! In the plan of creation, God's first choice is not to create man and woman, or all the living creatures of the land and sea, or plants and trees – God's first choice is put light in creation.

Why light, we might ask? Why didn't God create any of the other things first? Try to think for a moment what it would have been like to exist in a universe that is covered in darkness.

Have you ever experienced a blackout where you've had no artificial light, not even candle light? You may have found yourself hopelessly and cautiously stumbling around all sorts of obstacles, feeling quite unsafe, insecure and vulnerable, not knowing if danger was close by. You probably found yourself counting the seconds until the light came back on.

Imagine if we had to spend our whole life trying to get around in darkness. The thought of being stuck in darkness is not a very desirable one at all. There is no doubt that life in a world of darkness would be very different to what we experience it to be today.

Light, both natural and artificial, is something we take for granted today, yet we depend upon it for our whole existence. Not only does light allow us to see the beauty of creation around us but it also enables us to see and function in darkness and provides us with a sense of safety and security.

It is no wonder then that light was right at the top of God's creation plan! God never planned for man and woman to exist in a universe that was

'Let there be light'

covered in darkness, doomed to live a life full of fear and insecurity: God wanted us to be able to enjoy a universe filled with light so that we could see and delight in all the beauty of creation.

Yet even though we are living in a universe filled with light on the outside, both natural and artificial, it is possible that we may be living in a state of deep darkness within ourselves.

This state of deep darkness is one that survivors of abuse are familiar with from a very young age. It is what we lived and experienced day in and day out. With one single act committed by our perpetrator, it was as if our whole world of light suddenly disappeared or was stolen away from us and every time our perpetrator repeated the offences against us, this world of darkness we were thrown into grew even darker. Being forced to hold this tragedy secretly in our heart not only intensified this darkness but left us feeling totally desperate and afraid. I'm sure most of us would describe our experience as being in a very long dark tunnel where there is absolutely not even the smallest flicker of light to signal a way out.

Even though it may be years or even decades since the traumatic experiences occurred, we can still be living in a state of inner darkness. Perhaps there are many things that we still can't see clearly or make sense of. Perhaps we still experience that we are in the 'long dark tunnel' and wondering how we are ever going to come out of it.

But right now God invites us not to despair but to have hope because God is about to enter into our personal story and the very first thing that that presence will bring to our life is light, for 'God is light' (1 John 1:5). Today there is light in that very long dark tunnel and, yes, it is possible to come out of it because God who is light is there.

Imagine a big floodlight being turned on in a dark room: everything in that room becomes visible.

God's light is even more powerful than a floodlight: it is the most powerful light in the universe, so powerful that we are reminded in the Gospel of Mark that 'all that is hidden will be made visible and all that is secret will come to the light!' (Mark 4:22). God's light will permeate every corner, every crack, and every hole, even as small as a pinhole, of our story until eventually all darkness is banished from our life. What a powerful thought to hold on to, and what a much brighter story God promises us!

Today let us celebrate these words from Scripture in our heart – 'Let there be light and there was light.' Let us try to bring these words to mind repeatedly during the day and allow God to give us hope and encouragement through them, especially when we feel weighed down by our inner darkness.

Perhaps by the end of the day, even if it be in a very small way, we will be able to say: God said to me today (through the scripture reading), 'Let there be light', and, yes, 'there was light.'

'Let us make humankind'

Then God said, 'Let us make humankind in our image, according to our likeness …' God created humankind in his image, in the divine image God created them; male and female God created them.

Genesis 1:26a; 27

WE HAVE ALL HEARD OF THE SAYING 'Save the best for last'! What we see when we read the creation story in the book of Genesis is that God saves the best part of his creation for last. Man and woman were the final part of God's master plan of creation. Man and woman were to be so special to God that he wanted to set them apart from everything else in creation and God achieved this aspiration by doing something extraordinary – God created man and woman in God's image.

We have been carefully crafted by God and made in the divine image. This is what makes man and woman so unique in creation. God has imprinted in each of us the divine image; or, to put it in other words, we have the genes of divinity in us, the image of God who is Love (John 4:8). This is the essence of who we are; it is in our makeup, our truest and deepest identity: we have been made by God and in the image of God. God has clothed us with a very great dignity. So the natural thing should be that when we think about who we are and where we have come from we should feel proud, special and elated.

Identity can be an issue for many people, but it is more so for survivors of sexual abuse. Sexual abuse is an undignifying experience for the victims at many levels. Something that is commonly shared by survivors as we try to articulate our feelings connected to the abuse is that almost immediately we felt as though something deep within us had been stolen or violently taken away. This something deep within that we struggle to articulate is our dignity and identity. Consequently, as we grow and develop, so too do our problems with self-image as we are inundated with feelings of worthlessness, unimportance, not feeling valued, feeling as if we are 'nothing' and 'nobody'.

In this scripture reading from Genesis, God reminds us of who we are – we are created by God and made in the image and likeness of God. This is our true identity and our greatest dignity. No one person in our life (including our perpetrator), no experience, trauma or event in life, can ever take away, steal or change our true identity. Our identity is permanently ingrained in us: we have been hallmarked and branded as God's forever.

When you feel worthless, unimportant or simply like a 'nobody', let God remind you of who you really are. Let God say to you: 'Let us make [substitute your name here] in our image, after our likeness.' Remember the great image that has been sealed in you – God's image – which is why today and always you are worthy, honourable, valuable, important and someone very special. You are all this and much more to God and this is how God wants you to feel about yourself.

As you reflect on these words, also think about how happy God was to create you and how God must have delighted to make you in God's image.

Your story has a beautiful beginning. Quite often when we share our personal story we leave out the beginning yet it is the most essential part of our story because it goes to the very core of our being and reminds us of who we really are despite the fact that we may have passed through traumatic experiences. This beginning is crucial as we begin to process and interpret the traumatic events, because it reminds us constantly of our origins and how important, valuable, worthy and honourable we are. Believing in this facilitates us in our healing journey. As we open our hearts to our story's beginning – our true identity – we will begin to read it and tell it in a new way.

So, as you are working, relaxing, on the bus, or out walking today, spend time pondering this scripture reading and try to believe it with your

'Let us make humankind'

whole heart. The more we believe it the more we will experience that whatever was lost through the experience of sexual abuse will be recovered. It is the wonderful miracle that evolves from knowing who we are.

'Everything ... is very good!'

God looked at everything he had made and found it very good!

Genesis 1:31

DON'T YOU JUST ENJOY SEEING SOMEONE patting themselves on the shoulder and congratulating themselves for something that they have done well or are pleased with! When we read the creation story in the book of Genesis we have a glimpse of God doing this repeatedly as the creative work is in progress – God looks at the work and we read, 'God saw how good it was' (Genesis 1:10b; 12b; 18b; 21b; 25b). God is pleased with the outcome of this creative work: God finds it 'good'.

Yet, God's work gets even better – even God seems to think so. After the creation of man and woman, God looks at this new creation and we read in the scripture that God 'found it very good!'

God's greatest pleasure seems to come with this last creation, man and woman: God found it not only good but *very* good. God didn't create us just okay, or mediocre, or bad, but God created each person 'very good'. Even what some people may find humanly speaking imperfect, or 'a reject', or 'bad' – for example, a child born with a physical deformity – God finds even this person very good.

God's finding us very good is not based on our physical looks, or what we have done, or what we have or possess in life, it is based on the truth that, first, God made us, we are God's creation, and, second, that we are made in God's image – divine Love.

The goodness and value of every human being is founded

'Everything ... is very good!'

on this truth of faith. Our true self-esteem and self-worth come from knowing and believing this.

Unfortunately, what can happen as we grow and develop to adulthood is that we build our lives on false foundations outside ourselves, believing that these will be good for us and give us self-esteem. The danger is, if these things suddenly collapse and disappear – for example, we lose our physical capacities because of an accident – then so too does our self-esteem and we start to sink into waters of 'I'm hopeless', 'I'm no good', 'I'm a loser', and so on.

Survivors of sexual abuse struggle immensely with self-esteem, and trying to recover a healthy self-esteem is a journey in itself. One of the grave effects of sexual abuse is that it distorts the way we think and feel about ourselves and changing this is hard work because it involves undoing thinking patterns and beliefs we have repeatedly reaffirmed in ourselves as we developed into adulthood and beyond. For example, for many years I lived believing that 'I am bad'. I was convinced that the sexual abuse, the bad thing that happened to me, made me a bad person and happened to me because I was bad in the first place. This belief was often reaffirmed by the perpetrator who would tell me frequently, 'You are very bad.' Other survivors have been told far worse things. After years of secretly being indoctrinated by our perpetrator, it is not difficult to understand how this totally distorted and negative self-image becomes rooted deeply within us, destroying our self-esteem from an early age.

Recovering our self-esteem is a journey that requires us to go into our hearts. I like to imagine it like a gardening experience where we dig deeply, taking out all the weeds – the negative self-image that has been growing in us over the past years – so that we can plant new seeds, seeds of our true image. These are 'I am very good' seeds: the image that God himself affirmed right from the beginning of our existence.

We are very good! God has said so, right from the beginning of our personal story when we were created, and God continues to say so even now wherever we are on our healing journey. What God thinks and says about us goes way beyond whatever anyone else has ever thought about us or said to us

– including our perpetrator – or what we even say and think about ourselves. In the end, what God thinks and says is what counts.

So, we are very good! It is what we are! God invites us to listen to these words and to build our self-esteem on them, for they are the very foundation of who we are. By building our self-esteem on them, we cannot go wrong because we are building on the only true foundation in our life that will never change, crumble or disappear because it is the very core of who God says we are.

God constantly invites us to listen to these words from Scripture in the situations of our life, especially when we think negatively about ourselves and say such things as 'I can't do that, I'm no good!' or 'I'm such a disaster! I blew it again!' or 'I'm hopeless! I can't even say what I want' or 'They will never choose me, I don't deserve it anyway!' These are all opportunities to consciously stop and build on the true foundation of who God says we are – very good.

How different it is when we can manage to do this and truly believe what God says to us! How different it is to say 'I can do this ... I'm very good' or 'I blew it again, but I am very good' or 'I couldn't say what I wanted to, but I am very good' or 'They may choose me ... I am very good!' Whether things work out or don't work out for us, God's foundation of who we are never changes – we are 'very good'.

Let us dwell on this and believe it profoundly and experience how significantly it transforms our negative self-image and low self-esteem to a positive and healthy self-image and self-esteem, giving our personal story a new and strong foundation.

God has loved us first

You formed my inmost being; you knit me in my mother's womb. I praise you, so wonderfully you made me; wonderful are your works.

Psalm 139:13

GOD'S LOVE FOR US EXISTED even before we came to be. God didn't create us and then start loving us. God loved us first and, because of God's love, created us and gave us life (1 John 4:19). We are the product of God's love, no matter what others may say to us. God's love 'formed our inmost being', the parts of us we cannot see but we experience them – our feelings and emotions, our thoughts, the things of the spirit. God's love tenderly and carefully 'knitted us in our mother's womb' (Psalm 139:13), cell by cell, muscle by muscle, tissue by tissue, organ by organ, body part by body part. Even before our mother could cradle us in her arms, God was already holding us with loving hands, delicately putting us together in our mother's womb. What a mind-blowing thought!

We exist because we have been loved first by God and we continue to be profoundly loved by God. Every day, the fact that we have life and we wake up breathing as we open our eyes to see the new light of day, and we get up and start moving around – all this is because we continue to be loved by God.

This first love God had for us even before we existed, that brought us into being and that keeps us alive day after day, is something that will never change in our life. We have been loved by God in the past, we are loved by God now, and we will be loved by God into the future, even beyond death, forever.

God's first love for us is unchangeable; it doesn't change because of what others say or think about us, or because of what we say or think about ourselves; it doesn't change because of what others do to us, or because of what we do to ourselves.[2] God's love for us remains forever because God is love and God only loves (1 John 4:8).

God loves us profoundly, despite what we feel or believe about ourselves. Survivors of sexual abuse struggle to believe this and all sorts of questions come to mind revolving around the big question of *why*: 'If you love me God, why did you let this happen to me? Why couldn't you protect me? Why didn't you do something? Why couldn't you stop it?'

These questions lingering in our heart often act as obstacles that prevent us from believing that God loves us profoundly and they keep us at a distance from God. But what we will find helpful when these necessary questions arise is to remember that God is love and, being love, God's nature is no other than to love. God could never hate because it goes against God's nature. God could never wish any sort of evil upon anyone because it goes against God's nature.

Often we hear the saying, 'The last thing I want is …' For God, sexual abuse is not even the last thing that God wants for any person. It was never in God's plan and it never would be part of God's plan because sexual abuse is an evil act and it goes against God's nature of love. Sexual abuse is not and never can be an act of God who is love, but rather it is the act of a human being who is called to be love but instead chooses to act upon the evil that has seduced the human heart. It is the act of someone who has gone far away from being and living the true nature we are called to live – love. God is profoundly grieved by these acts of evil. God is even more grieved to see that the people who committed these evil acts were precisely the people that he planned to care for us and protect us from danger. God is also profoundly grieved to see that we have been terribly harmed by this evil act. God did not plan this for us.

But what is of prime importance to God is that we know and under-

---

[2] In no way am I insinuating that we should take advantage of God's love to cause harm to others or harm to ourselves.

God has loved us first

stand that, even with a history of sexual abuse, we have been and are profoundly loved by God and we always will be. God loved us first – before we were sexually abused, during the time we were being abused, after the abuse, and right now. God has never stopped loving us but, sadly, most of the time we are not aware of it.

Survivors often have other questions and doubts that come about because of how the trauma of sexual abuse made us feel about ourselves: 'How can you love me when I hate myself and only want to die? How can you love me when I only want to harm myself? How can you love me if I am dirty? How can you love me if I am bad and did bad things? How can you love me when my life is a total mess and I just can't pull myself together?'

It's just so hard for us to believe that God can love us profoundly when we feel that we are so unlovable. Even though we cannot love ourselves this is not the case with God! God loves us – yes, even more than we love ourselves!

I have met many survivors who have thought at some stage, 'I wish that I was never born [to experience the abuse]' or 'My life was just a mistake!' and these thoughts are usually accompanied by feelings of intense pain and despair. But our existence, according to the way God tells our story, is not a mistake. God knew very well what he was doing when he gave us life. We are not the result of an experiment, or a bad decision, or bad planning. We are here because God willed us to be here from long ago. God desired us first, long before we came to be, and even long before our parents desired us. It is because of God's love that we exist today. God's love is the essence of our whole being.

To know and believe that we are profoundly loved can be very powerful in our healing process. Knowing we are loved is what gets us up when we are down, moves us along when we are stuck, makes us persevere when we are ready to give up, empowers us to face a problem instead of running away from it – and much more. But we need to believe it.

This is what God wants to emphasize in his telling of your story today. You are loved by God, you always have been and you always will be.

Today, as we carry on with our lives, let us try to ponder on this core belief of our faith: You are profoundly loved, and you have been loved throughout your life from its beginning right to the present. There has not been a time in your life where you haven't been loved by God, even though you may be unaware of it.

An exercise that I found very useful in my own life and one that you may find helpful too is to try to be aware of the moments in your day when you feel unlovable. Perhaps it's when you let your temper fly, or when you are moody or feeling down, or when you are anxious, or angry. After you become aware of how you are and that you are feeling unlovable as a result, ponder on the fact that God profoundly loves you in the present. You may even like to confirm this with God by asking, 'Do you really love me, God, even now when I am moody, or angry, or down?' Let God's profound love affirm and reaffirm you.

You may like to repeat this exercise whenever you are feeling unlovable in your day. Don't worry about the number of times you need to do this: it may be a couple of times, it may be many more. If you find yourself struggling to believe that you are constantly loved then this is an exercise that you may want to practise regularly.

The more we repeat this exercise in our life, the stronger our belief in God's love for us becomes and although we may feel that this is a very slow process at times the beauty is that positive change is taking place within us even though we may not realize it. We will also begin to realize that even though we feel unlovable this it is just a feeling, because the truth is that we are loved.

So let us try to enjoy this day celebrating the reality that we are loved and always will be loved, even when we feel unlovable.

Our true Father[3]

'You are my son; today I am your father.'
Psalm 2:7

'I will be a father to him and he shall be a son to me.'
2 Samuel 7:14

'For I am a Father to Israel, Ephraim is my first-born.'
Jeremiah 31:9

'Ephraim, you are my favourite Son, the child I love best!'
Jeremiah 31:20

'When Israel was a child I loved him, out of Egypt I called my son.'
Hosea 11:1

'It was I who taught Ephraim to walk, who took them in my arms. I drew them with human cords, with bands of love. I fostered them like one who raises an infant to his cheeks; yet, though I stooped to feed my child, they did not know that I was their healer.'
Hosea 11:3-4

'Do not call anyone on earth "father", for you have one Father, and he is in heaven.'
Matthew 23:9

---

[3] The topic of God as 'Father' is a very sensitive one for those who have been sexually abused by their own father or by a priest who they referred to as 'Father'. The false images of God survivors have are a consequence of their experiences of 'father', parent or priest, and these false images are the greatest obstacles to re-establishing a relationship with God. I have tried to address some of these issues concerned with relating to God as Father. While our purpose here is to deal with these issues, we use the scriptural references to God as Father, and do not include gender-neutral language, for example referring to God as Mother. It is also important to note that where Scripture refers to 'son', 'son' is understood to refer to both masculine and feminine – 'son and daughter'.

CHILD, ARISE!

WHEN WE LISTEN TO GOD narrating our story through Scripture, one of the biggest realizations we may have is to discover that God – the one who has loved us first and carefully 'knitted us together in our mother's womb' (Psalm 139:13), giving us life – is our Father and we are his child. Long before our human parents held us at our birth, God had already 'fathered' us in our mother's womb. Even before we were named by our parents, we were already named as son or daughter by God.[4]

This does not minimize the role of our human parents in any way. On the contrary, our parents play a very important role because they are the people who bring us into the world and nurture and care for us as we grow. So, although we are firstly God's children, God entrusts us into the care of our parents. But there remains an eternal yearning in God's heart that one day we will be able to acknowledge him and call out to him 'Abba! Father!' as Jesus did.[5]

The Old Testament has many beautiful scripture verses that communicate this great truth of our faith where God is depicted as an all-tender, loving and caring heavenly Father who refers to us as his children. The significance of this is huge, especially for those who have been orphaned or are fatherless, because it means that every person has a Father – God is our Father.

It has been very moving for me in my ministry to witness people making the discovery that God is their Father for the first time, particularly in the atmosphere of a guided retreat where Scripture is used as a basis for prayer and reflection. I have seen people stirred with tears as their hearts are touched and captured by the intense joy, happiness, wonder, surprise and consolation that this truth fills them with.

Sadly, this is not normally so for those who have survived sexual abuse. Initially, the truth of God being 'Father' disconcerts us and shakes us to the

---

[4] See Jeremiah 1:5 – 'Before I formed you in the womb I knew you...' – and Ephesians 3:14-15 – 'For this reason I kneel before the Father, from whom every family in heaven and on earth derives its name.'

[5] See Mark 14:36: '"Abba, Father", he said, "everything is possible for you. Take this cup from me. Yet not what I will, but what you will." The truth of God being 'Father' was the core message of the Good News that Jesus shared with everyone he met. He made constant reference to God as Father.

Our true Father

very root of our being, especially if the perpetrator was our own father or a priest who we referred to as 'Father'. For us, the word 'father' is not charged with beautiful and positive messages but instead conjures up dark and negative images of a horrid monster who sought to destroy us. 'Father' for us paints the picture of someone we feared, someone who betrayed our trust, someone we did not feel safe with, someone who hurt us and caused us pain, someone who lied to us, someone who used us for their own pleasure, someone who robbed us of our dignity, and someone who we wanted to get out of our life and to leave us alone. Therefore when we survivors hear God being referred to as our 'Father' chaos and panic strikes us, all our alarm bells start ringing and all the red flags are raised!

It is amazing to see just how much our own personal experiences of 'father' influences the way we welcome and respond to the truth of God as 'Father' in our life. Whereas some will experience great elation at this discovery, we survivors experience great pain and even devastation to think of God as 'Father' and it is important for those who are accompanying survivors pastorally and spiritually to understand this.

For us, the thought of God being our Father can initially repulse us and we can have all sorts of reactions like, 'If God is Father, I don't want to go anywhere near him! I need to stay away from him! I need to get as far away as I possibly can! I can't let him touch me! I need to hide from him and not let him find me! I need to be careful because I can't trust him! I can't fall into his trap, he will hurt me and use me for his own ends and destroy my life even more.' At first, we may not even understand our own reactions, but what is clearly happening is that we are responding and reacting to God with the same feelings and attitudes that we had towards our own father or Father X. In psychology this is described as 'transference'.[6] We are unconsciously associating what belongs to our own father or Father X with God our 'Father' because this is the only image and experience of 'father' that we know.

---

[6] Sigmund Freud described transference as that part of therapy when the patient unconsciously substitutes the physician for a person from the patient's past. In our present context, this can mean transferring feelings and emotions associated with the traumatic past on to God.

No matter how much others try to encourage us with their own positive experiences of God as Father, it does not alter the initial grief and pain that is evoked in us when we hear that God is Father. For example, when someone who has not been abused reads, 'Ephraim, you are my favourite Son, the child I love best', perhaps their whole confidence and esteem will be boosted. But when a survivor reads this, their reaction will be, 'I don't want to be your "favourite" child or "the one that you love best" because that's what my father always used to tell me when he was abusing me – and I don't want to be God's favourite child!' Sadly, our initial reactions towards God as Father are yet another indication of how sexual abuse gravely harms and destroys the spiritual and faith dimension of survivors.

Beginning a spiritual journey in search of God involves healing spiritually. To be able to come to God and relate to him as a Father means correcting our image of 'father' which has been distorted because it is associated very strongly with sexual abuse. This means being attentive to what is happening within us as we try to be still in God's presence or as we read the Scripture. For example, when you try to listen to God speaking to you through the scripture verses above from Hosea 11:1, 'When Israel was a child I loved him ...', or Hosea 1:3-4, 'Yet it was I who taught Ephraim to walk, who took them in my arms ...', perhaps you will experience discomfort and the temptation to get up and run away and you are not even sure why you feel this way or what is happening within you. This is where the work of beginning to heal our relationship with God begins. It is a work that involves being able to separate who our father, or Father X, is from who God the Father is because what we do unconsciously is associate the two to be like each other when they are totally different. Consequently, we transfer all the behaviours, thoughts, feelings and emotions that belong to our own father to God the Father.

I have tried to include some steps below that I have found useful over many years in my own process of spiritual healing, particularly healing my image of 'father' to be able to relate to God as Father. Although doing this work requires courage on our part, it is mainly a work of God's grace and by persevering we will eventually be able to enjoy the fruits of a loving relation-

Our true Father

ship with God without doing transferences. It goes without saying that we need to be kind, gentle, patient and understanding with ourselves during this process because it does take time and even though there may be times when we feel that nothing is happening in our relationship with God, through God's grace, something is always happening!

Helpful steps in our healing process of relating to God as Father

(You may like to practise these steps when you experience difficulty in relating to God as Father.)

1. What happened when you tried to be still in God's presence or to read one of the scripture verses?

    Was there a particular thought that came to your mind or did you experience a 'flashback'?[7]

    Can you identify if there were particular words from the readings that may have triggered a reaction in you? What were those words?

2. Try to identify what you felt in God's presence or as you read the words from Scripture – for example, fear, anxiety, panic, unsafe, mistrust, sadness, paralysis?

3. Try to identify who these thoughts, flashbacks or feelings refer to? Are they associated with your own father or with someone else?

4. Once you have identified that your responses refer to your father or Father X, try to become aware of the present and that you are now with God and not with your own father or Father X, and tell yourself, 'It is okay! I am safe! I am not with my father but I am with God the Father! He is not like my father at all. They are different!'

5. God knows and understands what we are experiencing and God will help us. You can be honest with God and express whatever is going on in you as you try to sit with God's Word. For example, 'God, when you tell me that it was you who took me in your arms,

---

[7] 'Flashback': The re-emergence of a traumatic memory as a vivid recollection of sounds, images and sensations associated with the trauma. The person having the flashback typically feels as if they are re-living the event.

I feel so afraid because when Father X took me in his arms he abused me and I think that you may be like him and do the same thing. I get afraid to even come close to you because of this!' We don't need to pretend with God: God already knows what we feel.

6. Let God assure you that he is God and not [here we can put our father's name or Father X's name], as we are reminded in Scripture.[8]
7. Allow God to invite you again through Psalm 46:10 to 'be still, and know that I am God.'
8. After you are still again and aware that you are with God/Father and not with your own father or Father X, read the words of Scripture again.
9. Again, try to identify the words that are calling your attention and why.
10. Identify what feelings they are evoking in you? It does not matter if you still experience the same feelings associated with your own father for example, fear, panic, or sadness.
11. Repeat steps 5 to 7.
12. Do not lose hope if you were not able to experience progress or that your initial feelings changed in the time you tried to spend with God. Remember, we have lived through years of experiencing feelings, thoughts and emotions that are associated with the trauma of sexual abuse and it is normal that it will take more than one session of reflection or prayer to change all this.
13. God does not pay attention to external success but God pays attention to our hearts.[9] Today God celebrates our courage of heart in choosing to heal our relationship with him. Let's celebrate it too.

---

[8] Hosea 11:9b: '...nor will I turn and devastate Ephraim. For I am God, and not a man – the Holy One among you.'
[9] Samuel 16:7: 'The Lord does not look at the things people look at. People look at the outward appearance, but the Lord looks at the heart.'

God knows us deeply

'Lord, you have probed me, you know me; you know when I sit and stand; you understand my thoughts from afar. My travels and my rest you mark; with all my ways you are familiar. Even before a word is on my tongue, Lord, you know it all. Behind and before you encircle me and rest your hand upon me. Such knowledge is beyond me, far too lofty for me to reach.'

Psalm 139:1-6

BEING KNOWN BY ANOTHER can be a scary thought at times, and especially for survivors of sexual abuse because we fear that if people know us and the 'dark' part of our story they may reject, judge or label us, and our list continues. Consequently, we hold back from letting others know us, even though they are our loved ones and those who support us the most. If we decide to let others know us and what we are experiencing, what we hope for the most is that knowing us they will still love us.[10]

God fulfils our hopes to be known and loved. God knows us deeply and, knowing us, God loves us.[11] God doesn't reject, label or judge us, and never stops loving us. How could God who is love ever stop loving what he has created and given life to?

Even though we may have never told God about ourselves, God knows us deeply. God even knows what we don't know or understand about ourselves and for survivors the journey of knowing ourselves and understanding

---

[10] In no way am I insinuating that we should let everyone know us. Boundaries are essential when it comes to letting others into our life and story. As we go through our process we begin to know who we want to let in and who we feel it is safe to let in.

[11] 'To know' in the biblical sense means 'to love'.

the effects of sexual abuse takes time. But while there are things that we don't know or understand about ourselves, God knows us deeply.

This is what Psalm 139 alludes to: 'Lord ... you know me; you know when I sit and stand; you understand my thoughts from afar.' God knows when we sit. God knows we sit when we are tired or troubled or because we need to think carefully about something important. God knows when we stand. God knows what motivates and drives us to stand: as the psalm says, he 'understands our thoughts from afar, even the ones we cannot put into words.

God knows our travels. God knows where we go, what we do, and the reasons behind our travels. God knows what we are thinking as we sit on the bus, drive to work, wander in the shopping centre. God knows us when we rest. God knows what exhausts us and weighs us down. God knows the thoughts that are running through our minds as we lie on our bed at night or sit in front of the television. 'Even before a word is on our tongue', God already knows it. God knows why we say what we say, what made us say it and how we react after saying it, even though we might not even know ourselves. God knows everything about us – our thoughts, feelings, emotions, reactions, intuitions, movements. God is 'familiar with all our ways'. God knows us more than any other person on earth ever could.

God's deep knowledge of us should not make us feel afraid. In his first letter, St John says, 'There is no fear in love ... fear has to do with punishment' (1 John 5:18). If we are afraid of God knowing us it is because we do not know God for 'God is love' (1 John 4:8). Love is the true image of God, and yet for many survivors the image of a loving God may be very new. Whenever this handbook mentions God, it is referring to the God of love, a loving God.

To know that we are completely known by God should give us a great sense of peace and comfort on our healing journey. We all know how painful it is not to know or understand certain things about ourselves.[12] Quite often, as our memories slowly begin to return, often through flashbacks, they do

---

[12] Often, for survivors, a painful part of our journey is the reality of not knowing, in the sense of not being able to remember in detail what happened to us, and it can seem even more painful to realize that perhaps there are some parts of our story that we may like to know but may never know fully because we can't recall the memory.

God knows us deeply

not come in any chronological or sequential order; they are like small pieces in a huge jigsaw puzzle and we find ourselves confused and grappling to place these pieces in the puzzle of our life story. Not knowing how these memories fit together and what happened to us is agonizing.

Yet, even though we do not know and cannot recall, our body seems to know and remember the abuse very well and reveals it through reactions, thoughts, emotions and behaviours that increase our pain because we don't know where they are coming from and what to connect them to. All the not knowing can cause us to become anxious, but we need to be patient and gentle with ourselves and remember that coming to know the truth of the sexual abuse is a painstaking process that cannot be forced. When our body feels that it is safe and strong enough to handle the memories, and we are ready, the memories will come. Meanwhile, we need to remember that what we do not know God knows, and, knowing us, God loves us.

Today, let us try to ponder only one thought – we are completely known by God. When you experience that you are grappling with some unknown part of yourself, try to find peace and serenity in knowing that God knows it already – and, knowing it, God loves you. God doesn't judge, label or reject you. Think of God as holding this unknown part of you and taking care of it and loving you until you are ready to know it and recover the memory. God knows when we are ready. God knows our pain threshold better than anyone else, God knows what we can and cannot handle.

Perhaps there is someone presently in your life who does not understand you deeply and, based on your reactions, emotions and behaviour, they have made very wrong assumptions and conclusions about you, which causes you a lot of sadness; or perhaps there is someone who does know you more intimately, they know about the abuse and some of the effects that it has in you but you feel that they have judged or labelled you, or even rejected you. If this is your situation, then you might find it helpful to be aware that God knows you completely and loves you, even if others misunderstand you, misjudge you, label you, reject you or make wrong assumptions about you. God knows you and, knowing you, loves you, and at the end of our journey what God knows is what counts: what others think of us does not matter. This can offer us a great sense of peace and tranquillity in the middle of such distressing experiences.

So, take the opportunity to recall these words from the psalm during the day and let them give you peace and serenity particularly when you find that you are anxious about not knowing yourself: 'Lord, you know me; you know when I sit and stand; you understand my thoughts from afar; with all my ways you are familiar.'

God loves us

The Lord appeared to us in the past, saying: 'I have loved you with an everlasting love; I have drawn you with loving-kindness.'

Jeremiah 31:3

'You are precious and honoured in my sight and I love you.'

Isaiah 43:4

SOMETHING THAT IS COMMON to every person, no matter what our culture, language, age, social background or religion, is that we all yearn to be loved as we are, loved unconditionally, with all our experiences of life, ways of thinking, feeling, behaving, our opinions and our choices. Although our greatest longing is for this quality of love, all too often what we experience is a conditional love that is based on the power of 'only if you …' – 'I will love you only if you … do this … or don't do that …' or 'if you decide to …' or 'if you change …' So it can easily happen that because of our own insecurity and fear of losing love we find ourselves giving in to the power of these two words 'only if' and we do things or make decisions or behave in ways that are not being true to ourselves. This experience can be a very painful one that causes us suffering.

God's love for us is very different! It is not a conditional love. God will never say to us, 'I will love you only if you…' God says to us, 'I love you' – and that's all there is to it. God's 'I love you' is unconditional. God loves us as we are, with all our positives and negatives, in all our ups and downs, through our successes and failures, with all our gifts and limitations. It is an 'I love you' that is everlasting, as the Prophet Jeremiah points out in this beautiful reading: 'I have loved you with an everlasting love.' God has loved us from the beginning of our existence right up until now: there is not one moment in our life where God has not loved us.

The most typical question for survivors as we listen to these words from God is, 'What about during the time I was being abused? Did you love me then, God?' The answer is yes, even during that time God loved us. Automatically, we feel quite challenged to believe this and it can bring many painful questions to our mind and heart: If you loved me why didn't you do anything to help me or to stop the abuse from happening? Why didn't you defend me and protect me? Why did it feel like you abandoned me and left me all alone?

God knows all our questions, and even as we ask them I imagine God suffers immensely because all he ever wanted was for us to experience his loving care and protection. God also suffers greatly to know that the people who were supposed to be his human instruments and meant to show us his love and care instead caused us immense hurt and damage and left us feeling vulnerable, weak, alone and afraid. I imagine God has cried many tears over what we have suffered and understands better than anyone else where all our questions come from.

However, God wants us to know that even though these human instruments failed to show us love, care and protection, God was loving us even then, unconditionally. God never stopped loving us, either during that time or after. God's love was then, and is now, and will always be an everlasting love. Nothing can stop God's love for us: our past traumas can't, the effects of the abuse can't, the deep scars that we carry can't. God's love for us lasts through everything. It will never end.

Why does God love us with such an everlasting love? The answer is beautifully expressed in the Book of the Prophet Isaiah: 'You are precious and honoured in my sight and I love you' (Isaiah 43:4). These words sum up who we are for God – precious, honoured and loved. Each one of us is valuable to God, important, priceless, regarded with great respect and highly esteemed: we always have been and we always will be. This is a truth that

God loves us

will not change, no matter what others have told us in the past[13] or what they say to us in the present, no matter what we have felt, thought or believed about ourselves in the past or what we feel, think or believe about ourselves right now. No one, nothing – not even ourselves – can ever change the love God has for us.

St Paul in his letter to the Romans says, 'the love of God has been poured out into our hearts through the Holy Spirit that has been given to us' (Romans 5:5). From the beginning of our creation, when God made us in his image of love, up until now, 'the love of God has been poured out into our hearts.' This unconditional love of God goes to the very core of our being. It is a solid foundation in our life that will never collapse, crumble or be destroyed because it is the whole truth of who we are. True, part of our truth is that we are survivors of sexual abuse, but it is not the whole truth. The whole truth is that we are survivors of sexual abuse who are precious and honoured and loved unconditionally by God.

This deepest truth can have such incredible power in our life when we embrace it by listening to God and believing what God says to us: 'You are precious and honoured in my sight' and 'I love you.' As we do, we begin to experience that what we may have deemed lost forever through the sexual abuse, such as our self-esteem and dignity, returns in a gradual process!

It is a matter of being able to recall who we are throughout our daily life experiences, and in the depths of our being to listen to and believe God's words: 'You are precious and honoured in my sight and I love you'. For example, someone may be putting you down and speaking negatively to you and you begin to experience the negative impact of their words on you ... Stop and recall your deepest truth and God's words to you – 'You are precious and honoured in my sight and I love you' – and believe these words more than the negative words that were said to you. Allow God to repeatedly say them to you.

This simple process can be repeated and applied to all experiences of our life: when we fail at something, when we judge ourselves harshly, when

---

[13] Some survivors of clergy abuse have been told repeatedly by their perpetrators that God doesn't love them because they have been bad and have done bad things.

we experience our inability to do something, when we are at our lowest point, but also when we reach our highest point, when we are misunderstood, when we question the meaning of life. What we experience is only partially true, but there is always a deeper truth within us beckoning us to pay attention, listen and believe – 'You are precious and honoured in God's sight and God loves you.' May we never forget it!

God suffers with us

But the Lord said, 'I have witnessed the affliction of my people in Egypt and have heard their cry of complaint against their slave drivers, so I know well what they are suffering. Therefore, I have come down to rescue them from the hands of the Egyptians and lead them out of that land into a good and spacious land ... So indeed the cry of the Israelites has reached me, and I have truly noted that the Egyptians are oppressing them.'

Exodus 3:7-9

IN THE BOOK OF EXODUS, Moses is called to deliver God's people from their slavery under the Egyptians. When Moses experienced God's call, it was not from a God who was far away and disconnected from people or indifferent to their suffering. God was revealed as the opposite, for God had 'witnessed the affliction of his people' and 'heard their cry of complaint.'

God saw the pain and suffering of the people in Egypt: God didn't look away or turn a blind eye. God heard their cries: God didn't pretend not to hear them and walk away. If we read the full story of Moses' call there is no doubt that God empathized with the people who were suffering under their Egyptian oppressors. God saw and heard their cry, and was deeply affected by their suffering. God told Moses, 'I know well what they are suffering ... I have truly noted that the Egyptians are oppressing them.' God knew well what they were suffering, remaining close and connected to their personal story to the extent that God suffered with them.

Survivors often struggle to believe that God has been and remains close to us. It is even more difficult to believe that God has been close to us during the time that we were enduring the suffering of being abused. Perhaps at the time, some of us were crying out to God with all our heart – 'Please do something, God. Look how much I am suffering' – and we may have frantically wondered, 'Why isn't God doing anything?' In great turmoil and despair we may have cried secret tears to God: 'Don't you see what Father X is doing to me? Can't you hear me? Do something, please!' Eventually we may have given up, feeling that our cries were falling on deaf ears. Over the years we have probably made our own conclusions about God from such experiences: 'God is far away from us in our suffering … God doesn't care when we suffer … God is indifferent to our suffering … I cannot count on God in my suffering … I'm not important for God … God doesn't have time for me even when I am suffering', and so on.

The thought may also cross our mind as we read the call of Moses from the Book of Exodus, 'God, why couldn't you have sent me a Moses, someone who could have freed me from my offender?' The sad thing, one that causes God immense suffering and heartache, is that the one who was meant to have been a Moses figure in our story failed and instead turned out to have been precisely the one who carried out the evil offences against us. In the measure that we are able to recall our personal story we may even discover that during the time of the abuse perhaps God did send us others who should have been a Moses figure but instead they chose to turn a blind eye and a deaf ear to what was happening and walked away. Although they walked away from us, God did not. God 'truly noted our oppression' and 'knew well what we were suffering' and God continued to stay close and connected to us and involved in our personal story.

Although we may believe that God is far away from us, it is not true. God is always close to us even though we may not feel his closeness. God did not create us and then leave us here on earth to fend for ourselves and to figure out life on our own (even though we may feel this). The reality is that from the moment we come into existence, God remains close and connected to us. God is not uninterested in our life as some may believe. God is

God suffers with us

so interested in our life that he participates in it 24/7, and has done so from the beginning of our existence. God has never been disconnected from our personal story. God sees, feels, hears and experiences what we are suffering. God empathises with us in our suffering. Our God is not cold but a tender and loving God who feels and suffers for all his children – this is the God who shares our personal story.

God continues to be affected by our life today. God knows very well how we continue to suffer the consequences of the abuse and how it can still oppress us today. God continues to see us and hear our cries and suffer with us. God sends us people who act as Moses figures in our healing journey – counsellors, psychologists, survivor and advocacy support groups,[14] spiritual directors and pastoral care workers, family, medical doctors, specialists, and nurses – all helping to free us from the terrible oppression that we have lived under for years because of the effects of the abuse. Perhaps this can help us understand how God comes down to rescue us, leading us out of the land of oppression from the abuse 'into a good and spacious land' of freedom. It is these gifted and talented people who possess the special skills to support us on our healing journey. However, even if we find ourselves struggling, we are not alone – God still sees, hears and suffers with us. God remains connected to our personal story.

Today, let us try to connect with the God who is not indifferent to us but who sees, hears and suffers with us. When you are struggling with some effect or consequence of the abuse in your life, try to be aware that God sees, hears and suffers with you. You may find a simple conversation with God helpful, such as, 'Do you see what I am struggling with right now, God, and how after all these years the abuse is still affecting me? Can you hear me, God?' Try to allow God to respond to you through the reading from the Book of Exodus: 'I know very well what you are suffering.'

You may even want to go further and ask God, 'How are you going to help me? What are you going to do?' Again, allow God to respond to you through the scripture reading: 'I have come down to rescue you from this

---

[14] A list of some sexual abuse support groups can be found in Appendix 2 of this book.

land and to lead you to a good and spacious land.' If you feel comfortable, you can continue a conversation with God, trying to allow him to always respond to you through Scripture, remembering that it is by reading Scripture that we can learn to listen to God.[15] Otherwise, stop at the point you feel is right for you.

The most important thing is that you can feel comforted, peaceful and consoled knowing that God is very close to you in all your daily experiences (even though you may not feel this closeness, the reality of faith is that God is close to each of us) and that you are not suffering alone, for the God who created you, who gave you life, who loves you and knows you very well, is also suffering with you. God does not want us to feel alone in our suffering but holds our suffering with us, even more so when we feel it is too much for us to handle! It is always helpful to remember that God is God and although our suffering may be too much for us, it is never too great for God! Let us try to remember this when we meet suffering in our life today.

---

[15] Documents of the Second Vatican Council, *Dei Verbum, Dogmatic Constitution on Divine Revelation*, #25.

God does not abandon us

But Zion said, 'The Lord has forsaken me; my Lord has forgotten me.' Can a mother forget her infant, be without tenderness for the child of her womb? Even should she forget you, I will never forget you. See, upon the palms of my hands I have written your name; you are ever before me.

Isaiah 49:14-16

'I WILL NEVER FORGET YOU …' No one likes to be forgotten. Being forgotten, especially by someone we believe cares for us, can make us feel that we are unimportant and unloved; but, what is more, it can also make us feel that we have been abandoned.

These beautiful words from the Book of Isaiah came to the people of Israel after the fall of Babylon at a time when they were undergoing deep desolation and grief. They were a people in exile who were experiencing grave losses – the loss of a place to call home, loss of their possessions, loss of their livelihoods – and in the process they were struggling not to lose the one thing that gave them their true identity, their faith in God.

In this prolonged experience of pain and loss, the people of Israel were searching for God and asking him existential questions, 'Where are you, God? Why have you forgotten us, your people? Why have you abandoned us?' Clearly, the people of Israel did not experience God's presence and closeness in the middle of their misery but instead they felt that God had forsaken and forgotten them. After everything they had been through, it now seemed like the God they had put their faith in and who they believed loved them had abandoned them.

CHILD, ARISE!

I imagine that the experience of the people of Israel resonates with our own experiences as survivors of sexual abuse! At childhood, we begin to experience desolation and grief and as we journey into adulthood so too does our grief. Although we may not have lost our homes, or material possessions, we experience a profound loss of wholeness and well-being that was being quietly yet so violently shattered by sexual abuse and it is evident and felt at all levels: emotionally, psychologically, mentally, spiritually, and physically. Each survivor's list of loss will be unique at each one of these levels but some of the common losses that survivors manage to articulate include loss of dignity, self-esteem, innocence and trust in others.

In our prolonged experience of loss, we too, just like the people of Israel, ask existential questions in a desperate search for answers and an attempt to make sense of our past and present. If we have been brought up with religious beliefs, we turn to God and we call out to him from our deep despair. For survivors who have not been brought up with religious beliefs, it may be the point at which some do begin to search for what they may refer to as 'a Higher Power'.

Whatever context we are coming from, what we bring before God is a sense of abandonment as we desperately and at times angrily cry out, 'Where are you, God?', 'Why have you abandoned us?', 'Have you forgotten us, God, your people?' Even Jesus, just moments before his death, cried out to the Father: 'My God, my God, why have you forsaken me?' (Mark 15:34). It is normal that we ask such existential questions in our experiences of profound pain and suffering. Perhaps next time we do, we can remember that Jesus also knows what it is like to feel abandoned by God.

However, one thing is what we feel and another is our faith. Faith is 'being certain of what we do not see' (Hebrews 11:1). Although we do not always feel God's presence with us, it does not mean that God is not with us. God is with us even as we go through the darkest experiences of grief and loss.

This is the message of this beautiful reading from the Book of Isaiah: 'Can a mother forget her infant, be without tenderness for the child of her womb?' Unfortunately, in cases where the perpetrator has been the father,

God does not abandon us

some survivors do experience abandonment from their mother if she denies that the sexual abuse happened. The experience of being abandoned by a mother and unsupported in the healing process is devastating and distressing for the survivor. So, when God asks us, 'Can a mother forget her infant, be without tenderness for the child of her womb?' our answer may be, 'Yes, God, she can.'

God feels the devastation and distress that this causes us and does not want us to feel abandoned or be 'without tenderness', unsupported and alone. God wants us to know and to be sure that 'even should she forget you, I will never forget you.' How can God forget us? Remember, it was God who 'formed our inmost being' and 'knitted us together in our mother's womb (Psalm 139:13). God created us and gave us life. God loved us first and his love for us is unstoppable. 'Even if our mother forgets us', even if our siblings or our closest friends forget us, God will never forget us. God will always be with us and loving us.

Even though we may have felt abandoned in the past, the reality is that God has never abandoned us in all our pain and grief. God will never forget us, so much so that he has written our name on 'the palms of his hands'. Have you ever written something important down on your hand as a way of remembering it every time you glance down? We are so important and valuable to God that our name is permanently written on God's hand – whenever God looks at his hand what he sees and thinks about is us: 'we are ever before him.' What an awesome thought!

During the times when we feel forgotten, abandoned, alone, let us recall these words and allow God to say them personally to us, putting our name in place of 'Zion':

'But [Zion] said, "The Lord has forsaken me; my Lord has forgotten me. Can a mother forget her infant, be without tenderness for the child of her womb? Even should she forget you, I will never forget you. See upon the palms of my hands, I have written your name; you are ever before me."'

Try to allow God to repeat these words to you until they give you consolation. Believe them with all your heart. Whenever the feelings of being forgotten or abandoned or being alone return, come back to these words and allow God to comfort you again and again. As you continue on with your daily tasks, believe that God has not forgotten you but is with you in everything you do.

God comforts us

'Comfort, give comfort to my people', says your God.
'Speak tenderly to Jerusalem.'

Isaiah 40:1-2a

WHEN ANY PERSON EXPERIENCES grief and pain, regardless of their age, what they naturally long for is to be comforted. Our God, who created us, knows this very well! God knows how vital it is for our human heart to be soothed and consoled when we are distressed and despairing.

Isaiah was one of the major prophets of the Bible.[16] The Book of Isaiah is divided into two parts and this particular scripture verse comes from the second part, referred to as the 'Book of Consolations'. The prophet spoke these words to the people of Israel at a time when they were passing through deep heartache and distress. This reading reveals the heart of a loving God who longs to comfort his people in their distress.

What we feel behind the words of the prophet is God's sense of urgency to reach out to his people and console them, in the same way that a mother would console her young child in distress. We catch a glimpse of the maternal and nurturing side of our loving God who is very attentive to his people. He reveals himself as a shepherd, who 'gathers the lambs in his arms, carrying them gently close to his heart and leading them with care' (Isaiah 40:11). These words connect us with the maternal characteristics of God, one who is warm, loving, gentle, tender, caring, compassionate, protective, consoling,

---

[16] A 'prophet' in the biblical sense of the word was a spokesperson for God. The role of the prophet was to communicate God's message to humankind. The divine message the prophet spoke came through divine illuminations and referred either to the past, present or future. Some of the great prophets in the Bible were Isaiah, Jeremiah, Ezekiel and Daniel.

life-giving. This is the God who reached out to the people of Israel; not an angry, punishing, condemning, cold, vengeful, cruel or brutal God (which may correspond to some of the false images we too have of God). This is a God who desires to speak tenderly to his people, with words straight from a heart full of compassion. God does not want to speak harshly, or in a cold, condemning or merciless tone. God speaks 'tenderly'.

Our God is a comforting and tender God who feels great compassion towards us. Isn't this what we have longed for as survivors – comfort and tenderness? The comfort and tenderness of our compassionate God soothes and consoles us. As young children who were victims, this is what we needed most, yet, because we were forced to keep the abuse a secret by our offenders, we were denied the chance of receiving comfort and tenderness from any other source. While we were experiencing the abuse and the distress was building up in us, all we ever wanted to do was to make ourselves feel better. In an attempt to cope with and survive the trauma we looked for ways to comfort and soothe ourselves (self-soothing).[17] Every time we experienced the intense feelings and emotions that were consequences of the abuse, we would turn to these ways of soothing ourselves.

As adult survivors, we continue to experience our wounds and the constant need to be comforted and consoled. Our God knows our story and feels and suffers with us, and is waiting for us with open arms like a shepherd who wants to gather his lambs in his arms and carry us gently, close to his heart, and lead us with care. God wants to soothe us in our distress with his tender words of love.

When you find yourself getting distressed about something and you experience the need to be comforted or consoled, try to recall that God is waiting for you, like a shepherd, wanting to speak to you tenderly with words of love. How can we listen to God speaking to us tenderly? We listen to God's words when we read Scripture.[18] So, in times of distress, when we read a scripture reading we are listening to God.

---

[17] When a child does not receive comfort or reassurance then they may look for other ways to provide it.

[18] Documents of the Second Vatican Council, *Dei Verbum, Dogmatic Constitution on Divine Revelation*, #25.

God comforts us

When you want God to comfort you with tender words, choose one of the scripture verses that you have found resonates with you and when you read it put your name at the beginning of the verse. As you read these words, remember that it is God who is speaking to you. Re-read the verse over and over again and allow the words to sink into your heart more each time, trying to believe what God is saying to you through the words.

Once these words have offered you some consolation, try to carry them in your heart as you move on to your daily routine and activities. Keep trying to recall them in the silence of your heart as you are walking, or working, or sitting, or lying in bed, and allow God to comfort you through them.

When you next find yourself in distress, you may like to choose a different scripture verse and repeat the steps of this exercise. As you do this over time, you will begin to experience that our God comforts us and speaks tenderly to us with words of love!

God is with us always

'When you pass through the deep waters, I will be with you; and when you pass through the rivers, they will not sweep over you. When you walk through the fire, you will not be burned; the flames will not set you ablaze. For I am the Lord your God, the Holy One of Israel, your Saviour.'

Isaiah 43:1-4

LIFE IS MADE UP OF ALL SORTS of experiences. Some give us joy, pleasure, happiness or excitement while others cause us to suffer and can generate fear, anxiety, desperation or sadness. In these painful experiences we find some consolation knowing that there is someone nearby to strengthen us and help us get through. It scares us in these experiences to feel that we are totally alone.

Yet, no matter how much others genuinely love us and care for us, their intervention will always be limited because they cannot be with us 24/7 and accompany us every step of the way.[19] However, where human intervention is limited, God's presence is unlimited. God can and does walk every step of the way with us through these experiences, even though we may be unaware of it. God is with us 24/7. God has been with us in the past. God is with us now and will be with us always in the future. God has never abandoned us even though we may have felt so at times. Even though everyone else may abandon us, God will always stay with us through the thick and thin of our life.

As survivors walk through the healing process, it is like 'passing through deep waters' in all aspects – emotionally, physically, psychologically and spiritually – and our greatest fear is drowning beneath waters that seem

---

[19] 'Others' refers to those who accompany us externally on our journey: family, friends, counsellors, psychologists, support groups ...

God is with us always

to be so much bigger and more powerful than we are. Initially, we can find that we are struggling with our own denial, and time and time again we try to tell ourselves that we are okay and that we can go on with our life not having to deal with the effects of the abuse. This is our way of by-passing these deep waters and the fears we have, until we find courage within ourselves and make a decision to go through the healing process.

Through these beautiful words from the Book of Isaiah, God promises to be with us every step of the way, even when the deep waters turn into a roaring 'fire' fuelled by our personal circumstances and intense emotions. 'Even when you walk through fire', God says, 'you will not be burned; the flames will not set you ablaze. I am the Lord your God, your Saviour.' No one else can be with us as God is, no matter how much they love us.

Learning to believe this will make a huge difference during our healing process because we will begin to experience that we are never alone. But this will not happen magically: it is the result of exercising our faith in the very real situations of our daily life, especially the 'deep water' experiences. It is then that we call out to God: 'God, look at me, I am in deep water and I am afraid ... where are you?' Allow God to speak to you through the words of Scripture: 'When you pass through deep waters, I will be with you.'

Perhaps you need more reassurance, and God doesn't mind if you ask for confirmation – 'Are you really with me? I can't see you and I can't feel you God?' Allow God to respond to you again through Scripture: 'I am with you as you walk through deep water.' Try to believe God as you would believe someone who you know loves you, and then continue on with your daily routine believing God's words. If at any time you feel the waters are getting deep again, try to let God's word from this scripture verse resound in your heart as you carry on with your activity. Most importantly, believe God's word, even though you may not feel or experience God's presence. This is what it means to practise faith.[20] The more we practise our faith, the more we will experience that we are never alone because God is with us unconditionally throughout our personal story.

---

[20] Faith is the practice of believing without seeing. In John 20:29, Jesus said to Thomas, 'You believe because you have seen me. Blessed are those who believe without seeing me.'

God strengthens us

'Do not fear, for I am with you; do not be dismayed, for I am your God. I will strengthen you and help you; I will uphold you with my righteous right hand ... For I am the Lord, your God, who takes hold of your right hand and says to you, do not fear; I will help you.'

Isaiah 41:10,13

HOW FITTING ARE THESE WORDS for our personal story. God is encouraging us, 'Do not fear ... do not be dismayed' for 'I am with you' and 'I will strengthen you.'

Survivors of sexual abuse are very acquainted with weakness on our journey towards healing. Often on our journey, the experience of being plagued by fear, dismay, disillusionment, loss of courage or apprehension, leaves us feeling as if every little fibre of energy has been sucked out of our body until we have been drained of all our strength and we collapse. Fully immersed in this state of weakness we worry despairingly about how we are going to get up again and keep walking our journey and where our strength is going to come from.

God hears our silent cries for help and responds to us through these words from the Book of Isaiah. First, God says, 'Do not fear, for I am with you; do not be dismayed, for I am your God.' Our God, the all-powerful Creator of heaven and earth, and everything that exists and has life, is with us so we don't need to be afraid or dismayed. God tells us, 'I will strengthen you and help you; I will uphold you with my righteous hand.' God knows when we don't have strength and feel too weak to continue on our journey and says to us, 'I will strengthen you.' In other words, don't worry about

God strengthens us

how you are going to summon up the energy and strength to keep walking; 'I will strengthen you and help you. I will uphold you with my right hand.., for I am the Lord, your God, who takes hold of your right hand and says to you, do not fear, I will help you.'

We are not alone in our weakness; our all-powerful God is with us, not passively but actively – upholding us with his right hand and taking hold of us. Often survivors, because of our experiences of the past, are afraid to accept a helping hand and risk being hurt or betrayed again. Perhaps we have rejected a helping hand in the past and preferred to try and get through our struggles on our own.

We may find that we have exactly the same reaction when God extends his hand to us and says, 'I will strengthen and help you.' But there is a difference; the hand that is offered to us is not a human hand – one that is able to hurt, harm, damage and destroy when evil is at work – but it is the hand of God,[21] a hand of Love (1 John 4:8) that knows only how to genuinely love us.

God's hand strengthens us and empowers us to get back up on our feet again and not to let fear control us or have the last word in our lives. Our God is with us to help us and we don't need to be afraid. God's hand is a mighty hand and the strongest hand that we will ever be offered in life, but God will leave us free to take it or to reject it. God does not demand or exert any force on us and if we do reject it, it will remain extended to us in case we change our mind in the future.

When we are weakened by fear or dismay, let us remember that God's hand is always extended to us. God says to us personally, 'Do not fear ... do not be dismayed ... I will strengthen you and help you.' God offers us his strength, a strength beyond human strength, and assures us, 'I am with you ... I will take hold of you ... I will help you.'

---

[21] I am in no way implying all human help should be mistrusted. There are many good people who are genuine in offering us help and showing concern for our welfare, especially family, close friends, counsellors, psychologists, doctors, those who accompany us spiritually. I am referring here to the mistrust we may experience when it comes to accepting human help that is born from having been sexually abused by someone we trusted which is why I make reference to 'when evil is at work'.

If we want, we can be strong again with God's help! The more we learn to trust God and to accept God's helping hand, the more we will experience that 'we will find new strength'– a strength that does not diminish but that enables us to 'run and not grow weary' and 'walk and not faint' (Isaiah 40:31).

To the end of our life

'I will be your God throughout your life time – until your hair is white with age. I made you, and I will care for you. I will carry you along and save you.'
Isaiah 46:4

HOW REASSURING ARE THESE WORDS from the Book of Isaiah! God promises to be with us faithfully right to the end of our personal story, 'I will be your God throughout your life time, until your hair is white with age.'

Generally, we are afraid of being abandoned, whether it is by a spouse, a parent, a sibling, a child, a friend or someone who has been a major support for us. Perhaps some survivors have found that, when they finally plucked up the courage to reveal to someone they had been sexually abused – someone they felt they could trust and expect support from – they were shattered by the shocking response of not being believed or supported and then being abandoned altogether by the person. Perhaps people who initially showed care and support gradually withdrew, leaving them feeling abandoned.

God, however, gives us the security of his unfailing and unconditional presence right to the end of our life: 'I made you, and I will care for you.' The God who gave us life and initiated our personal story tells us, 'I will care for you.' God's care will sustain us throughout our lifetime and often we will experience that care 'through cords of human kindness.'[22] These cords of human kindness may be healthcare professionals, support workers, advocacy groups, spiritual and pastoral care workers, or social and community

---

[22] See Hosea 11:4: 'I led them with cords of human kindness, with ties of love. To them I was like one who lifts a little child to the cheek, and I bent down to feed them.'

workers. Through their care we can experience God 'carrying us along' on our journey and 'saving us' time and time again.

But if there are times in our life when these cords of human kindness are lacking, God continues to care for us by 'bending down to feed us' through the Word of Scripture – speaking to us tenderly with words that nourish us spiritually and renew us with energy, courage and hope for our journey. As God speaks to us, we feel ourselves carried along our way, through the 'deep and stormy waters',[23] and through the 'fires',[24] over what are seemingly high mountains and hills for us,[25] through darkness[26] right until our 'hair is white with age'.

Yes, God is with us right to the end of our life! Even in death, we can have the security that God will not abandon us.[27] As our personal story on earth draws to a close, God will continue to carry us along safely into eternity where we can look forward to a new life in God's presence.

This is what God invites us to believe today. Let us allow God to speak to us in our personal circumstances. Perhaps you find yourself thinking, 'God, why should I go through another day of trying to face my pain? What is the worth of it all? What for? Who really cares? Who cares if I get through all the obstacles of today?'

In these circumstances, God's words from the Scripture can fill us with reassurance and security: 'I made you and I will care for you.' Try to listen to God speaking deeply in your heart, saying, 'I care for you today, I care that you get through all your obstacles, I care when you experience pain. I care for you and I will carry you along. Be sure of it.'

---

[23] See Isaiah 43:2 and Matthew 14:25-27: 'And in the fourth watch of the night Jesus came to them, walking on the sea. But when the disciples saw him walking on the sea, they were terrified, and said, "It is a ghost!" and they cried out in fear. But immediately Jesus spoke to them, saying, "Take heart; it is I. Do not be afraid."'

[24] Isaiah 43:2.

[25] Matthew 17:1: 'After six days, Jesus took with him Peter, James and John the brother of James, and led them up a high mountain by themselves.'

[26] Psalm 23:4: 'Even when I walk through the darkest valley, I fear no danger because you are with me. Your rod and your staff – they protect me.'

[27] Romans 8:38: 'For I am convinced that neither death nor life, neither angels nor demons, neither the present nor the future, nor any powers, neither height nor depth, nor anything else in all creation, will be able to separate us from the love of God that is in Christ Jesus our Lord.'

Through the gift of Jesus

God so loved the world, that he gave his one and only Son, that whoever believes in him shall not perish but have eternal life.

John 3:16

THE LAST THING THAT GOD EVER WANTS for any of us is to perish. The God we put our faith in is a God of life, not death, and what God desires for us most is that we live forever. God accomplishes his utmost wish for us through the gift of Jesus, his one and only Son.

In the person of Jesus, God became flesh and blood and took on our humanity so that he could dwell with us.[28] Through Jesus, God knows what it is like to be human[29] and to experience joy and gladness,[30] suffering,[31] exhaustion,[32] anger,[33] betrayal by a close friend,[34] hunger,[35] abuse and

---

[28] John 1:14: 'And the Word became flesh and dwelt among us.'
[29] Hebrews 2:17: 'For this reason he had to be made like them, fully human in every way…'
[30] Luke 10:21: 'At that time Jesus, full of joy through the Holy Spirit, said, "I praise you, Father, Lord of heaven and earth, because you have hidden these things from the wise and learned, and revealed them to little children."'
[31] Mark 14:3: '"Abba, Father", he cried out, "everything is possible for you. Please take this cup of suffering away from me. Yet I want your will to be done, not mine."'
[32] John 4:6: 'Jacob's well was there, and Jesus, tired as he was from the journey, sat down by the well.'
[33] John 2:15: 'And when he had made a scourge of small cords, he drove them all out of the temple, and the sheep, and the oxen; and poured out the changers' money, and overthrew the tables.'
[34] Matthew 26:49: 'He came to Jesus, and said, "Hail, master"; and kissed him.'
[35] Luke 24:41: 'And while they still did not believe it because of joy and amazement, he asked them, "Do you have anything here to eat?"'

condemnation,[36] and so on. No matter what emotion or experience we are dealing with, God understands our humanity through and in the person of Jesus. God understands the discomforts of our human experiences and even understands our fear of perishing better than anyone else.

In this verse from the Gospel of St John, God promises that, through the gift of Jesus, 'we shall not perish but have eternal life.' God does not give us Jesus to condemn or judge us,[37] or to kill and destroy us[38] but, on the contrary, so that we can have life and have it to the full.[39] However, people may have misconceived perceptions of Jesus and these can become an obstacle for welcoming the gift of his presence into their life.

Survivors of abuse are among those who can have these misconceived perceptions, and this is even more so when a survivor has been abused by a member of the clergy. How is it possible for us to believe that God does not want to condemn, destroy, or even kill us, if someone who claimed to be a servant of God has condemned us to a life sentence of destruction and spiritual death through the act of sexual abuse?

As mentioned earlier, it is extremely difficult for survivors to disassociate the perpetrator of the abuse from God or Jesus, especially in the case where he was a priest or other member of the clergy, since our own faith formation as young children taught us that the two (priest and God) are connected – the whole reason why we trusted the perpetrator in the first place. It is not difficult to understand how a survivor's own faith and spirituality is

---

[36] Luke 23:33-39: 'When they came to the place called The Skull, there they crucified him and the criminals, one on the right and the other on the left. But Jesus was saying, "Father, forgive them; for they do not know what they are doing." And they cast lots, dividing up his garments among themselves. And the people stood by, looking on. And even the rulers were sneering at him, saying, 'He saved others; let him save himself if this is the Christ of God, his Chosen One.' The soldiers also mocked him, coming up to him, offering him sour wine, and saying, 'If you are the King of the Jews, save yourself!' Now there was also an inscription above him, 'THIS IS THE KING OF THE JEWS.' One of the criminals who were hanged there was hurling abuse at Him, saying, 'Are you not the Christ? Save yourself and us!'

[37] John 3:17 'For God did not send his Son into the world to condemn the world, but to save the world through him.'

[38] John 10:10 'The thief comes only to steal and kill and destroy; I have come that they may have life, and have it to the full.'

[39] John 10:10.

Through the gift of Jesus

gravely shattered, devastated and damaged as a consequence of sexual abuse at the hands of a member of the clergy.

Trying to regain and reclaim our faith in God and heal spiritually is not an easy labour – in fact it is extremely painstaking – but it is possible. It requires attentiveness to what we think, feel and believe when we try to engage with God, whether that be through Scripture, nature, song or praise. If we become aware that we think, feel or believe that God is and must be like our perpetrator, saying to God 'I can't trust you!' or 'I can't believe that you want the best for me', then we need to stop and do the labour of consciously undoing that association in our mind and heart.

First, we need to acknowledge to ourselves: 'No! My perpetrator was like that, but I want to believe that God is *not* like that. God is different because God is Love. After we have acknowledged this in our heart we can acknowledge it to God by being honest and saying, 'God, I am finding it hard to trust you because I think you are like my perpetrator. But I want to believe that you are different.' Or, 'I am finding it hard to believe that you want the best for me, God, because that's what my perpetrator told me. But I know that you are not my perpetrator, and that you are God and I want to believe that you do want the best for me.'

When we try to become aware of what is going on within us as we try to engage with God, maybe we will be surprised to discover that we are constantly doing these transferences[40] with God and associating God with our perpetrator. If we want to begin to heal our relationship with God, then each time we become aware of this, we are invited to consciously do the labour of undoing that association in our mind and heart and separating our perpetrator from God because God and our perpetrator are very different.

This labour will eventually be fruitful, because when we can change the way we think about God and the image we have of God then we will find that our faith in God will begin to grow. But we need to be patient and not expect that this is going to happen overnight. Initially, we may feel

---

[40] See footnote 6, page 41.

as though nothing is happening and that it is all fruitless, but over time we will experience the fruit of God's grace working in us as we do this labour of faith.[41]

Perhaps, as we spend time reflecting on this verse from St John's gospel, we will find that we are struggling with these transferences. Perhaps we will find ourselves thinking, 'How can I believe that you do not want me to perish, God? Fr X who was supposed to be like you did a terrible thing to me and since that time I have been perishing! How can I believe in you?' This is when we are invited to do the labour of undoing the association we are making in our mind.

First, we need to acknowledge it to ourselves: 'My perpetrator and God are different. Fr X is not God and God is not Fr X. Father X did something to me to make me perish, not God.' Second, we need to acknowledge it to God: 'God, I need to believe that you and Father X are different. He was supposed to be like you and what he did to me caused me to perish, so now I find it hard to believe in you. I really want to believe that you will not do anything to me to cause me to perish, but I am struggling.'

Without doing this labour, we will find it extremely difficult to have a heart-to-heart connection with God. However, as we begin to acknowledge our transferences and work through these thoughts in our mind (by acknowledging what belongs to our perpetrator and what belongs to God) we will also learn how to listen to the personal message God is speaking to us through his Word.

For example, this scripture passage has a beautiful message, but we will only be able to appreciate the wealth of it if we can get past our transferences. God promises us that if we believe in Jesus we will not perish but have eternal life. This is a message that is very relevant to survivors of sexual abuse. We often feel we are going to perish, but God is saying to us through this verse, 'I have loved you so much that I have given you the gift of my Son, Jesus. If you believe in him you will not perish.' It is a call to believe God deeply – believe God wants you to have life and not to perish: 'You will not

---

[41] Philippians 2:13: '... for it is God who works in you to will and to act in order to fulfil his good purpose.'

Through the gift of Jesus

perish in despair, grief, disappointment, anger, rage, loneliness, negative thoughts, exhaustion or tragedy, but you will have life forever.'

What a promise God makes us! Whenever we are afraid of perishing, God says to us, 'You will not perish.' It is a word that will nurture us existentially if we can come to believe in it. Let us recall these words of God in times when we feel we are perishing and try to believe that through the gift of Jesus we will have life.

*They shall mount up
with wings like eagles,
they shall run
and not be weary,
they shall walk
and not be faint.*

                    Isaiah 40:31

PART II

Working through our issues with a loving God

Time out

TAKING TIME OUT TO CARE for ourselves and look after our own needs is very important. Yet, through my conversations with survivors of abuse, it is noticeably something that we find difficult to do. At the time of the abuse, many of us were only young children so we did not learn how to care for ourselves, and to be self-nurturing. Taking time out (especially from our perpetrator) would have been impossible and we certainly couldn't express our need for it. On the contrary, most of us may well and truly have found that, just when we thought we had reached our coping limit, it was stretched a little further by the continuing offences of the perpetrator.

By the time we are adults, we can be so accustomed to stretching ourselves that we struggle to identify our own limits. We may not know the point at which we need to say to ourselves and to others, 'This is as far as I can go right now!' or 'I cannot go beyond this point!' Learning to identify our physical, emotional and psychological limits is essential in learning to voice the call for time out.

Taking time out is about being self-nurturing and self-loving. Learning to be nurturing and loving with ourselves first is also the key for learning how to nurture and love others. Some survivors I have accompanied have equated taking time out to being selfish or ego-centred and they express feeling guilty when taking time out. Others have said that they don't take time out because they don't feel they deserve it or are worthy of it. Others have said that they avoid time out because they perceive that this is when their issues may surface (or re-surface) so they choose to keep on going. My case was that I didn't know how to take time out because I never learnt to as I developed into adulthood.

Taking time out should not be about whether we feel we deserve it, and it certainly should not be confused with being selfish. Time out is about taking care of ourselves and responding to our personal needs. If we do not learn to take care of ourselves and continue pushing ourselves beyond our limits we run the risk of collapsing with exhaustion from an overload of stress on our bodies. Taking time out is not only a precautionary measure but it is essential for our general well-being.

Taking time out allows us to process and assimilate what is happening in our life. It gives us a space to acknowledge, accept and embrace whatever it is that is causing us stress, as well as giving ourselves the space we need to be re-energized, renewed and re-created. Time out is essential.

Jesus understood the importance of taking time out very well. Often, Jesus retreats (sometimes alone and at other times with his disciples) from the demands of huge crowds that followed him, seeking to find a quiet spot where he could pray and process his life experiences with his Father. In reality, taking time out was so essential for Jesus that it was an integral part of his mission and ministry.

Jesus can teach us how to identify our limits and how to take care of ourselves by taking time out. In the two scripture readings below, we see Jesus taking time out with his disciples.

The scripture reading

At daybreak, Jesus left and went to a deserted place. The crowds went looking for him and when they came to him they tried to prevent him from leaving. But he said to them, 'To the other towns also I must proclaim the Good News of the Kingdom of God because for this purpose I have been sent.'

Luke 4:42-43

We know from the passage prior to this (Luke 4:40-41) that the night before was a very busy one for Jesus. He had cured many sick people who were brought to him. We can imagine that as Jesus attended to these people he would have listened to many stories of great sadness and suffering. There is no doubt that, as he listened to the people, he was also deeply affected by their pain. Perhaps, as he listened to their stories, a deeper restlessness was stirred in his heart, perhaps what they had shared with him led him to ask some deeper questions about his own calling in life, or perhaps making himself available to them had come with some sort of personal cost whether physical or emotional.

Whatever went on within Jesus' heart the previous night, it is very interesting to see the first thing Jesus does the next morning. He does not get up and, like a machine, carry on with his ministry but at daybreak he 'left and went to a deserted place' where he knew he would not be disturbed.

Before carrying on with his ministry, Jesus feels the need to take time out. He goes to a deserted place to pray and converse with God his Father. You may want to ask Jesus in your prayer, 'Why did you take time out to pray? … Why was it important for you to do it? … What did you talk about with the Father during your time out?'

By the time the searching crowds find Jesus, he is not only renewed but he also has some new light and clarity about the direction of his life and what he was being called to do: 'To the other towns also I must proclaim the Good News of the Kingdom of God because for this purpose I have been sent.'

When we too are deeply affected and stirred up by events or encounters in our life or when we experience that something we do comes with a big personal cost to ourselves either physically, emotionally, mentally or psychologically, Jesus invites us to take time out to pray just as he did.

Taking time out for Jesus meant coming away from the stresses and demands of his ministry and finding a new and quiet space where he would be uninterrupted and alone to attend to and find response to the deeper questions in his heart through prayer.

Taking time out for us will also mean coming away from whatever we find demanding and stressful and going to a new and tranquil space where we can be quiet and uninterrupted. Perhaps it will be a space in nature where we feel safe, or a house we can retreat to, or somewhere in the country, or by the sea, or simply taking a long and gentle walk. In this space we too can attend to and find response to the deeper questions in our heart.

Not only will we come away from taking time out feeling renewed and re-energized, but like Jesus we may even experience some new light and

Time out

clarity about a particular situation we are facing or understand a new direction we are being called to take.

Praying the scripture reading

1. Be still and try to be aware of God's presence in you.
2. As you read the Word, try to imagine the scene. It is daybreak and Jesus is getting up and leaving where he is ... You follow him to see where he is going ... Then you stop and contemplate Jesus as he prays.
3. As you imagine the scene, what is it about Jesus that calls your attention? It may be his ability to rise early; it may be the freedom he has to just leave everything behind and go; it may be the fact that he looks for a 'deserted place' and not a busy place ...
4. Try to identify what this evokes in you – feelings, questions, thoughts, reactions. Try to begin a conversation with Jesus about this. For example, 'What drove you to take time out? Did you reach a personal limit? Was there some restlessness in your heart?' Or, 'Jesus, why did you choose to leave at daybreak? Why not a little later?' Or, 'Why did you find such a deserted spot to take time out?' Or, 'What was going on in your heart in that deserted spot? What were you sharing about with your Father in prayer?' Try to listen to Jesus' response in your heart.
5. You may like to ask Jesus: 'Is there something you are trying to communicate to me about taking time out through this scripture reading?' Try to listen to Jesus' response through his Word. You may like to share with Jesus what it is that prevents you from taking time out, or what makes it difficult for you to do so. After you have shared this, try to listen to Jesus' response.
6. At the end of your prayer, try to make some resolutions with Jesus around taking time out. You may like to ask him, 'How are you inviting to me take time out? When do I need to take time out?'
7. As you go on with your daily life, try to remember this Word of

Jesus in your heart, especially during the times when you feel yourself reaching your limit. It is then that Jesus invites you to put this scripture reading into practice.

The scripture reading

The apostles gathered together with Jesus and reported all they had done and taught. He said to them, 'Come away by yourselves to a deserted place and rest a while.' People were coming and going in great numbers and they had no opportunity even to eat. So they went off in the boat by themselves to a deserted place.

Mark 6:30-32

The scripture reading prior to this one gives an account of the death of Jesus' cousin, John the Baptist, who was beheaded under the order of King Herod (Mark 6:17-29). So we can imagine that as Jesus' apostles gathered together with him part of their report was giving Jesus the sad and disturbing news of his cousin's beheading and burial. We can certainly imagine that Jesus would have been deeply affected and grieved by this news.

Nevertheless, even though Jesus is sad, he remains sensitive to the needs of his disciples. He sees that they are tired and is aware that they have not even had time to eat because they have been so busy attending to the needs of the crowds. Jesus knows that his disciples have reached their limit.

We see in Jesus a beautiful display of his humanity and compassion. He does not push his disciples beyond their limit, expecting them to keep soldiering on and working like machines. Jesus makes the call for time out for them, inviting them to 'Come away to a deserted place to rest a while.' It is without doubt that Jesus also would have felt the need to have some time and space to process the tragic death of his cousin. Jesus invites his disciples to recognize their own limits and to learn to take time out to nurture and care for their physical, spiritual and emotional needs.

Jesus invites us to learn to do the same when he says to us today: 'Come away to a deserted place to rest a while'. It is a lesson in self-care and learning to have a healthy self-love. If we neglect this in our own journey, we will find it very difficult to care for and love others properly.

So when we experience that we have reached our limit, let us recall these words of scripture and Jesus' invitation.

Praying the scripture reading

1. Be still and try to be aware of God's presence in you.
2. As you read the Word, try to imagine the scene. Perhaps you may imagine that you are one of the apostles coming back to Jesus to report all the things that you have been doing. Imagine Jesus and how he is as you come towards him. What do you notice about Jesus?
3. Try to be aware of what is happening within your heart as you imagine this scenario. Perhaps you are feeling excited as you come to Jesus, or it could be that you are feeling exhausted from all that you have done, perhaps you are coming to Jesus stressed and anxious or tense about a current situation in your life. When you notice Jesus, do you feel happy or peaceful? Once you identify what you are feeling, try to begin a conversation with Jesus about this. For example, 'Jesus, why are you so excited to see me?' Or, 'Why are you patiently waiting for me to hear about what I have done?' Or, 'Jesus, I am so stressed lately about what is happening in my life.' Or, 'Jesus, I believe I have reached my limit with this situation because …' In all that you share with Jesus, allow him to speak and try to listen to him.
4. Now imagine the scene again … Jesus stands in front of you and says to you personally, 'Come away by yourself to a deserted place and rest a while.' What is it about Jesus that calls your attention as he invites you to take some time out? It may be his sensitivity to what you are experiencing, his caring attitude, the fact that he knows what you need and are longing for, or his gentleness and love. This may stir questions or thoughts or reactions in you that you may like to share with Jesus. For example, 'Why do you care

about me Jesus?' Or, 'How do you know that I need time out? Have you seen me reaching my limit? What do I do that tells you this? Is it in the way I react or behave?' Try to listen to Jesus' response in your heart. You may want to write down your conversation.

5. When you hear from Jesus, 'Come away by yourself to a deserted place and rest a while', notice how you react. What is it that you feel? Afraid, hesitant, insecure, happy, yearning for what is being offered by Jesus? Try to have an honest conversation with Jesus about it. For example, 'Jesus, I know that you are inviting me to take time out because you care for me, but when I feel that people want to care for me I find it difficult to trust.' Or, 'Jesus, I am so happy that you are inviting me to take time out with you, but can you tell me first where this 'deserted place' is? Will I be safe? You know how I need to feel safe!' Try to wait and listen to Jesus' response to you.

6. You may like to ask Jesus, 'Is there something you are trying to communicate to me about taking time out through this scripture reading? For example, it may be to take time out to pray and spend time with Jesus processing your experiences.

7. As you finish prayer, try to make some resolutions with Jesus around the theme of taking time out. When will you do it; how will you do; what will you do?

8. As you go on with your daily life, try to hold this Word of Jesus in your heart, especially during the times when you feel yourself reaching your limit. It is then that Jesus invites you to put this scripture reading into practice.

The scripture experienced in my life

From time to time my auto-immune disorder unexpectedly flares up, and during these periods deep fatigue kicks in and I have no other choice but to rest. Normally, my body would respond well to this and in a given time

Time out

I would be back on my feet again and carrying out my apostolic ministry which is quite full on.

However, this time it was different. I experienced an intense flare where it became clear to me that I had reached a physical limit. I was totally fatigued and exhausted as I tried to deal with a whole array of symptoms that sent me crashing to the ground. It was like my body was crying out to me 'Stop! You have to seriously stop!' and all the red light signals around me were flashing. I knew the time had come for me to heed this call otherwise my health was going to pay the consequences.

I prayed this scripture reading and Jesus' voice was loud and clear, 'Come away by yourself and rest a while!' Jesus had invited to me to do this on many occasions in the past, but this invitation was distinct. Jesus was not inviting me to come away for a few hours or for a couple of days to retreat with him in prayer. He was inviting me to take a much longer period of time out from the stresses and demands of my apostolic ministry and the intensive and fast paced life-style that I had been living for so many years, so that I could take care of my own health needs and regenerate physically and spiritually.

Perhaps it would have been easy for another person to ask for time out. For me, it was one of the most difficult things I have ever had to ask for. Time away from my community and my ministry meant time away from what had given me so much joy and meaning for the past twenty-two years. Coming away from this was not an easy experience at all. On the other hand, asking my religious leader for some time away because of health reasons helped me to acknowledge, accept and embrace that I had reached my physical limits.

By heeding Jesus' call, I have been able to discover at a deeper level the immensity of God's love and tender care. Not only does God understand our human limitations but God wants to attend to us by inviting us to come away and take some time to rest.

Jesus is not like some bosses or managers in today's workplace who push their colleagues to the limit, only concerned about the amount of work that is produced. Jesus is the opposite. He does not look at any person for what he can get out of them or for what they can produce: he looks at us to see what we need and seeing what we need he loves and cares for us. Taking time out has reaffirmed this experience in my life over and over again!

The scripture experienced in your life

Were you able to experience the scripture reading in your life today? If so, how did this happen? You may like to write down your own account.

Keeping faith as we process trauma

PROCESSING THE MEMORIES and trauma of childhood sexual abuse is a very overwhelming experience for any survivor. Although our present circumstances and contexts may be very different to those of our childhood, and even though we may be surrounded by people who love and support us, when our body remembers the trauma of the sexual abuse, it is as though we are reliving the event in all its aspects – physically, emotionally and psychologically. For any survivor, this is a terrifying experience and it is not unusual in the process to feel or think, 'I must be going crazy' or 'I think I'm losing it!'

When my memories of the sexual abuse first began, on many occasions I would say to my psychologist, 'I think I'm going insane!' At the time, I was a missionary immersed in full-time ministry, so I had commitments and responsibilities. Externally, the adult in me managed to function but, internally, the child in me was in deep distress. It was as though I was living two worlds at the same time – the world of the functioning adult and the world of the child who was in turmoil and chaos and deeply distressed. At times, it reached a point where even though the adult wanted to function the child was stronger and more dominant. The child was saying to the adult, 'I need you to listen to me and to attend to me and to understand what it was like for me physically, emotionally and psychologically. I could never tell anyone but I feel it's safe to tell you now. Can you have compassion and gentleness with me?'

If the adult part of us chooses to cooperate with the child in us, survivors may experience that there are days when the child comes to the forefront of our lives. When this happens, we can feel that we have lost or are losing the adult part of ourselves. Our whole world is thrown into the chaos of the child who was abused and is reliving the fear, silence, lack of trust, isolation, anxiety, desperation, hurt and anger. For a while we feel as though we are stuck again in this part of our past childhood, never to recover the adult. What is happening is that this part of our past childhood trauma is crying out to be integrated into our present life. It is like the child saying to the adult, 'I feel safe now to let you know about me!' Believe it or not, if we are on this path, crazy as it may seem, we are on the path to healing. We are not on the road to insanity but on the road to sanity.

One of the greatest tools that we can have in this process is the gift of faith, although we will have days when we experience that we are unbelieving and losing faith. However, Jesus never loses faith in us. He remains very close to us, whether we feel his presence or not. He walks with us as we process our past trauma and work to integrate it in our lives as adults, and he will strengthen our faith on this journey just as he did with the father of the young boy in the scripture passage below.

The scripture reading

Immediately on seeing Jesus, the whole crowd was utterly amazed. They ran up to him and greeted him. He asked them, 'What are you arguing about with them?' Someone from the crowd answered him, 'Teacher, I have brought to you my son possessed by a mute spirit. Wherever it seizes him, it throws him down; he foams at the mouth, grinds his teeth, and becomes rigid. I asked your disciples to drive it out, but they were unable to do so.' They brought the boy to him. And when he saw him, the spirit immediately threw the boy into convulsions. As he fell to the ground, he began to roll around and foam at the mouth. Then he questioned his father, 'How long has this been happening to him?' He replied, 'Since childhood. It has often thrown him into the fire and into water to kill him — but if you can do anything, have compassion on us and help us.' Jesus said to him, 'If you can! Everything is possible to the one who has faith.' Then the boy's father cried out, 'I do believe, help my unbelief!'

Keeping faith as we process trauma

Jesus, on seeing a crowd rapidly gathering, rebuked the unclean spirit and said to it, 'Mute and deaf spirit, I command you: come out of him and never enter him again!' Shouting and throwing the boy into convulsions, it came out. He became like a corpse, which caused many to say, 'He is dead!' But Jesus took him by the hand, raised him and he stood up.'

Mark 9:15-18, 20-27

I believe the story of this son and his father will strike a chord with all survivors of sexual abuse. As the child in me re-lived the trauma of the abuse, I could certainly feel identified with the son in the reading who experiences a 'mute spirit'. Family and friends can be around us at the time, trying to talk to us, even calling us by my name: 'Can you hear me?' We can hear them externally but we are not present to them because the child in us is reliving something of the past. It is as if the world of our past takes over the present and, even though the adult part of us wants to speak out, we cannot because it is the child now who has come to the forefront. Perhaps even the child in us wants to speak out and break the silence but cannot.

The child in us has been temporarily seized again by the power and control of the abuse. The child in us is 'thrown down', as the trauma surfaces just as with the boy in the reading. The child starts to feel what it did at the time of the abuse – dirty, shameful and guilty all over again. The child in us can begin to 'foam at the mouth' like the boy in the reading. We can try to speak to those who love and support us but we can't articulate anything. Our speech becomes that of a young child struggling to put two words together. We can sit around or lie in bed at night 'grinding our teeth' like a young frightened and terrified child. We can become 'rigid' and 'numb' as a way of protecting ourselves from feeling more hurt or pain.

Perhaps as the child in us comes out, so do the behaviours of the child during the time of the abuse, whether it was rolling on the ground in despair, rocking for some consolation, fainting and falling to the ground because of dizziness and disorientation. If the child began to self-harm during the abuse, then we can once again find ourselves in this destructive behaviour. So, even though we do not know what caused the boy in the reading to be like this, what the boy experienced is very close to home for survivors of sexual abuse.

Then there is the father in this story, who experienced helplessness, despair and hopelessness. Aren't these feelings also very real for survivors? Not only do they arise in the process of assimilating trauma but they may also re-surface as we go through other events during our life. Perhaps this father is like the adult part of us that is trying to make sense of what is happening during the process and struggling to believe that healing will eventuate.

In the reading, Jesus stops and listens to what the father has to say to him about his son. When Jesus sees the son, he is moved with compassion and asks the father 'How long has this been happening to him?' 'Since childhood', the father answers, and he shares some more detail with Jesus. In the conversation, Jesus attends to the father's faith only after the father asks him to help his unbelieving side. It is at this point that Jesus turns to the son and asks the mute spirit to come out of the boy. At that, it looks like the boy is getting worse as he begins shouting and going into convulsions. He is even described as looking like a corpse. Doesn't this process resonate with us? At times we feel as though we are getting worse or going backwards though we are actually getting better. It is in this state of appearing dead that Jesus takes the boy by the hand, raises him up and helps him to stand on his feet.

When we pray this reading today, we may find that we identify with both the father and the son. Perhaps the father represents the adult part of us that wants healing but needs more faith and perhaps the son represents the child in us that is experiencing the very real effects and consequences of the trauma of the abuse. Perhaps the adult part of you can initially come to Jesus today talking to him about the experience of your inner child and how you view what happens to your child through your adult eyes. Perhaps Jesus will also say to you, 'How long has this been happening?' In other words, 'How long have you been going through this suffering? How long have you been enduring this?' Jesus cares about what you are suffering. He wants to listen to you. Talk to him honestly.

Perhaps the adult part of you will start to plead with Jesus just as this father did: 'If you can do anything, have compassion on us and help us!' You

Keeping faith as we process trauma

may get surprised because Jesus may get taken aback a little as he did with the father and he may also say to you 'If you can!' Of course Jesus can do something for the father! Of course Jesus will have compassion with both this father and son and help them. But what is essential is that the father believes in Jesus and has faith in him. Perhaps after so many years of watching his son suffer and feeling helpless, the father is losing faith but it is precisely at this time when the man's faith is lacking that Jesus challenges him and says, 'Everything is possible for the one who has faith!', to which the father responds, 'I do believe! Help my unbelief!'

As we relive the trauma, no doubt there will be days when we too feel we are losing our faith in Jesus because we feel the suffering has been going on for too long and we can't take any more. But if we open up our hearts to Jesus as this father did and beg him – 'I do believe but help my unbelief!' – Jesus will increase our faith in him so that we can believe that he is much more powerful than our past and the abuse we suffered as children.

Jesus will then empower the child in us with his very same power. He will ask whatever is distressing the child in us to come out and not to enter us again. If it is a terrifying memory, he will ask it to come out and not to enter us again, if it be a deep despair, he will ask it to come out and not to enter us again. In the process of prayer, we may get exhausted and finish up looking like we are dead but Jesus will not leave us for dead for he came so that we 'have life and have it to the full' (John 10:10). He will take the hand of our child and help us to get up and stand on our feet. Seeing and experiencing this, our faith in Jesus will increase.

No matter how many times the child in us comes to the forefront, reliving the trauma of the past, Jesus will not abandon us but will give us the strength to get up and stand on our faith. He will help us to keep our faith in him as we continue to process the trauma in our life.

Praying the scripture reading

1. Try to be aware of Jesus' presence with you and, as you read the reading very slowly, image the scene unfolding.

2. Which character in the reading resonates with you: the father, the son, or perhaps both? If it is the father, try to put yourself in the shoes of the father (that is, imagine that you are presenting the trauma of your 'child' (from your childhood) to Jesus. Try to be aware of what you are feeling (helplessness, frustration, hopelessness …) and let Jesus know this.
3. If you identify more with the son who is experiencing the power of the 'mute spirit' in his flesh and blood (for us it is the power of the memory of the abuse), come to Jesus as you are and tell him your situation just as you experience it. For example, 'Look at me, Jesus! I feel a mess. I can't sleep at night because I am so frightened. I find that I can't trust anyone because I am afraid that they may hurt me. I just want to be alone and isolated from everyone because it's the only time I feel safe …'
4. Let Jesus respond to you through his Word. If you identify with the father, let Jesus say to you the words he said to the father: 'Everything is possible for the one who has faith.' Try to continue a conversation with Jesus around this.
5. Likewise, if you identify with the son, try to imagine Jesus taking you tenderly by the hand and raising you to your feet. Express yourself with Jesus from your truth and reality. If you are frightened to take his hand, tell him what you feel and listen to what he has to say. Experience how free Jesus will allow you to be. Let Jesus reassure you of his genuine love that wants you to be well and to have fullness of life.
6. Try to experience how Jesus' Word can empower you and increase your faith.
7. As you prepare to continue your daily routine, try to keep the words from this reading in your heart. If you find yourself low in faith during the day or struggling with traumatic memories, recall this Word and let Jesus empower you.

Keeping faith as we process trauma

The scripture experienced in my life

As I was getting ready for an appointment, I heard a knock at the door. I thought it may have been my brother coming to visit, so I called out his name asking if it was him. The voice that came from behind the door was not his but instead a man I was not familiar with. He said he was from the gas company and that he needed to change the gas meter.

At the time, I was home alone and I began to have terrible memories of when my perpetrator forced himself through the door of my bedroom. I was no longer the adult but the extremely frightened and paralysed teenager who was trying to keep her perpetrator outside. I knew I needed to say something to the man. I had to force the words out of my mouth: 'I'm sorry, but I have not received any letter or phone call about the gas meter. Please get the office to call me to arrange a time.' At least then I could arrange for someone to be home with me next time he came around. He left very upset. I was a mess at all levels.

This incident in the present had taken me right back to a very traumatic memory. I just wanted to lock myself in my room where I could feel safe from the world. Instead, I stopped and remembered this reading. As I was sitting in the lounge chair, with my arms and legs trembling like jelly, I imagined Jesus saying to me, 'Fear, come out of her and don't enter her again! … Helplessness, come out of her and don't enter her again!' and I told Jesus, 'But I still feel afraid!' Jesus kept repeating his words and eventually he invited me: 'Stand up!' I did. I really experienced that I was not alone but that Jesus was with me and helping me in that very moment. I got to my feet and continued to get ready for my appointment. I experienced the power of Jesus' Word in my life in a very practical way.

The scripture experienced in your life

Were you able to experience the scripture reading in your life today? If so, how did this happen? You may like to write down your own account.

Stability in instability

SURVIVORS OF SEXUAL ABUSE YEARN for stability. As young children, not only did we try to survive the chaos of our own emotional world but we were also trying to deal with the unpredictable behaviour of our perpetrator and their erratic changes of mood which created a world of instability. Unfortunately, as we develop and grow we can become accustomed to being unstable. As adults we are invited to attend to our instability otherwise we will always have the sense that we are never in control of our own emotions, our behaviours, our moods or our reactions.

Apart from this, when our external circumstances that we believed to be stable unexpectedly change – for example, we lose a job, we lose a partner, we lose the support of a long-time friend, our counsellor or psychologist tell us that they are moving to another place – we feel as though our whole world is crumbling because what appeared to be stable and unshakeable in our life is about to disappear.

This external experience moves us to internal instability. We feel as though the ground has opened up beneath our feet and we have nothing to stand on. Instability makes us feel as though our whole world has caved in and we are sinking.

Experiences of instability make us feel the need to hold on to something stable, unchanging and eternal. When we can manage to do this, it is like finding a solid ground or foundation that we can stand on. God offers us a ground in our lives that is unshakeable, unbreakable, unchangeable and most of all eternally faithful. When we stand on God's solid ground, we find stability.

When we experience sudden instability, the scripture reading below will empower us with the stable, unconditional loving presence of our God.

Stability in instability

The scripture reading

Though the mountains leave their place and the hills be shaken,
my love shall never leave you, nor my covenant of peace be shaken,
says the Lord, who has mercy on you.

Isaiah 54:10

In this reading from the Prophet Isaiah, God promises stability in the midst of instability.

Believing that a mountain can 'leave its place' or the 'hills being shaken' is quite impossible for us! A mountain or hill is not something that we would expect to suddenly disappear. They are seemingly immovable. However, even nature experiences instability. When a massive earthquake shook Taiwan in 1999, huge mountains that were inhabited by many poor people crumbled and disappeared in a matter of seconds. It was a great tragedy that not only claimed the loss of a large number of lives but it also changed the landscape forever.

In a similar way, there may be mountains and hills in our life that we think are stable, immovable and unshakable. There are the external ones – the supporting presence of a family member, a partner or spouse and their intimate love, a friend or a therapist, a job or career, a place to live in, our physical health. And there are the internal ones – our emotional and mental well-being and health. Each one of us can make our own list. We get used to these things being secure and stable in our lives day in and day out. We do not expect them to suddenly disappear.

However, just as the Taiwanese people experienced the harsh reality of nature's instability in a matter of seconds, we too can experience the same. Our external and internal world can come tumbling down just as quickly as it did for those earthquake victims. Family, friends or other people who have always been a stable supportive presence can suddenly disappear from our lives, a job can come to an end, we can become ill and our physical, emotional or mental health are shaken up. The stable world that once offered us comfort and security has been shattered. As we are thrown into a world of instability and chaos, we experience the ground beneath our feet is crumbling.

It is precisely in these times of crisis and personal instability that God offers us the stability of his loving and peaceful presence. God promises us through this scripture reading: 'My love shall never leave you, nor my covenant of peace be shaken.' God's love is stable. People can leave us or abandon us, our circumstances or situation may change, we can lose our physical or mental health through an accident or, in our case, a trauma, but God promises that he will never leave us. We need to remember that when God says 'never', God means never. God's love is faithful, unchanging and immovable. God is the one stable presence in our life that we can be certain will never disappear.

So, when we experience that the ground beneath us is breaking up and our life is thrown into turmoil, let us lay down the true rock foundation of God's stable and loving presence in our life and stand firm on his solid ground. Let us also allow God to remind us during these times that his love will never leave us. The more we come to believe these words of God from Scripture the more we will experience stability in instability.

Praying the scripture reading

1. Try to be still and aware of God's presence with you.
2. Read the scripture reading slowly, putting your name at the beginning of each phrase.
3. Are there particular words that call your attention in this scripture reading? You may want to tell God what these words evoke in you or how you react to these words.
4. Try to have a conversation with God around these words, asking questions or sharing your thoughts. For example, if it is the words, 'My love shall never leave you', you may want to ask God, 'Why do you never want to leave me? ... What if I abandon you. Would you still not leave me?' Try to listen to God's response in your heart.

Stability in instability

5. Can you identify the 'mountains' or 'hills' in your life that have left their place or been shaken? You may like to share this with God and also how this caused you instability.
6. In response, let God repeat his words to you from the scripture reading: 'My love shall never leave you, nor my covenant of peace be shaken.' You may want to talk more with God about this until you experience that his Word is consoling you.
7. You may like to ask God how it is possible for you to experience his stable presence while you are experiencing instability.
8. As you prepare to continue your daily routine, try to have as your goal calling to memory these words from Scripture every time you are feeling unstable. Every time we do this and believe in God's word we are laying down rock foundations in our life and standing on God's solid ground.

The scripture experienced in my life

In June 2012, I became very ill with my auto-immune disorder and asked my leader for leave of absence from my community for health reasons.

At the start of my period of absence from the community, it was like a 'mountain' had been shaken in my life. For the previous twenty-two years, I had lived each day surrounded by members of my community and fulfilled in my ministry. When I stepped aside from the two because of illness it felt as though my whole inner and outer world was shaking. I had always imagined that my community and my ministry would be sure and stable in my life.

When the instability seemed too much to bear, I would recall these words of God again and again: 'My love shall never leave you, nor my covenant of peace be shaken.' Every time, I recalled what God was saying to me: 'Although you feel that your whole life and future has been shaken up, I will never leave you. I will be with you forever. I am a stable loving presence that you can always count on!' I tried to allow God to keep repeating his Word to me until I experienced his consolation. I then tried to continue my day believing the Word God had spoken to me.

It has been so amazing to experience how, over time, this particular Word has provided me with a source of stability. I am forever grateful to God and I know through my life experiences that with him I stand on a solid ground that can never be shaken and that will give me stability even in the midst of instability.

The scripture experienced in your life

Were you able to experience the scripture reading in your life today? If so, how did this happen? You may like to write down your own account.

Panic attacks – 'Quiet! Be still!'

IT WAS PEAK HOUR AND I WAS CATCHING the bus to go home. As I got on, there were still quite a few people getting on behind me. I was nearing the back of the bus and all the seats were taken. The people behind me were pushing me down as far as we could go. There was only one seat right at the very back. I sheepishly took the seat. The bus was full to capacity. The driver called, 'No more!', and revved up the engine and we began to move. As we did, I began to feel suffocated. I began struggling for breath.

There were no windows that could be opened and the heating was on. I could feel my whole body breaking out into a sweat. I was very hot and clammy. Suddenly my heart started racing and I could feel every one of its deep pounds within my body. I felt as though I was going to have a heart attack. My mind was going as quickly as my heart.

I began to have flashbacks[42] to when my perpetrator abused me on the back seat of a bus. In that moment, my body began to re-experience that terrifying occasion. I felt trapped, paralysed, as though I could not escape. My hands and legs felt like jelly.

My panic increased when I noticed that I was surrounded by men. Alarm bells rang in my mind. 'I've got to get out of here! This is unsafe! I don't want to be here! How can I get out?' I felt as though I was going to pass out as I tried to gasp for breath. Fear built up in my body: I could feel it freezing. I looked for the back door of the bus. I could barely just see it among the people but it seemed too far away. All my energy had been zapped from me. Even if I wanted to, I could not make it to the door.

Panic attacks are associated with post-traumatic stress disorder. A panic attack can be a terrifying experience. In the moment we feel as though

---
[42] See footnote 1 page 2.

we are going to die because the physical symptoms are so intense. The challenge of any panic attack is calming the inner turmoil and reaching a state of peace and stillness again. Panic attacks are the perfect opportunity to learn to 'wake up Jesus' in our life and to experience how he can quieten us down again.

The scripture reading

Leaving the crowd, they took him with them in the boat just as he was. A violent squall came up and waves were breaking over the boat, so that it was already filling up. Jesus was in the stern asleep on a cushion. They woke him and said to him, 'Teacher, do you not care that we are perishing?' He woke up, rebuked the wind and said to the sea, 'Quiet! Be still!' The wind ceased and there was a great calm. They were filled with great awe and said to one another, 'Who then is this whom even the wind and sea obey?'

Mark 4:35-40

Imagine the sheer panic of the disciples as this violent squall hit them and waves began entering their boat. They must have been terrified. They must have been thinking 'What can we do? How can we come out of this alive?' Until they suddenly remember – 'Jesus! We have Jesus with us. The one who has performed so many miracles!' They wake him up in absolute terror, crying to him, 'Don't you care that we are perishing?' Jesus wakes up and the disciples experienced his great power as he calms the wind and the sea.

Panic attacks are like these violent squalls in life. They come upon us unexpectedly, quite often in situations where we feel unsafe. The physical symptoms we experience – our racing heart and thoughts, our difficulty to breathe, the heat in our body, our arms and legs becoming like jelly, our body freezing – are like waves breaking within us. The challenge is to remember that when we are having a panic attack we are not alone – Jesus is in the boat with us (the 'boat' can represent our life). What we need to do is to wake him up because he may be sleeping in our life as he was with the

Panic Attacks – 'Quiet! Be still!'

disciples. Panic attacks are the perfect opportunity to wake up Jesus in our life and to let him act.

The next time you are in a state of panic, try to remember to wake Jesus up. Tell him what you experience. Ask him as the disciples did: 'Don't you care that I am about to die?'[43] Let Jesus start speaking to you in the midst of your panic. Listen to him saying, 'Quiet! Be still!' Let him say to your mind, 'Quiet! Be Still!' Let him say to your racing heart, 'Quieten down!' Let him say to your trembling arms 'Quiet! Be Still!' and the same to your legs 'Quiet! Be still!' Let him ease your breathing, saying, 'Quiet! Be still!' Let him tell you, 'You are safe: it is okay!' Experience how Jesus can bring about a 'great calm' once again in your body and move you from a state of panic to a state of stillness and peace. Just like the disciples, we too will be amazed and left in awe.

Praying the scripture reading

1. Every time you experience the onset of a panic attack, try to recall this passage
2. Use your panic attack as an opportunity to 'wake up' Jesus. Call out his name.
3. Ask him to show you his power working in your life.
4. Let him speak to every part of you that is in panic – your mind, heart, breathing, arms, legs … Let him say to every part 'Quiet! Be still!'
5. Let Jesus repeat these words to you as long as you need to hear them.
6. Let Jesus reassure you that you are safe.
7. Let yourself be amazed and in awe at who Jesus is in your life.

The scripture experienced in my life

This reading was fresh in mind when I had the panic attack on the bus, and

---

[43] 'Die' – I am not referring to the word in the physical sense but I am using it in the sense of what we feel is happening to us when we have a panic attack. The physical symptoms are so real that we can feel like we are going to die.

it came to my mind in my panic-stricken state. Experiencing that I was in the middle of a 'violent squall', I called out to Jesus in my heart and began telling him of my trouble: 'Jesus, help me out here. I am about to die! My heart is thumping and racing so fast, my mind can't stop, my whole body is trembling. I feel like I can't help myself!'

Then I recalled Jesus' words. He was saying to me, in the middle of my panic attack, 'Be still!'

I tried to let Jesus speak to every part of my body that needed to become still. He said to my heart, 'Be still', and to my mind, 'Quiet! Be still!' and to my trembling body, 'Be still!' and to my legs that were like jelly, 'Be still!'. I recalled his words a second time and a third time, until, eventually, I experienced his grace. I became quiet and still. What an amazing grace! This Word of Jesus has not failed me yet. May the power that Jesus has to quieten us and make us still not remain sleeping in our life.

The scripture experienced in your life

Were you able to experience the scripture reading in your life today? If so, how did this happen? You may like to write down your own account.

Revealing what is concealed

I HAD BEEN FOLLOWING THE MEDIA'S coverage about the scandals of sexual abuse in the Catholic Church by members of the clergy. There had been daily coverage about fresh cases that were unfolding. Victims, survivor groups, and advocates for childhood sexual abuse had been pushing hard for a Royal Commission to look into the church's response to sexual abuse claims. Then a very brave police officer, Detective Chief Inspector Peter Fox, who was previously involved in the investigations of Catholic priests for sexual abuse claims and later dismissed from the investigations, went public and spoke from his inside knowledge of how child sexual abuse was covered up by the Catholic Church and criticized how the police were handling cases.

Several days later, in November 2012, the Prime Minister at the time, Julia Gillard, announced a Royal Commission into Institutional Responses to Child Sexual Abuse. It was a historic day and a great celebration for so many victims, survivors and advocate groups of child sexual abuse who had been crying out for a Royal Commission for decades, seeking justice. Finally, survivors of institutional child sexual abuse were now being welcomed to have a voice and to tell their stories within the safe context of a Royal Commission and their claims would be taken seriously. This was of ample importance to many survivors of sexual abuse whose claims had either been unsatisfactorily dismissed in the past or who had been asked or paid by authorities to keep silent.

Back in late 2002, I personally experienced how the Catholic Church had been attempting to investigate and respond to victims of sexual abuse by Catholic clergy after I decided to report my case to the church's Professional Standards Office. I was asked to make a statement of claims for my case and this initiated me into the Towards Healing process. Part of the role of this process is to investigate claims of sexual abuse.

Although my mother had previously reported my perpetrator – a Catholic priest – to Catholic Church authorities back in 1987, I had never come forward personally to those authorities to make a formal complaint or statement. My mother's attempt to report the perpetrator seemed to fall on deaf ears. She was never able to speak to the Cardinal personally and only got as far as the Cardinal's secretary. She was never guaranteed that the matter would be looked into and she never received a return telephone call. There was no indication or accountability on the church's part that something serious had happened and that the perpetrator would be dealt with.

So, more than two decades after I was sexually abused by the offending priest and after a long journey of confronting and dealing with sexual abuse by a family relation, I felt that the time was right to deal with the perpetrator's abuse and to formally report the matter to the appropriate church authorities.

Personally, I did not find the church's response at the time satisfying – perhaps others have experienced a more satisfying response. I was granted a personal interview through the Professional Standards Office, where I made a complaint. After this I called the office several times to find out how the matter was proceeding. I was called back for a second session where I was told very little about the perpetrator. I never heard again from anyone in the church after that session. I did not have any guarantee, neither was I given the assurance that the matter would be dealt with appropriately by church authorities. I had experienced first hand, how undergoing the Towards Healing process meant that survivors became very vulnerable as they opened up their deep wounds and recalled the horrific events and how they would consequently experience re-traumatization.

After personally experiencing what this process involved, my dissatisfaction and deep frustration arose from experiencing that the church did not seem to take responsibility for what had happened or to hold itself accountable. I never received an apology from any church official for what had happened. Just like my mother's experience of over two decades ago, I too experienced that my claim had fallen on deaf ears. I was deeply disappointed and somewhat distressed by the experience. I did not pursue the matter fur-

Revealing what is concealed

ther at that time, since I was a consecrated member of a Catholic religious missionary community and the time was not favourable for me to do so.

Now, ten years later, a Royal Commission into Institutional Responses into Child Sexual Abuse has been established. The aim of the Royal Commission was to investigate how institutions, including the Catholic Church, had responded to abuse claims in the past, to discover what the systemic failures were in those institutions, and to see what needed to be implemented to improve these systems in the future so that such atrocities would never happen again and so that our institutions would become safer places for children.

My current personal circumstances were now very different from what they were in 2002 when I decided not to pursue the matter. Currently, I was not living within the context of my religious community for health reasons and I was free of ministry commitments. As the Royal Commission invited survivors to come forward, I saw my personal circumstances at the time as part of God's plan. I was now in a context where I was freer to pursue this matter and felt empowered to do so.

I felt as though I was being called personally to tell my story, even though I perceived that this would be traumatic for me, and to make my contribution to this very significant moment in Australia's history. I felt that the voice of every survivor coming forward was important if the institution of church was to be purified and if positive systemic changes were to be implemented to prevent sexual abuse from happening in the Catholic Church in the future. It was even more vital to let our voices be heard so that, if our perpetrator had not yet been apprehended and was still offending and causing grievous harm to other children, the appropriate civil action would now be taken and justice would be done for these victims too, and, we hope, save many other children from the life-long suffering of the effects of sexual abuse.

For some days, I struggled with the thought of re-living the trauma of the abuse, but I saw clearly that I needed to do it one day when I was praying the following scripture.

The scripture reading

'Therefore, do not be afraid of them. Nothing is concealed that will not be revealed, nor secret that will not be known. What I say to you in the darkness, speak in the light; what you hear whispered proclaim on the housetops.'

Matthew 10:26-27

Jesus spoke these words in the context of persecution. He was trying to encourage his listeners to be courageous in the face of persecution. His first words are consoling – 'Do not be afraid of them.' 'Them' is referring to the persecutors.

Among the survivors I have shared with, one of the reasons why we concealed the sexual abuse and keep it locked away in the closet for so many years is because we have a deep fear of being persecuted: persecuted in the sense that we are told, 'It can't be true! So-and-so has always been such a lovely person.' Or, 'I'm sure it didn't happen like that, you must be exaggerating! You always had a bit of a wild imagination.' Or, straight out, 'I don't believe you!' Or, 'Perhaps you need to see someone; I've noticed you haven't been well for a while' (trying to imply that we are mentally ill). Or perhaps some will even fear being banished or shunned altogether by family and friends. These experiences make us think long and hard about revealing our secret.

However, Jesus does not want us to experience the burden of carrying such a deep secret, nor does he want us to experience the damaging and destructive physical, emotional and psychological effects that holding this secret can cause us over time. Our well-being depends on revealing our secret, but we can only ever do this if we feel that we are in the right environment, one where we feel safe, there is trust, we feel we will be listened to, and that our secret will be held with respect.

Through this scripture, Jesus supports and encourages us not to be afraid to reveal what we have concealed perhaps for decades. Wrong has been done to us by others and Jesus encourages us to reveal this. Institutions will only change their responses to abuse claims in the future if there are enough brave people who speak out and reveal their secret. It is powerful to listen to many voices speaking the same truth and as a group these voices can generate change.

'What I say to you in the darkness, speak in the light! What you hear whispered, proclaim on the housetops.' Jesus never silences us or asks us to be silent. On the contrary, in cases where a wrong or injustice has been done, he always invites us to 'speak in the light', in other words, bring it out into the open so that something can be done to address it.

What Jesus says next is not to be taken literally and survivors need to be careful to understand it correctly. When Jesus says, 'What you hear whispered, proclaim on the housetops', he doesn't mean proclaim on the housetops that we have been abused. Sexual abuse is a sensitive issue and it needs to be treated with sensitivity and delicacy. What has happened to us is deeply personal and intimate and not everyone needs to know about it. Choosing who to reveal it to calls for discretion, and creating boundaries for ourselves to feel safe is important when it comes to revealing our story. In fact, many survivors may only chose to share their story with a small number of people over a life time and even then there may be certain details of their story that they choose never to reveal. What Jesus wants to emphasize when he says 'proclaim on the housetops' is letting our secret out and making it known so that it no longer destroys us from within.

Revealing our inner secret is essential to begin our healing process. When we do, it is like opening the inner window of our heart and letting out the putrid and bad odours that have been suffocating us for most of our life and finally letting some fresh air come in to our life, perhaps for the first time in decades. Opening that window and revealing the secret is the key to the beginning of change in our life and personal story.

Praying the scripture reading

1. Read this scripture passage slowly, putting your name at the beginning of each sentence so that you can experience God speaking personally to you through his Word.

2. Which words or phrase call your attention and why? (You may like to write these down.)
3. Jesus says, 'What I say to you in the darkness, speak in the light!' What is it that Jesus is saying to you in the 'darkness' of your heart? How do you think that Jesus is inviting you to bring this out 'in the light'? Is there someone he wants you to say this to?
4. What can you do to put this into practice? (You may like to write it down.)
5. Don't finish your prayer without allowing Jesus to reassure you through his words: 'Don't be afraid' because 'I am with you'. Try to hold these words of Jesus in your heart today as you carry on with your routine. If you experience fear and find yourself lacking courage at a time when you feel you are being called to speak out, allow Jesus to repeat these words to you.

The scripture experienced in my life

After experiencing the continual promptings of the Spirit through all the media coverage, and also through the words of this reading, I decided that it was time to deal with the unfinished business that I had begun through the Professional Standards Office back in 2002. I found and called the telephone number of the Royal Commission into Institutional Responses to Sexual Abuse and told them I would like to tell my story. I was asked several general questions and I was told that I would be called at a later date and given an appointment time for a private hearing with a couple of the commissioners. I was reassured that the commissioners really wanted to listen to my story as well as those of many other survivors so that they could get to the bottom of the systemic failures that permitted the abuse to continue over decades.

I was fully aware that going through a private hearing was not going to be easy. In fact, I knew it would be quite traumatic, but I experienced the power of Jesus' Word in the Scriptures. Jesus was constantly encouraging me, 'Don't be afraid!' He wanted me to speak out, even if it meant speaking out against someone who was supposed to be a Servant of God – a priest.

Revealing what is concealed

Jesus understood how challenging this was because he confronted the religious leaders of his time and spoke out against their hypocritical ways, and now he was inviting me to also speak out against the priest who had caused me (and very likely others) grave harm. Jesus was urging me to bring this 'darkness' into the 'light' and I was now provided with the appropriate place to do it – the Royal Commission.

The scripture experienced in your life

Were you able to experience the scripture reading in your life today? If so, how did this happen? You may like to write down your own account.

Facing trouble with courage

WHEN I MADE MY INITIAL CONTACT with the Office of the Royal Commission into Institutional Responses to Child Sexual Abuse and expressed my desire to make a submission, I was asked if anyone else was aware of the abuse and if it was ever reported to any church officials or hierarchy at the time. I advised them about my mother's attempt to report it and my own process of reporting it to the Professional Standards Office back in 2002.

I also informed them that I believe it may have been reported by one other person to a different diocese back in the late 1980s. I was asked if I still had contact with the person I believed reported it and I said 'No'. I was asked if I knew how to get in touch with that person and I said 'Yes'. I was asked if it was safe to get in touch and I said 'Yes' but explained that it would be awkward for me because it had been more than twenty-four years since I had been in touch with the person. They suggested that if I was comfortable enough to get in touch with them to find out some information before my private hearing it would be helpful for my session – mainly, who the abuse was reported to, when it was reported, and if any action was taken as a result of the report.

For several days, I experienced apprehension at this task but at the same time I understood that finding out this information would be important and of use for the Commissioners. I also knew that speaking to this person was going to be like bringing back a ghost from my past who was associated with my memory of the abuse. Before I made the call, I wanted to make sure that I was in a good and right space internally to deal with whatever may resurface in me as a consequence. Several days passed. It seemed a simple task – making a phone call – yet it led me to experience so much trouble.

During these days, I began to have flashbacks and memories of the abuse. I recalled the dilemma I experienced at the time of wanting to tell this particular person that I was being abused by Father X in the hope of finding help, but I was so afraid of what Father X would do to me if he found out. I remember how my perpetrator sensed what I was thinking and how he mentalized me against this person, and now, more than twenty-four years later, all this was coming back to my mind and I felt as though I was re-living that same dilemma.

But there was a difference this time. I could take back my power, speak out and reveal the secret. Praying the scripture reading below gave me courage in this middle of my trouble.

The scripture reading

'In the world you will have trouble, but take courage, I have conquered the world.'

John 16:33

Some people think that because Jesus was God he did not suffer as we do. If we think about it, this belief rejects Jesus' humanity.

The gospels, however, reveal to us a very different picture of Jesus. Not only do they present Jesus as a divine being but also a human being. While they show us Jesus' divine power, might and grace, they also show us his humanity and we see him tired, weak, angry, grief-stricken and totally vulnerable. Jesus did not escape human troubles for the fact that he was divine. In the gospels we see that Jesus was well acquainted with trouble, so much so that he understands and identifies with us in our trouble. He understands all the human emotions that we experience when we are in trouble. He knows what it is to experience pain, grief, loss, sadness, disappointment and hurt.

For this reason, in the middle of our troubles Jesus tells us, 'Take courage.' What is the courage that Jesus is talking about? It is the same courage that emerged from him when he found himself in the hands of his enemies. It is the inner strength that emanated from within Jesus' mind, heart and spirit, empowering him to face the impossible circumstances and danger that lay ahead of him with total self-possession.

CHILD, ARISE!

Today Jesus says, 'Take courage. I am giving you courage as my gift so that you will have inner strength in your mind, heart and spirit to go through all your troubles that overwhelm you and seem impossible.'

In the next part of the reading it is as if Jesus is saying to us, 'You can do it!' He says, 'I have conquered the world.' He invites us to contemplate him, particularly in the light of his Passion.[44] 'Look at me and see what I have passed through: the hardships, the suffering, the injustices, the sorrow. If I could come through it all, so can you! Don't forget, I have conquered the world – and the troubles that you are passing through. Take courage! I will be with you and help you.'

Our troubles are not the end but they are a means to experience the gifts that we have in Jesus. One of those gifts is courage. In our process and journey, let us not forget to 'take courage' to help us in our troubles.

Praying the scripture reading

1. Try to be aware of Jesus' presence with you.
2. Read the scripture reading slowly putting your name at the beginning of the phrase.
3. You may like to share with Jesus the trouble you are experiencing in your life at the moment. (You may like to write it down.)
4. Now that you have shared your trouble with Jesus, listen to him saying to you: '[put your name] take courage. For I have conquered the world.' As you listen to Jesus' words, what do you feel in your heart? Tell Jesus. (You may like to write it down.)
5. Try to understand how Jesus is inviting you to be courageous in your current troubles. Is there something you experience he is inviting you to do? Is he inviting you to have a different attitude? Or is there something unresolved in your life that he may be inviting you to attend to? (You may like to write it down.)
6. Before you finish your prayer, try to resolve how you can put this into practice.

---

[44] The suffering and death of Jesus.

Facing trouble with courage

The scripture experienced in my life

After praying this reading, I felt encouraged by Jesus to get in touch with the person who could provide me with extra information for the Royal Commission. I was not successful in speaking directly with the person: I got as far as a personal assistant. Before she could pass my message on, she needed information about who I was. I had difficulty with this because of the sensitive issue involved and because I wanted to be discreet and keep my boundaries. I kept recalling Jesus' Word and listening to him telling me 'Courage!'

The personal assistant assured me my message would be passed on, however, she could not guarantee that I would be called back, since that was not her decision. Ten days passed and I had still not heard anything. My private hearing session was in seven days' time. I wondered what the reasons may have been not to return my call. Could it be that the PA took down my number incorrectly? Could I have missed the call? Perhaps this person did not want to bring up things from the past? I wanted to call again but I felt timid. Again, I recalled the words of Jesus 'Courage! I have conquered the world.'

With these words, I picked up the phone and dialled again. This time the PA I had spoken to was away for two weeks and I was told to follow up my query with her when she returned. I began calculating in my mind. Two weeks would be too late! My private hearing would be over by then.

Although, it appeared that my attempt to speak directly with this person and get some answers to my questions was in vain, at least I was able to experience that Jesus gave me the courage to overcome the negative thoughts that accompanied me on my way. What a gift that was!

I have tried to make this normal practice in my life every time I feel I lack the courage to do something, I listen to the words of Jesus inviting me to 'Take courage!' and I am constantly surprised at how this courage empowers me in my troubles.

The scripture experienced in your life

Were you able to experience the scripture reading in your life today? If so, how did this happen? You may like to write down your own account.

Grieving and consolation

EVERY PERSON WILL EXPERIENCE GRIEF at some stage in their life whether it be in the form of the loss of a job, the loss of health or faculties through sickness or an accident, moving house, children leaving home, the disintegration of a dream or long-time project, or the death of a loved one.

When survivors of sexual abuse experience any type of loss in the present it is very likely that the experience will trigger feelings of loss from childhood. Grief is a natural response to loss and betrayal, and an essential part of healing from traumatic experiences is to be able to express and share our feelings.

As young children we were unable to do this, particularly having been sworn to secrecy by our perpetrators which denied us of the opportunity to find comfort, support, healing and resolution. Quite often survivors learnt to deny emotions by repression or dissociation, which can leave us with a sense of chronic sadness and grief.

The process of grieving invites us to feel what we did not allow ourselves to feel as young children: sadness, anger, guilt, self-reproach, anxiety, fear, loneliness, pain, sorrow, hurt, confusion, despair, fatigue, betrayal, helplessness, shock, abandonment, yearning, bitterness, relief, numbness, resentment, revenge.

The process of grieving plays an important role in recovery from loss. If we continue to bury our grief we limit our capacity to experience joy, spontaneity and life.

Experiencing grief is healthy: it humanizes us and makes us whole. Even Jesus (Son of God) experienced grief in his earthly life. In the gospels we can learn from Jesus that accepting our grief, feeling the pain of it and expressing it externally is part of the grieving process.

Grieving and consolation

The scripture reading

When Mary met Jesus, she looked at him, and then fell down at his feet. 'If only you had been here, Lord', she said, 'my brother would never have died.' When Jesus saw Mary weep and noticed the tears of the Jews who came with her, he was deeply moved and visibly distressed.

'Where have you put him?' he asked. 'Lord, come and see', they replied, and at this Jesus himself wept. 'Look how much he loved him!' remarked the Jews, though some of them asked, 'Could he not have kept this man from dying if he could open that blind man's eyes?'

John 11:32-37

This scene is full of emotion. Lazarus, Mary and Martha's brother and a close friend of Jesus, has died and been buried now for four days. Jesus, after receiving the news, has come to see Martha and Mary. Mary comes to meet Jesus and as she falls at his feet weeping she opens her grieving heart to him: 'If only you had been here, Lord, my brother would never have died.' We get the sense that Mary is blaming Lazarus' death on Jesus' absence and she feels that she was abandoned by Jesus. These emotions are typical of grief.

Perhaps there is something in Mary's words that strikes a chord with us. It may be that like Mary we too have felt this way on occasions of personal loss: 'If only you had been here, Lord, I would not have died ('died' in the spiritual sense of the word – in our case, a death through sexual abuse).' Or, 'I would not have [whatever the loss is – this sickness, the loss of my job, the loss of a friend …].' In other words, 'If you had been here, Lord, perhaps things would have been very different in my life today and I may not be spiritually dead as I am now. Perhaps I would not be as broken as I am. Why did you abandon me, Jesus? Why did you leave me and let this happen to me?' Perhaps we are still experiencing some degree of grief.

When Jesus sees Mary weeping, he does not say to her: 'Don't cry … Be strong … Cheer up! … Get over it! … Move on!' Jesus is not indifferent to Mary. On the contrary, he is fully present to her, listening to her as she expresses her grief, so much so that Jesus connects with her intimately. He feels her pain and heartache to the point that he is 'deeply moved' and 'visibly distressed'. Perhaps we have imagined Jesus to be a 'superman', immune from experiencing intense human emotions. Even though Jesus was divine (being God), we often forget he was also human like us, meaning that he experienced his humanity as we do. We see this clearly in this gospel where Jesus displays his sorrow publicly.

Jesus then asks the crowd who is accompanying Mary, 'Where have you put him?' Jesus wanted to see where his friend Lazarus was buried. He was not afraid to confront the reality of death even though he knew that this would cause him pain, sadness and sorrow. Jesus could have avoided the pain by not asking to see where Lazarus was buried but he didn't. Jesus chose to face his pain. The crowd invited Jesus to come and see, and with this Jesus begins weeping. Jesus doesn't repress his pain but he feels it in his heart and he expresses it externally through weeping.

Jesus responds to our grief in the same way. Whenever we come before him weeping, he will never say to us, 'Stop crying … Be strong … Get over it … Move on … Cheer up!' On the contrary, Jesus will be fully present to us. He will listen to our pain and sorrow as we express it to him, feeling it with us to the point where he too is deeply moved and distressed.

Jesus does not want us ever to feel that we are alone or abandoned in our grief (even though we may have felt that way in the past). He wants to be a supportive constant presence that we can count on as we pass through our grieving process. In the same way that Jesus desired to see where his friend Lazarus was buried, he desires to see where we are 'buried' (in the spiritual sense) and he will ask us too, 'Where are you buried?' In other words, 'Let me see you even though you feel dead spiritually.' Jesus is asking permission to come into our heart and to see our grief. Perhaps we are buried deep in sadness, sorrow, confusion, darkness and emptiness. We may find that we are hesitant and feel uncomfortable to let Jesus see where we are buried but at the same time perhaps we will find ourselves being deeply moved that Jesus cares enough and desires to see where we are in our grief.

Grieving and consolation

What we need to remember is that our situation or emotional state is never too overwhelming for Jesus. As soon as we invite Jesus to 'Come and see' our grief we will find him close to us, so close that we will experience that when we weep he weeps with us. Our loss is his loss, our pain is his pain.

Allowing Jesus to come into our hearts and see our grief facilitates us to go through the grieving process. As we reveal our grief to Jesus in prayer and experience his intimate and loving support, we will find that he enables us to accept our grief rather than deny it and he helps us to feel the pain and express it externally in a healthy way rather than to repress it or avoid and escape it.

While it is true that all our losses are very real and very painful, they are not the ultimate reality. We grieve, but not hopelessly. We weep, but not endlessly – thanks to Jesus who wept and felt pain in his earthly life but proclaimed victory over it through his resurrection.

Praying the scripture reading

1. Try to be still and aware of Jesus' presence in you.
2. Read the scripture reading slowly. As you do, try to imagine the scene. Imagine Jesus and Mary meeting. You may like to imagine that you are one of the crowd who is following Mary.
3. What is it about Mary in this encounter that calls your attention? Can you identify with Mary in some way? (You may like to write it down and express it to Jesus.)
4. What is it about Jesus in this encounter that calls your attention and why? (You may like to write it down and express it to Jesus.)
5. Are there some words from the encounter between Mary and Jesus that move you within, that cause you to feel identification, sadness, sorrow, pain, a memory from the past? (You may like to write this down and express it in conversation with Jesus.)
6. If you are able, try now to put yourself in Mary's place. Imagine that it is you meeting Jesus and your support crowd is following

you. If you feel comfortable enough, try to express your grief to Jesus as Mary did. (You may like to write it down.)

7. After doing this, try to be aware that Jesus is not indifferent to what you have shared with him. He is also 'deeply moved' and 'distressed'. Try to grasp Jesus' compassionate and tender presence with you as you grieve. How does Jesus' presence make you feel? (You may want to write it down in conversation with Jesus.)

8. Imagine that Jesus is now asking you, 'Where have you put him?' or, speaking to you personally, 'Where are you buried?' – meaning 'Let me see where you have died spiritually?' The crowd responded 'Come and see?' Are you also able to say, 'Come and see'? If you are, then let Jesus 'see' you profoundly. Let him see the emotions that have buried you. Feel free to express them to Jesus if you want. If you want to write them down, you can. Perhaps you have no words but only tears, so feel at peace to cry all you need to with Jesus. He is fully present to you.

9. Try now to notice Jesus. Jesus is not indifferent to your tears or to what you have shared with him. He weeps with you, just as he did with Mary. He feels your sorrow and pain deeply. Try to be aware of Jesus' compassionate presence with you. You may want to tell Jesus how his presence makes you feel, for example, consoled, thankful that you are not alone, strengthened ...

10. In what way has this encounter with Jesus helped you to process grief? (You may like to write this down in conversation with Jesus.)

11. What would you like to take away from your encounter with Jesus today and practise in the future as you work through your grief? (You may like to write it down in conversation with Jesus.)

The scripture experienced in my life

Earlier today I had a session with my psychologist in preparation for my private hearing with the Royal Commission. I was recounting how I had been sexually abused by Father X and how utterly powerless and helpless I was to

Grieving and consolation

do anything at the time. I could sense so much emotion building up inside me and I felt myself holding back from expressing it in my session. Sure enough, by the time I arrived home I could feel the tears welling up in my eyes. I went to my room and I broke down in tears and I could not stop sobbing.

As I was sobbing, I remembered this gospel reading and I thought this was an opportunity to experience grieving with Jesus. I opened up my Bible and I began to read this gospel passage very slowly. I then imagined that Jesus was with me in my room and standing right in front of me. I began to pour my heart out to Jesus in the same way that Mary did in the gospel and I cried to Jesus, 'Jesus, if you had been with me, I would not have been abused and had to suffer the horrible consequences and effects of it for all these years. If you had been with me, Lord, I would not be experiencing this spiritual death now!'

I experienced Jesus saying to me, 'Let me see where you are buried?' I said to Jesus, 'Look, see, Jesus! See how deep my pain and sorrow is. See my sadness and desolation. See how much the abuse has damaged me as a person.' I poured my heart out to Jesus and told him how crippled I felt because of the abuse and how many other losses I experienced as a result of it. I really experienced Jesus' presence in my heart and that he was listening to me.

After I had no more tears to cry, I imagined myself looking up at Jesus and when I did Jesus was weeping. I was very moved to see Jesus weeping and I asked him, 'Jesus, why are you weeping?' The answer was clear, 'Because of you and for all that you are experiencing because of the abuse!' Jesus was feeling my pain and sorrow deep in his heart. His compassion, tenderness and personal love for me made me sob again. We sat there together weeping. We did not have the need to exchange any words. Everything was understood in this sacred silence. It gave me great consolation in my grief to know that I was not alone and that there was someone with me who knew me, and was feeling my pain, and who loved me.

I cannot deny that something beautiful and sacred took place that afternoon as I grieved. God, through his divine grace, had entered into my sorrow through Jesus and there he wept with me. I cannot precisely sum up the experience but there was something uniquely distinct about the unity I experienced with Jesus that afternoon and I cannot compare it to any other human relationship. I accepted this as one of God's gifts that we receive when we grieve with Jesus!

The scripture experienced in your life

Were you able to experience the scripture reading in your life today? If so, how did this happen? You may like to write down your own account.

Hopelessness – the power to transcend it

HOPELESSNESS. SURVIVORS OF CHILDHOOD sexual abuse are very familiar with it. Haven't we all had mornings where we wake up and experience that there is not a single thing we can look forward to or hope for as a new day dawns upon us. This is even more typical when we are passing through the process of dealing with painful traumatic memories – memories our body has stored away over a long period of time until it feels that we are ready to handle them. As these repressed memories begin to come out, our body begins to re-live or re-experience what we went through during the abuse both physically and emotionally. Many of us find ourselves trying to deal with overwhelming emotions that we never knew how to process as a child. Each one of us would have coped with these overwhelming emotions as a child in different ways. Like me, some may have tried to block these emotions by numbing ourselves so that we didn't have to feel the pain of what was being done to us. It was our way of coping with and surviving something that was and is so traumatic for a child.

So, for adult survivors of childhood sexual abuse, hopelessness is one of the emotions we can find ourselves dealing with. In the process, there are days when we feel totally hopeless. Knocked down and beaten about by not only the memories and flashbacks, but also the emotions that arise with these, and we can begin to think, 'I can't go through this any more! It's all too hard! I've had enough! It's too much! What is the purpose of all this? Where is it all going? I'm over it!' We feel like we're in a very dark tunnel and all the lights are turned off! We feel utterly hopeless. It is a very uncomfortable emotion to acknowledge and to sit with.

But in our hopelessness there is hope. The scripture reading below gives us great hope.

The scripture reading

May the eyes of your hearts be enlightened, that you may know what is the hope that belongs to his call, what are the riches of glory in his inheritance among the holy ones, and what is the surpassing greatness of his power for us who believe, in accord with the exercise of his great might, which he worked in Christ, raising him from the dead and seating him at his right hand in the heavens, far above every principality, authority, power and dominion, and every name that is named not only in this age but also in the one to come.

Ephesians 1:18-21

In this reading, St Paul is inviting us as believers in Christ to experience the hope that Christ gives us.

If we feel that we are caught in a dark hole, unable to see even the smallest flicker of light, that we have nothing to hold on to and nothing to give us even a glimmer of hope for the future, then we are in the perfect condition to experience the hope that Christ gives.

It is precisely in this dark hole that we can come to know 'what is the surpassing greatness of God's power for us who believe' and 'the great might of God' which he 'worked in Christ, raising him from the dead ... far above every principality, authority, power and dominion, and every name.'

St Paul is inviting us to keep believing in Christ, even while we are in this dark hole and seeing everything painted black. It is a call to believe that the great might of God is working within us, even though we can't see it or feel it. We also need to remember that we are not talking here about human might that is limited, we are talking about the might of God that is unlimited and goes far beyond any human might. God proved the power of his might by raising Jesus from the dead.

When we feel hopeless, God invites us to believe that the same might that raised Jesus from the dead will also work in us, if we believe, and raise us from the death we experience in this very dark hole. As with Jesus, God will raise us too, 'far above every principality, authority, power and domin-

Hopelessness – the power to transcend it

ion, and every name that is named.' For survivors, this means that God will raise us far above the power of a nightmare, flashback or memory. God will raise us far above the dominion of fear and the dominion of thoughts of self-harm.

Most of all, the might of God will raise us far above the name of our perpetrator and all other names that threaten to keep us dead and buried in this black hole. God will raise us far above all these experience so that they no longer have authority, power and dominion over us. This is the hope that all survivors can have in Christ and this hope will never fail us.

Today let us hold on to our hope in Christ which gives us light in our darkness. Let us look forward to this new day as an opportunity to experience our hope and in the darkest moments of our day, and when we feel the power, authority and dominion of the abuse, let us practise our hope by saying to God, 'I believe that you can raise me far above the power that this memory has over me' or 'I believe that you can raise me far above the despair that I am going through' or 'I believe that you can raise me far above the dominion of these words that my perpetrator used to say to me.'

By believing in God's might, in the practical moments of our darkness, we will 'come to know our hope in God' and we will experience God's might working in us to raise us from the dead.

Praying the scripture reading

1. Try to be aware of God's presence with you. Read the reading very slowly putting your name at the beginning of the verse (this will help you to be aware that God is speaking to you through his Word).
2. Stop at the words or the phrase that strike you or call your attention in some way. It could be, for example, 'the surpassing power of his greatness' or 'raising him from the dead' or 'far above every principality, authority, power and dominion' or other words). The important thing is to stop because God is trying to say something to you through these particular words.

3. Try to identify what these words make you feel (hope, wonder, doubt, enthusiasm, joy ...). Tell God what you feel. If you have questions, ask them. Try to listen to God's response through the words from the scripture.
4. Don't be afraid to also let God know if you feel 'dead' inside (in the sense that you have no life from within) and what you feel is keeping you in this state of death. If you are feeling that the trauma of the abuse still has power, dominion and authority over you, tell God about it.
5. Let God speak to you through his Word and assure you, 'My might is working in you. For just as I raised Christ from the dead, I will also raise you from the death that you are experiencing in your black hole and I will raise you far above the power, authority and dominion of the abuse.'
6. Let God continue to reassure you through his Word until you experience that you are feeling more hopeful.
7. During the day, if you experience that there is some aspect of the abuse that is overpowering you or dominating you (a body language, something you read or saw, and it brought something to memory) and you feel that the dark hole is getting even darker, recall God's Word from this reading to assure you, 'I am working in you in this very moment' and 'I will raise you far above the power and dominion of this memory. Believe in me.'
8. After recalling God's word, try to continue about your daily routine believing that God's might is working in you and raising you up from your hopelessness.

The scripture experienced in my life

I was driving my car home and I had the radio tuned in to a talkback station. The radio announcer was talking about a call that he took off air because he said that he knew that if he aired the call a lot of people would have been offended. It turned out that the call was from a friend of a perpetrator of child sexual abuse who was trying to convince the announcer of how much suffering the perpetrators of sexual abuse go through and that the public cannot understand this. I was outraged hearing this and it made me recall how Father X also tried to tell me that he was 'suffering' during the time he was abusing me. At the time, this caused me so much confusion because he didn't look like he was suffering, and I knew *I* was definitely suffering. I used to get angry when he said these things but I could never tell him I was angry because he used to get violent.

By the time I reached home, I felt as though I was being sucked deeper and deeper into my black hole. Hopelessness surrounded me. Once again I felt that I was being overpowered by the memory of the abuse. I made a conscious effort to recall God's Word and I tried to listen to those words in my heart 'I am working in you' and 'as I raised Jesus, I will raise you.' I asked, 'How are you going to do this, God'? 'With my might', God replied. I felt God inviting me, 'Believe in my might!' I told God, 'I believe in you, but please raise me far above the power of this memory. Don't let it keep me here in this hole.'

I continued to do my work that afternoon believing that while I worked God was also working to raise me above this terrible memory. I had the most amazing experience. Normally such a memory had the power to keep me feeling hopeless for at least a day, but that afternoon I was even able to work on the assignment for my class. I was blessed to have a glimpse of God's might raising me from my hopelessness.

The scripture experienced in your life

Were you able to experience the scripture reading in your life today? If so, how did this happen? You may like to write down your own account.

A boost of confidence

CONFIDENCE IS DEFINED as the 'feeling or belief that one can rely on someone or something; firm trust' or 'the state of feeling certain about the truth of something.' It is understandable why survivors of abuse struggle to gain confidence. When a child has been traumatized by sexual abuse, their confidence is shattered. Normally, the one who has caused their trauma is someone they thought they could firmly trust. They no longer feel certain that what a person says can be true: for example, 'This person says that they love me, but is it true?' or 'This person says that this is good for me, but is it true?' or 'This person says that they will not hurt me, but is it true?'

This shattered confidence is something that becomes very evident to all adult survivors through the circumstances and events of our life. It is very tangible in our life and it is something that we need to restore as we rebuild our lives.

Today I have experienced my lack of confidence. It is the day before my private hearing for the Royal Commission. I feel the uncertainty arising within me and the thoughts racing through my head: 'Can I really trust that I will be listened to? Am I going to be dismissed again? Can I trust that it is safe to tell my story? Will harm come to me again through this? Will the outcome be a good and fruitful one for me and for all other survivors and those who are still victims of abuse?'

I should have expected this lack of confidence, but it always seems to startle and unsettle me in a new way each time. I find the best way to deal with it is to acknowledge it by calling it by its name: 'Hello, shattered confidence!' Then I turn to God in prayer and I ask for a boost of confidence. The reading below always achieves this for me.

A boost of confidence

The scripture reading

I am confident of this, that the one who began a good work in you will continue to complete it until the day of Christ Jesus. It is right that I should think this way about all of you, because I hold you in my heart, you who are all partners with me in grace.

Philippians 1:6-7a

St Paul wrote this letter to the community of the Philippians from prison. In his letter, Paul expresses gratitude to the Philippians for their concern and help in the continued progression of the Gospel. It is a letter that expresses his deep joy, human sensitivity and tenderness. In these particular verses, St Paul is expressing his confidence in the community of Philippi that God, 'the one who began a good work' in them, 'will continue to complete it until the day of Christ Jesus.' I'm sure that St Paul would have first listened to these words from Christ and experienced them in his own life before writing them to the community in Philippi.

I imagine that when St Paul's letter was read out loud at one of the communal gatherings, even if there were some in the community who were feeling low in confidence and doubting that God could be doing 'a good work' in them, these words would have given them a big boost in confidence. Through the words of St Paul, they would have experienced the confidence that Christ himself had in them as a community to keep on going with the good work that God was doing in them, confident that Christ would be the one to bring it to completion.

Perhaps from where we stand currently, completing our journey can seem like such a long task because we experience the effects of the trauma in all the dimensions of our life – physical, emotional, psychological, spiritual and social. It may feel like we are doing a lot of internal work but that not much change seems to be happening on the outside. Perhaps we even feel as though we haven't achieved anything yet. Perhaps we get a lot of encouragement and support from other people but we ourselves are not convinced and we lose confidence.

Today, let us try to listen to these words from Christ through St Paul's letter, for it is Christ himself who is saying to us, 'I am confident of this, that the one who began a good work in you, God your Father, will continue to complete it until the day of Christ Jesus.' Even though we ourselves can lose confidence on our journey, Jesus maintains a strong confidence that 'God, who began this good work in us' – a good work of letting the darkness come to light and making our truth known, healing from the effects and consequences of the abuse, creating awareness and prevention of abuse in the future – he 'will continue to complete it' until the end of our days when we come face to face with Christ.

As we pray this reading today, we need to remember, we are 'very good'! God himself said it when God created man and woman (Genesis 1:31): 'God looked at everything he had made and he found it very good!' What is bad for survivors is the evil of sexual abuse we suffered at human hands. It is so important to make a differentiation here. The evil we experienced does not mean that we are an evil person. We are good people who have experienced something evil in our lives. Believing this is critical for our own well-being.

When God looks at our life today, God still finds us 'very good' even though we have experienced and endured such evil in our lives. But God does not want this evil to have the last word in our lives. God wants to work with us to eradicate the effects of this evil. This is the good work God has initiated in us and God will not abandon us until it is complete.

Today let us listen to the full confidence that God has in us and let us allow this confidence to help us take the small steps that are all part of the good work that God will complete in our lives.

Praying the scripture reading

1. Try to be aware of God's presence. Read the scripture verses slowly, putting your name at the beginning of the verse.
2. Try to be aware as you read these words that it is God saying to you that 'he is confident'. What do these words evoke in you? Express

A boost of confidence

this to God (You may want to write it down.) For example, perhaps these words make you realize your lack of confidence. If this is so, tell God.

3. You may want to ask God, 'Why are you so confident? How long have you had this confidence in me? Why is it, Lord, that I don't always feel your confidence?' Try to listen to your heart and what God may be trying to reveal to you there. (You may want to write it down.)
4. You may also want to ask God more about the 'good work' that he is initiating in you. For example, 'What is the good work, God, that you are doing in me? How long have you been doing it for? Is it possible that a good work can come out of my life, God? Is this good work progressing from the day you initiated it, God? How do you see that, God? Why is this good work so important?' Take time to listen to God in your heart. (You may want to write it down.) Try to enjoy listening to God.
5. In conclusion, you may like to ask God what is the good work that he is confident he will complete in you today?' (If you want, write it down.) If you lack confidence, then let God share his confidence in you once again through these words.
6. Make a resolution with God to put step 5 in practice today.

The scripture experienced in my life

After prayer, I held on to the words Jesus had spoken to me through St Paul's letter to the Philippians: 'I am confident of this, that the one who began the good work in you will continue to complete it until the day of Jesus Christ.' After prayer, Jesus gave me the confidence that going ahead with my private session for the Royal Commission was a 'good work' that God himself had initiated in me. This meant that I could trust in it and believe in the good work that the Royal Commission had set out to do. If our institutions were to change their responses to child sexual abuse and, as a society, we were to become willing to do more to prevent it, then going ahead with my private session was an opportunity that God was giving me to play my part in history. So today I continued to confidently prepare my responses to the questions that were going to be asked of me. Although I still got a little anxious when I thought about how affected I may be after the session, I found that Jesus kept reminding me, 'If you are affected, I will continue to complete my work in you! Be confident!' I really did experience a boost of confidence today.

The scripture experienced in your life

Were you able to experience the scripture reading in your life today? If so, how did this happen? You may like to write down your own account.

Being gentle with self

OFTEN WE LEARN BY EXAMPLE. Children are a good demonstration of this. Frequently they imitate what they see their parents doing or hear them saying and they learn to imitate their attitudes and behaviours.

Unfortunately, it may be the same case for survivors of sexual abuse in regard to their perpetrators. It is possible that as young children we also learnt some of the destructive attitudes and behaviours that belonged to our perpetrator. As we grow into adulthood so too can these destructive attitudes and behaviours grow until we become aware of their harmful effects on us and make a conscious decision to work at changing them.

Being hard on ourselves, beating ourselves up, either through self-harming actions or destructive negative self-talk, is one of these learnt attitudes that is not only damaging to ourselves but also affects others.

We all know how it goes — we might fail a goal we set for our day, make a mistake, fall into a temptation, have an out of proportion reaction to something, be triggered by an event and, bang! The self-harming attitude we learnt at the time of the abuse automatically erupts in us. Even before we can catch ourselves doing it, we are already beating ourselves up for what we have done and telling ourselves how stupid or hopeless or no good we are. We bury ourselves in self-blame and self-hatred talk which in some cases can be followed by self-harming action.

For many of us, the attitude of being gentle with our self is foreign. Yet it is an attitude that is so vital in the process of healing and one that will help us overcome many of the issues we find burdensome in the process.

Jesus, who knows us so well and loves us unconditionally, invites us to learn from him how to be gentle with our self.

The scripture reading

'Come to me, all you who labour and are burdened, and I will give you rest. Take my yoke upon you and learn from me, for I am gentle and humble of heart, and you will find rest for yourselves. For my yoke is easy, and my burden light.'

Matthew 11:28-30

This is a beautiful invitation that we don't need to feel afraid to respond to. Jesus is clear about the intention of His invitation – 'I will give you rest'. He does not have any hidden agenda or any personal or self-interest. His invitation is a response to our deepest need for rest. Jesus is not referring here to physical rest but to a deeper, spiritual, rest – a rest from all the attitudes that break our spirit and make us exhausted: being hard with ourselves, beating ourselves up, self-blame and self-hatred. Not only do we long for this 'rest' deep within ourselves but it is vital on our healing journey.

Jesus knows this very well. He knows, more than anyone else, all the internal labour that is involved in the process of healing from sexual abuse. He knows how heavy our burdens are and he suffers when he sees us being hard on ourselves and getting so exhausted.

In this reading, he invites us to take his yoke upon us and learn from him, for he is gentle and humble of heart and he promises us that we will find rest for ourselves.

Like me, you may also say to Jesus, 'But it sounds like you are giving me more work, Jesus – taking up your yoke. I already have a heavy yoke just trying to go through this healing process!' But Jesus is not talking about giving us more to carry or to be burdened with. On the contrary, Jesus wants to make our load much easier and lighter. When he asks us to take his yoke upon us, he is inviting us to learn the secret of how to make our burden easy and light like his.

'I am gentle and humble of heart.' As we saw previously, Jesus is not only divine in nature but he is also human. He lived his earthly life in a

Being gentle with self

human body. He experienced the limits and weaknesses of his own humanity (particularly manifested in his passion and death), just as we do. When we realize all the human experiences Jesus passed through during his earthly life, we may ask, 'How did he manage to stay above ground level? How did he keep moving forward?' Jesus shares the 'how' with us in the scripture verse, 'I am gentle and humble of heart.' Jesus knew how to embrace his limitations and weaknesses as part of his own humanity and, more importantly, he knew that these limitations and weaknesses did not change who he was for God.

Jesus knew that in spite of his human limitations God continued to embrace him with an unconditional love and acceptance. I imagine that Jesus would have been caught up in the constant dynamic of going to God in prayer, expressing his human limitations, and listening to God reaffirming him with the words, 'You are my beloved Son, with whom I am well pleased' (Matthew 3:17). So we can imagine that this prayerful experience taught Jesus to be gentle with himself when he struggled with his human limitations, but it also provided Jesus with a source of gentleness, which we know from the gospels he embodied in his life and shared with all those he ministered to.

Jesus knows that the rest we are looking has a lot to do with adopting an attitude of being gentle of heart. For this reason, Jesus invites us to come to him and to learn from his gentleness. In the measure that we experience Jesus' gentleness towards us, we can learn to be gentle with ourselves and then gentle with others. To achieve this, we may want to try to get into the habit of going to Jesus, especially when we experience our own limits through failure, a mistake we have made, an opportunity we have blown, a reaction that is out of proportion, falling into temptation ... all the experiences that cause us to be hard on ourselves and start beating ourselves up with self-blame and self-hatred, to the point of exhaustion and self-harm. It is precisely in these moments that Jesus invites us to sit with him and pray and learn how to make our yoke easy and light.

Perhaps we will say to Jesus, 'Oh, I hate myself! I'm stupid! I'm hopeless! I feel like disappearing!' If we listen to Jesus through his words in

Scripture he will say to us, 'No. You are my beloved son or daughter, with whom I am well pleased' (Matthew 3:17; 17:5).' Perhaps we won't believe it the first time and we will keep repeating what we think to Jesus, but if we listen hard enough to our heart Jesus will keep affirming us: 'You are my beloved son or daughter, with whom I am well pleased.'

Learning how to be gentle with our self from Jesus takes time but once we learn it and practise it we can begin to experience the fruit of the inner work we are doing. Even though we are carrying a heavy burden due to the effects of sexual abuse, the process seems to be easier and lighter through the experience of Jesus' gentleness working within us. To top off this experience, we find the long-awaited rest that we have yearned for in our hearts!

We always win when we are gentle with our self.

Praying the scripture reading

1. Try to be still and aware of Jesus' presence in you.
2. Try to imagine Jesus sitting either in front of you or beside you (don't worry if you find it difficult). Now read the scripture reading slowly, putting your name at the beginning of each phrase.
3. Try to notice what you experience in your heart as Jesus invites you to come to him (joy, wonder, surprise, anxiety, fear, distress, curiosity ...) You may want to write it down and express it to Jesus.
4. Can you identify your 'burdens' and what causes you to labour from within? It could be an issue that you are currently dealing with in your process. Once you have identified it, allow Jesus to invite you through the scripture reading to come to him. Listen to Jesus telling you that he wants to give you rest. If you have any questions, thoughts or feelings that arise, you may want to write them down and express them to Jesus. For example, 'How are you going to give me rest? What sort of rest are you talking about, Jesus? How do you know I am tired, Jesus? I would really love a

Being gentle with self

good rest from all this chaos, Jesus!' Try to listen to what Jesus may be saying to you in your heart.

5. Allow Jesus to invite you to 'take his yoke upon you' and to learn from him as one who is 'gentle and humble of heart'. Express your thoughts, feelings or questions to Jesus and once again try to listen to his response through the words of Scripture. For example, 'I don't know if I can carry your yoke Jesus! I can barely carry my own! What is your yoke, Jesus? And why are you asking me to carry it for you? Is it too heavy for you? Do you need help? What is this being gentle all about? Why is it important to be gentle? I have never been gentle Jesus! I've always been a hard and rough around the edges sort of person.' Try not to rush your prayer.

6. If you are able to, try to deepen on the topic of being gentle by contemplating Jesus' life and asking him questions. For example, 'Jesus, how were you gentle in your heart when you were being persecuted? How were you gentle in your heart when people didn't believe in you? What about when you were betrayed by your close friend Judas? How did you manage to remain gentle in your heart? What about when you got tired from carrying your cross? How were you still being gentle in your heart Jesus?'

   The more we ask Jesus questions, the more we come to learn from him about being gentle. As you ask Jesus questions, remember to try to patiently wait for him to speak to your heart. (You may want to write down your conversation with Jesus.)

7. As you contemplate Jesus in his gentleness, you may see your own hardness of heart with yourself and how different your attitude is compared to Jesus'. You may like to express this to Jesus.

8. In conversation with Jesus, try to identify the events or situations that provoke you to be hard and beat yourself up. (You may want to write this down.) You may want to ask Jesus, 'How do you feel when I am like this and do this to myself?' Try to listen to Jesus' response in your heart. (You may want to write it down.)

9. Ask Jesus, 'What do you want to tell me in these events or situations?' Listen in your heart for his response. (You may want to write it down.)
10. Conclude this prayer by making a resolution to be more gentle. When events and situations arise in the future, where my automatic response would be to be hard on myself and beat myself up, how would I like to respond? How can I practise being gentle with myself? Is there something I learnt from Jesus about this in today's prayer? Is there a Word of Jesus that I can bring to mind to recall this?
11. Try to remember your resolution and practise it next time you are being hard with yourself.

The scripture experienced in my life

My day was going well until I went out to my local shopping centre. I saw someone from a distance that I knew and the encounter took me back to some traumatic memories of the abuse. All those feelings associated with the abuse came flooding back to me. I suddenly began feeling dirty, shameful, ugly, like rubbish! It's amazing just how quickly our body remembers those feelings. But this time, instead of immediately being hard on myself and filling myself with destructive thoughts of self-hatred and blame, I recalled Jesus' words, 'I am gentle of heart.' It was Jesus himself reminding me, 'Be gentle with yourself'. So instead of listening to all my harmful thoughts, I let Jesus reaffirm me by telling me repeatedly as I walked through that shopping centre, 'You are my beloved daughter, with whom I am well pleased.' I would have listened to him repeating this at least twenty times as I continued to do my shopping.

What a difference it made to be gentle with myself! Instead of coming home and feeling heavy and exhausted, I came home feeling light and easy, which even surprised me. Being gentle with self really does give us a deep rest!

Being gentle with self

The scripture experienced in your life

Were you able to experience the scripture reading in your life today? If so, how did this happen? You may like to write down your own account.

Walking through fire

TODAY IS THE DAY THAT I HAVE my private hearing with the Royal Commission for Institutional Responses to Child Sexual Abuse. I could not have reached this day without the help and support of so many people – my family, my psychologist, my spiritual director, my health professionals, the organization ASCA (Adults Surviving Child Abuse), and I cannot forget the help of God through daily prayer.

Although I had been anticipating this day for some months, and was eager to share my story as a means of preventing child sexual abuse in the future, particularly perpetrated by priests, I found myself procrastinating as I woke up on this cold winter morning. I lay in bed struggling. My mind was saying to my body, 'You must move and get up! Today is the day to speak out and say the truth about what happened to you. You can't be late.' The more I told my body to move, the less it wanted to. The same fear that I experienced at the time of the abuse was overwhelming me once again.

Not only that, I also had to struggle against the voice of my perpetrator sounding in my ears again: 'If you say anything, I will kill you! Don't say this to anyone.' Even though it was more than twenty-five years since the abuse had taken place, the fear that this priest instilled in me was overpowering me again. This was part of the re-traumatization that I was preparing myself for and part of the cost of coming forward to tell my story. This is part of the reason why it is so difficult for victims of sexual abuse to tell someone about what has happened to them and to speak out publicly.

The only way I could get out of bed and start getting ready was by listening to Jesus repeating the words from Scripture again and again, 'Don't be afraid, I am with you' (Matthew 28:20).

As a way of preparing myself spiritually for my private hearing, I recalled and prayed these scripture verses from the Prophet Isaiah.

Walking through fire

The scripture reading

Thus says the Lord, who created you, O Jacob, and formed you, O Israel.
Fear not, for I have redeemed you, I have called you by name, you are mine.
When you pass through water, I will be with you, in the rivers you shall not drown.
When you pass through fire, you shall not be burned, the flames shall not consume you.
For I am the Lord, your God, the Holy One of Israel, your saviour.

Isaiah 43:1-3

When we read the Scriptures, we need to be aware that Jesus, the Son of God, is the fulfilment of all the promises God made to the People of Israel through the prophets of the Old Testament.

In this reading from the Prophet Isaiah, God promises the people that no matter what they are passing through God will not abandon them, for they are God's children, created and formed by God.

This promise comes true in the person of Jesus, the Son of God. Jesus knew very well what it was to pass through deep water and fire! The gospels paint the picture for us at various times throughout Jesus' public ministry: he stands in deep water and fire when he publicly condemns the hypocritical practices of the religious leaders of his time and is persecuted for it; he breaks with some of the cultural and religious practices of his time making himself vulnerable to criticism; he is betrayed and handed over to the religious authorities by one of his close friends; he is arrested, abused physically, and condemned to death.

But, being in the middle of this water and fire, Jesus is not totally consumed and burned by flames of death. The faithful love of God saves Jesus, and, in a powerful demonstration of grace, Jesus emerges through the flames alive and with a gift in hand for all who believe in him – a much stronger life, an Eternal Life that will never end.

So, when the time comes for us to pass through fire, let us try to remember Jesus' promise, 'You will not be burned, the flames shall not consume you.' Naturally, we will experience the fear of fire, and the heat that comes from it, the discomfort, how it leaves us parched, dry and desolate, but let us believe in God's Word, that these flames will not consume us. Jesus promises us that he will save us from the flames, and that as he came through them alive, so too will we and, in the process, we will become much stronger in our inner selves than we were. It sounds ironic, doesn't it! Passing through fire makes us stronger people! It can be true if we believe in God's promise.

Praying the scripture reading

1. Try to be still and aware of God's presence with you. Read the scripture reading slowly substituting your name where the reading refers to 'you'.
2. Try to notice what you are feeling in your heart as you read God's Word. It may be encouragement, a sense of strength, anxiety, peacefulness ... Try to express what you are feeling to God. (You may want to write this down.)
3. Now read the words that refer to 'passing through fire' slowly. Try to remember that it is God who is speaking to you through these words from Scripture.
4. As you read these words, what do they make you feel? You may want to express these feelings to God.
5. Is there something you would like to ask God about these words? For example, 'What will stop me from getting burned God? How is it possible that I will not be consumed? Is it necessary to pass through the fire? Why or why not, God?' After you have asked God your question, try to listen deep in your heart to what God may be saying to you. You may like to write it down.
6. You may like to ask God, 'How do I know that you are with me and haven't abandoned me?'

7. As you prepare to 'pass through fire', remember these words from Scripture. As you recall them, let them give you strength to pass through the fire and go beyond your fear. You may even get a surprise to experience that you have been strengthened inwardly by God's grace.

The scripture experienced in my life

Thanks be to God, I was able to 'walk through fire'. I am referring to my private hearing session. I certainly experienced the intensity of the fire, even though I was in a safe environment and sitting before two very sensitive commissioners and a Royal Commission officer. When I was asked to give a summary of the events that took place, it was as if I went back to that time and place, feeling all the terror and horror of it again. My whole being trembled as I tried to recount the events and I was stifling my words. I felt as though I was the small child again, struggling to articulate my own personal tragedy. I just couldn't find the appropriate vocabulary. Throughout the hearing, my body trembled with immense fear, stress and anxiety. The heat of the fire was so strong, but the amazing thing was that the fire did not consume me.

There was a brief moment in the session when I thought, 'I'm not going to make it out of this alive', and I paused. Right at that time, these words from Scripture came to me, 'When you walk through fire, you shall not be burnt, the flames shall not consume you, for I am the Lord, your God, the Holy One, your Saviour!' I found the strength to continue telling my story to the end.

I would say that I definitely came out with some heat exhaustion! My arms and legs were like jelly, I was very hot and clammy, I had difficulty regaining my normal breathing rhythm, and I was emotionally exhausted – all normal for what I had just gone through. After my session, I spent time talking with one of the counsellors who were available about putting in place some self-care strategies and also making sure I had the right support to help me get through the trauma I was presently experiencing. I was grateful for the care, kindness, compassion and sensitivity that I was able to experience within the whole context of my private hearing session from beginning to end. The experience in itself was healing for me, despite the trauma that telling my story produced in me.

As I got up to leave the building, I was still quite unsteady and I tried to take control of my body as best as I could. I began nurturing my hurting inner child with tender self-talk as we walked out the door. I knew that with God and my support network, and a lot of self-care, I would be able to come through this. When I returned home, I had time out for the rest of the day. I was aware that I was quite traumatized, yet there was something to celebrate – the fact that I experienced God's words from Scripture as true: 'When you walk through fire, you shall not be burned, the flames shall not consume you.' Thank you, God.

The scripture experienced in your life

Were you able to experience the scripture reading in your life today? If so, how did this happen? You may like to write down your own account.

Difficult decision making

DURING MY PRIVATE HEARING SESSION for the Royal Commission, I was informed that my matter was a case for prosecution. Prior to the hearing, I had not intended to proceed in this manner, however, the whole setting of retelling the horrors of my story and what I had lived through, experiencing the trauma of the event in my body again, and being taken seriously by the two commissioners in front of me, re-affirmed for me that the offences involved were criminal. Could my private hearing be the important catalyst for taking further steps towards justice?

I asked what this would involve on my part, and I was told, first, I would need to have an interview with the police to make a formal statement and then, if the matter did go to court, I may need to bear witness in a court room. At the time, I was so overwhelmed with intense emotions from recalling the trauma that I felt my brain struggling to focus on what was being said to me and I was unable to ask more questions. Even though I heard what the commissioner was saying, my brain could not process the information. Not being clear headed at the time, I asked for some time to consider this. The commissioners were very kind and understanding and informed me that a commission officer would be in touch with me at a later date to find out if I would like to proceed with prosecution or not.

Sure enough, more questions came to me during the next days: Would I need to sit in the same court room with my perpetrator? Would I need to get legal representation? If so, what costs am I looking at? What would happen if my perpetrator was now living overseas? Is it still possible to prosecute? What sort of time frame does prosecution involve – months, years …? Would my safety from the perpetrator be guaranteed?

Other questions arose from the fact that I am a member of a religious community: I needed to find out if there was any reason why I could not proceed with civil prosecution. Am I able to prosecute being a Catholic missionary? Is permission from my leaders required? Would it involve my religious community in any way?

Perhaps the most important question for me, one that meant being very honest with myself, was, am I ready and strong enough to deal with the physical, emotional, psychological and spiritual implications of proceeding with prosecution? Would I have the sufficient support networks around me so that I wouldn't feel alone or isolated while coping with these impacts?

All these unanswered questions made it very difficult for me to reach an informed decision. I did not want to enter into prosecution blindly and naively; I wanted to find out more information and to have my questions answered. I knew that if I proceeded there would be a huge personal cost for me so I felt that I could not be superficial in making the decision.

However, to think about not prosecuting also raised some very hard and deep questions of conscience that required a lot of soul searching and prayer. What if the perpetrator is still offending and harming others? Would I be able to live peacefully knowing that I could have done something to stop him and didn't? Is it right that the perpetrator is not brought to justice for criminal offences and can continue to live believing that he got away with it? Is it justice, for me and for the other victims of the perpetrator who may still be living in silence and for all survivors of sexual abuse, not to proceed with prosecution? Is my not pursuing prosecution continuing to give the perpetrator power to keep offending? Then there were questions that pertained more to my personal religious beliefs and responsibility as a member of the church and making the church a safer place for children in the future. I felt that these questions required a deeply personal response that I could live peacefully with. I am aware that from one survivor to another the response to each of these questions may be very different because even though we may suffer the same effects of sexual abuse we are very likely to have different limitations and what we can and cannot do may be very different.

With all these questions, I was beginning to feel like the helpless little child I was in the past and clearly the helpless child in me needed empowering.

The Holy Spirit guided me to the reading below. It responded perfectly

Difficult decision making

to both the helpless child in me as well as the surviving adult who was trying to make an informed decision.

The scripture reading

'Ask and it will be given to you; seek and you will find, knock and the door will be opened to you. For everyone who asks, receives; and the one who seeks, finds; and to the one who knocks, the door will be opened.'

Matthew 7:7-8

In this scripture reading, Jesus invites us to be active in our relationship with God by asking, seeking and knocking. In order to know and discern God's will in the situations of our life, God invites us to turn to him in prayer and ask for guidance: 'God, what do you want me to do in this situation? What is the best for the common good? How do I know that this is your will?' Apart from this, we can actively seek God's will by being attentive to the events or circumstances that are unfolding before us in our daily life. And we may need to knock on doors that we are not very familiar with; perhaps people that God directs us to in prayer or organizations that may be able to help us with information.

When we have an active attitude of faith, Jesus promises us that our prayers will be answered, because 'everyone who asks, receives; and the one who seeks, finds; and to the one who knocks, the door will be opened.'

Asking, seeking and knocking means coming out of our comfort zone but it is a sure way of moving forward in our lives, particularly in situations where we meet a crossroad and need to decide which direction to go.

Asking, seeking and knocking are steps that empower us during the process of difficult decision making. Not only will we be able to make difficult decisions but we may also experience new and unimaginable doors are opened in our life.

Let us see today if we can take up Jesus' invitation to ask, seek and knock.

Praying the scripture reading

1. Try to be aware of Jesus' presence in you.
2. Read the words of the Scripture slowly, putting your name at the beginning of each phrase.
3. Are there certain words that call your attention, like the word 'ask' or the word 'seek'? What do these words evoke in you? You may want to write this down.
4. Try to begin a conversation with Jesus around this word, expressing your own questions or thoughts or reactions to his Word. You may want to write it down. For example, 'Jesus, I don't even know what to ask you for. There are several things happening in my life at the moment but the one thing that is concerning me the most is … What should I do Lord?' Try to be practical in your conversation with Jesus applying his Word to your life and remember to take the time to listen to Jesus' response in your heart.
5. If you have understood that Jesus is inviting you to put something into practice during the day, try to resolve how and when you can do this. You may want to write it down.

The scripture experienced in my life

After praying this reading I felt quite empowered to begin asking, seeking, and knocking on doors to find answers to my questions. I wrote down a list of people and organizations who could potentially answer my questions in regard to prosecution.

I began by calling ASCA (Adult Survivors of Child Abuse) and I spoke with a very helpful counsellor. She connected me to another lady who was part of the team organizing a legal advisory service for sexual abuse victims who were coming forward to tell their story to the Royal Commission. It was also suggested that I get in touch with the Royal Commission call centre to see if they had established an office for this legal advisory service (which is known now as Knowmore) and if there was a particular person who was

Difficult decision making

already available for victims who had completed their private hearings. I called the Royal Commission call centre and my enquiry was passed on to the Commissioner's office.

Several hours later, I received a phone call from one of the officers of the Royal Commission who was assigned to follow up my decision about prosecution. We had a conversation and I relayed all my questions to him. Unfortunately, he could not give me all the answers I wanted but he told me that he would speak to the commissioners who were involved in my private hearing and call me back.

The next day I received a phone call from the same officer, who provided me with answers to all my questions plus extra information. He suggested that I speak to some other people who could give me further details.

Jesus' word is true. I spent a couple of days speaking to different people, asking questions and seeking answers. I knocked at the door of ASCA, the Royal Commission call centre and the Commissioner's office and, yes, the door was opened and I found answers to my questions.

Asking, seeking and knocking certainly helped me make an informed decision. Although I still needed to find out more information, at least now I had more information at hand than when I concluded my private hearing session.

Asking, seeking and knocking are attitudes that are definitely worth remembering and practising when we are trying to make difficult decisions and discern God's will.

The scripture experienced in your life

Were you able to experience the scripture reading in your life today? If so, how did this happen?

Running on empty ...

THIS IS A REALITY THAT MANY survivors are familiar with, especially while we are processing and dealing with traumatic memories. You can wake up in the morning and you feel like a tonne of bricks has fallen on top of you and you are crushed beneath them. You try moving your body but you just can't. The slightest movement causes you to ache all over. It seems impossible to get up. Your head begins to pound as you think of the responsibilities and commitments that await you, whether it is your medical or healthcare appointments, study, work, domestic duties, or whether it is the needs of your partner/spouse or children, or social activities.

From your perspective, getting through the day seems impossible because, even before you start, you have no energy – physically, emotionally, mentally, intellectually, spiritually – your gauge is clearly marked 'empty'! All your resources have been dried up. You feel that you have nothing left of yourself to give. Only a miracle can get you through this day!

Miracles are possible. When I have felt like this, the scripture reading below has been very helpful.

The scripture reading

As the day was drawing to a close, the twelve approached him and said, 'Dismiss the crowd so that they can go to the surrounding villages and farms and find lodging and provisions; for we are in a deserted place here.' He said to them, 'Give them some food yourselves.' They replied, 'Five loaves and two fish are all we have, unless we ourselves go and buy food for all these people.' Now the men there numbered about five thousand. Then he said to his disciples, 'Have them sit down in groups of about fifty.' They did so and made them all sit down. Then taking the five loaves and the

Running on empty ...

two fish, and looking up to heaven, he said the blessing over them, broke them, and gave them to the disciples to set before the crowd. They all ate and were satisfied. And when the leftover fragments were picked up, they filled twelve wicker baskets.

Luke 9:12-17

This is one of Jesus' famous miracles – the feeding of the five thousand! It's awesome to see how this miracle comes about.

Jesus and his disciples were surrounded by a huge crowd they had been attending to. As the day draws to a close, the disciples ask Jesus what seems to be quite logical: 'Dismiss the crowd so that they can go to the surrounding villages and farms and find lodging and provisions.' The disciples are obviously exhausted and believe they don't have the resources to cater for the needs of this huge crowd. They are thinking, 'Where on earth are we going to get food for so many at this time of night? It's impossible!' And not only that but, 'Where are we going to get the energy to do this?'

Isn't it easy for us survivors to understand what the disciples were experiencing? We can understand that feeling of being surrounded by a crowd of responsibilities and commitments, and things that need to be attended to but we are exhausted and we experience that we don't have any resources left. We are running on low! The tasks before us seem impossible.

Jesus listened to the disciples' request but he responded to them with a challenge: 'Give them some food yourselves!' Imagine what went through their heads. They must have thought 'Jesus, you've got to be kidding! Are you for real?' The disciples tried to make Jesus aware of just how little they had: 'Five loaves and two fish are all we have, unless we ourselves go and buy food for all these people!'

Jesus isn't bothered by the reality of how little his disciples have. He is happy, even though they consider what they have to be too little. Jesus uses what they believe is too little to perform a miracle. He takes what the disciples have, looks up to heaven, blesses the food and breaks it and gives it to the disciples to set before the crowd. The five thousand eat and are all satisfied and there is even a lot left over. It is amazing! But this miracle would not have come about if the disciples didn't hand over the five loaves and two fish. I guess they were the first ones in awe at this miracle. I'm sure they learned the lesson: miracles can happen, even when we feel we have nothing to offer and are running on low.

This scripture reading can say a lot to survivors. Perhaps we have woken up this morning feeling like we've been crushed by a tonne of bricks and that there's absolutely no way that we can attend to our responsibilities because we have nothing left to give! And if we express this to Jesus, all he will say to us is, 'Give them some food yourselves!'

Perhaps we find ourselves just like the disciples thinking 'Jesus, but don't you see my reality. Can't you see that I don't have it in me today to accomplish these commitments!' Our surprise will be that Jesus will say to us, 'Give this to me!' He will give thanks for that 'little bit of energy', he will bless it and he will make it multiply and he will set it before us so we can go out and deal with the crowd of commitments and responsibilities that need attending to today!

Yes, in a short conversation, where we are able to surrender to Jesus the little that we have, Jesus can perform a miracle. All he needs is a little, no matter what this little is. It could be a little hope, disappointment, courage, anger, sadness ... The little we have, no matter what it is, is miracle material for Jesus if we just surrender it. Once we hand it over to Jesus, he and the Father will work with it and we will experience a miracle taking place in us.

Never be afraid when you experience that you are running on empty. Just think, 'It's time for Jesus to perform a miracle!'

Praying the scripture reading

1. Try to be still and aware of Jesus' presence with you. Read the reading very slowly and, as you do, try to imagine that you are one of the disciples with Jesus. Imagine the huge crowd. Perhaps you may like to write down what this crowd is for you today – personal commitments, family responsibilities, social commitments.

Running on empty ...

2. You may like to express what you feel about the crowd to Jesus just as his disciples did. They wanted to dismiss the crowd and send them away. You may feel the same: for example, 'Jesus, I wish all these things to do would just go away. I wish work would go away. I wish I didn't have to get up now to attend to my family ....' (You may like to write this down.)
3, Listen to Jesus saying to you personally, '[your name], give them some food yourself!' (Write down what these words evoke in you. What are your feelings and thoughts? Express these to Jesus)
4. The disciples were honest with Jesus about the little they had, 'Five loaves and two fish is all we have.' You too can be honest with Jesus and name the little you have today without feeling embarrassed about it. For example, 'Jesus all I have is a little bit of hope' or 'a little bit of insight' or a 'little anger', or a 'little bit of faith'... (You may like to write it down.)
5. Try to imagine Jesus taking the little you have, looking up to heaven, blessing it and breaking it and setting it before you. Imagine that what you see before you now has now been multiplied! You may want to express to Jesus how this make you feel. (You may like to write this down.)
6. Now imagine that Jesus sends you out today to attend to the 'crowd' (your responsibilities and commitments), but with your new supply of resources. Picture yourself doing the tasks of this day. How do you feel? (You may like to express this to Jesus.)
7. As you finish your prayer, remember the miracle that Jesus performed in you and that you are not finishing your prayer the same way you began, 'running on empty'. You have been refuelled by the miracle of Jesus' love working in you.
8. Try to recall this miracle today as you carry on with your commitments and responsibilities.
9. Let yourself be in awe at the miracle that Jesus has worked in your life today.

The scripture experienced in my life

Today when I got up, I actually did feel like a tonne of bricks had fallen on top of me. Not only was I dealing with post-traumatic stress after my private hearing at the Royal Commission but I was also knocked over by a nasty flu. My body was aching and my head was pounding with a terrible migraine. Outside was a very wet and cold winter morning. What did I have to offer Jesus on this new day?

The only thing I could find was a little bit of self-pity. I couldn't believe it when I told Jesus what I had. He didn't reject it but said, 'Give it to me!' I felt so light after I imagined myself giving it to him. Jesus looked very prayerful with my little package and when he gave it back to me it was an absolutely huge package – but not of self-pity! It seemed that Jesus had transformed my self-pity into a package of enthusiasm. The transformation I experienced was a miracle and so was the abundance of what Jesus gave back to me. Jesus asked me to share it with the crowd. Part of my crowd is writing this reflection for my book. Even in sickness, Jesus gave me the enthusiasm to listen to his Word and to share it with my fellow survivors so that it can be a little bit of 'bread from heaven' for you! But the credit goes to Jesus, it's his miracle not mine! It truly is amazing what he can do when we are running on low.

The scripture experienced in your life

Were you able to experience the scripture reading in your life today? If so, how did this happen? You may like to write down your own account.

Re-establishing healthy boundaries

PERSONAL BOUNDARIES ARE GUIDELINES or limits that we create to identify for ourselves what are reasonable, safe and permissible ways for others to behave around us and how we will respond when someone steps outside those limits. They include physical, mental, psychological and spiritual boundaries, involving beliefs, emotions, intuitions and self-esteem. Boundaries guard and protect the dignity of our person. They operate in two directions, affecting both the incoming and outgoing interactions between people.

We are not born knowing personal boundaries. They are something we need to be taught from an early age and continue to learn as we grow and develop into adulthood.

Unfortunately, personal boundaries are not always respected. In the case of children who have been sexually abused, personal boundaries have been disrespected and broken at all levels – physically, mentally, psychologically and spiritually – affecting the most sacred part of the dignity of the person.

Consequently, victims of sexual abuse struggle to re-establish boundaries as they grow into adulthood. As a child, the lines that marked a limit and made us feel protected were erased by the intrusion of our perpetrator leaving us vulnerable to further abuse. Re-marking these lines in our life and re-establishing healthy boundaries is very important otherwise there is the danger that we will become victims of abuse again.

Learning to re-establish personal boundaries is not an easy task because the lines we want to mark as limits are not even clear to ourselves: we question, 'Where do I need to draw the line?' Like young children, we need to re-learn the basics. Learning to do this is a key part of our healing and enables us to live as a functioning and whole person.

It is possible to learn how to re-draw these lines in our life through prayer. As we try to make a sacred space in our life for God, we come to learn and understand more about personal boundaries as we begin to identify what we will allow to come in to our sacred space and what we want to stay out of our sacred space.

Initially, I found the scripture reading below very challenging because of the word and image associations that connected me to my past trauma. However, as I overcame this, God began to speak to me about re-establishing healthy boundaries in my life. God also began to teach me how to do this through prayer.

One of the personal benefits of learning boundaries through prayer is that they can easily be transferred to our daily life. So, even though you may find the scripture reading below challenging (for the same reason I did) try to move beyond the associations to perceive God's invitation. It may help us to remember that God will never hurt us, for 'God is Love' (1 John 4:8).

The scripture reading[45]

> 'When you pray, do not be like the hypocrites, who love to stand
> and pray in the synagogues and on street corners so that others
> may see them. Amen, I say to you, they have received their reward.
> But when you pray, go to your inner room, close the door and pray
> to your Father in secret. And your Father who sees in secret will
> repay you.'
>
> Matthew 6:5-6

In these verses, Jesus is teaching his disciples about prayer. He invites his listeners not to be like the hypocrites who pray in public just so that they will be noticed and appear to be 'good' before others.

---

[45] This reading refers to God as 'Father'. I have tried to address the issues around this in my explanation of the scripture reading and I am mindful that for some survivors the reading may cause traumatic memories. I will leave it up to the discretion of the reader and their knowledge of self to discern whether they feel ready to proceed with it or not (See also footnote 1 on p. 2.)

Re-establishing healthy boundaries

Jesus invites us to find a private space when we pray so that we can have an intimate face-to-face and heart-to-heart dialogue with God. He reminds us that our Father, who sees in secret that we are praying will repay us by responding to our needs. For this quality of prayer, Jesus invites us to 'go to our inner room' – the deepest and most sacred part of our being where we find ourselves alone with God. Perhaps in your prayer you may want to ask God, 'How do I get to my inner room? What will I find in this inner room? Why do I need to meet you there? Why not somewhere else? Will I be safe in this inner room?' Or you may have your own questions.

Another important step that facilitates intimacy with God in prayer is 'closing the door' (the door of our heart). A door creates a physical boundary and keeps unwanted visitors outside. If we leave a door open, anyone and anything can enter. When a door is closed it communicates to those who are on the outside 'Do not enter' or 'Do not interrupt'. It marks a limit, saying, 'This space is private and personal.'

When Jesus says 'Close the door', he is not referring to a physical door but to a spiritual door. In the same way that physical doors create physical boundaries to keep unwanted visitors outside, a spiritual door creates spiritual boundaries to keep unwanted visitors, intruders or robbers out of our heart during the time we are praying. Learning to practise spiritual boundaries when we pray is just as important as learning to practise physical boundaries in our relationship with others.

When we try to go to our inner room, it is not unusual for us to experience that intruders and unwanted visitors – in the form of bad memories, thoughts or feelings from the past, or things that people have said to us in the past, judgements that people have made about us, problems, worries or unresolved issues in our life – attempt to invade our sacred space and make it very difficult for us to enjoy the fruits of being alone with God.

Jesus understands our struggles and this is why he invites us to go to our inner room and close the door. It's an invitation to practise spiritual boundaries. If we are praying and a bad memory enters into our space with God, close the door and say to this bad memory, 'Stay out! You're not wanted here!' Or perhaps we are trying to savour some words from Scripture and some destructive words that our perpetrator used to say come out of nowhere – that's when we can put up a spiritual boundary and say, 'You are not welcome in my space. Get out and leave me alone.' If it helps, imagine that you are closing the door on that voice. Or the face of your perpetrator may be in front of you – again, put up a spiritual boundary. Imagine that you are getting him or her out and closing the door. You can say whatever you would like to say to him or her: 'You are never going to come into my life again!' The more we practise spiritual boundaries, the better we will become at it and the more empowered we will be through prayer.

Practising spiritual boundaries is a fruitful exercise because we can apply what we learn in prayer to help us re-establish healthy physical, emotional, psychological and mental boundaries in our life.

Praying the scripture reading

1. Find a quiet place where you know that you will not be interrupted.
2. Try to be still and aware of God's presence with you.
3. Read the scripture reading slowly, putting your name at the beginning of each phrase.
4. Try to visualize that you are going to your 'inner room' – the most sacred part of your being – where God and the fullness of God's love dwells. Imagine yourself entering this room. What do you feel? What do you think? How do you react being in this room? What do you notice happening within your heart as you enter? Talk to God about whatever you experience.
5. Now picture a door at the entrance of your inner room and Jesus inviting you to close the door so that no one or nothing will interrupt your sacred time with God.
6. Try now to focus on having a dialogue with God as you sit with him in your sacred space. You may want to ask God, 'How long have you been waiting here for me? Why did you want to meet me here? Is there something else that I should know about my inner room, God?' or whatever questions may come to mind.

Re-establishing healthy boundaries

7. If you find that unwanted visitors enter and intrude on your sacred space, interrupting your dialogue with God, mark a spiritual boundary: tell them, 'You must leave now.' Imagine yourself opening the door to see them out and once they are out close the door again. By doing this in prayer, you are already empowering yourself to do this in your daily life.
8. Keep repeating this step as many times as necessary. It is a step that is necessary to practise every day in your prayer if your goal is to experience an intimate sharing with God. As you do, you will notice that the quality of your prayer will improve day by day.
9. You may want to talk to God about your experience of 'closing the door' in this session of prayer. Perhaps you have found it hard to do or perhaps you got tired doing it or perhaps you have found that your intruders are much stronger than you are. Express whatever you have experienced to God. For example, 'God, did you see how that destructive thought just came in to our sacred space? I didn't know how to deal with it and get it out. I just let it hang around but it totally ruined my time to be alone with you. I felt it invaded me.' Try to listen to God's response in your heart. You may find God gently encouraging you not to give up. You may find that God tells you that he will help you to practise 'closing the door' and setting boundaries.
10. To conclude the prayer, you may like to ask God, 'What do you want to teach me from this prayer for my life?'
11. Finally, you may want to ask God 'Are there any physical, emotional, psychological or mental doors that you want me to close in my life today? When and how are you inviting me to practise that?'

The scripture experienced in my life

After prayer, I made further phone calls to gather more information around the question of prosecution. My final call was to the Commission officer who was waiting to know that I had gathered the information I needed. Despite that, I was not yet 100 per cent certain and a small part of me was still holding back. I felt I needed time and space to come to terms with what the implications of my decision would be, whichever way I decided to go. I felt it was necessary to establish a mental boundary to provide myself with the time and space to think things through calmly on my own and to assimilate the information I had been given. I asked the Commission officer whether I could have more time: I would call back when I was ready? 'Yes, of course!' he replied.

In the past, I would have found it very difficult to establish such a boundary but through the gift of prayer and dialogue with God I have come to learn that establishing healthy boundaries empowers us to be who we are called to be – God's children – and they teach others to respect us.

The scripture experienced in your life

Were you able to experience the scripture reading in your life today? If so, how did this happen? You may like to write down your own account.

The terror of the night (sleeplessness)

A LONG DAY HAS PASSED. You are exhausted after a very long and emotional day. Your body is craving a healthy and well-deserved night's sleep to recover and be ready for another day's work. Once the lights go out and you are in complete darkness you become hyper-vigilant to all the sounds you hear, whether they be loud and close by or faintly heard in the distance. You want to switch off from it all but you can't! It's as though the volume in your head is turned up to maximum.

You hear the voices outside as partying youths stroll by your house, some sounding as though they have had too much to drink. You hear the young girl screaming further down the street. Your mind begins racing one hundred kilometres per hour. 'Does she need help? Oh my gosh! Is she okay?' Those voices you heard apparently walking past the house seemed to have stopped outside your place. You listen out a bit more. 'Are they entering my gate? Am I safe?'

There are the sounds of cars driving up and down the street. 'Wait!' There is one pulling over right outside my place. The engine turns off. A car door opens and after a couple of seconds you hear it shut again. You hear footsteps. Then they stop. You hear the neighbour's front door opening. 'Oh, it's all okay!' Then, after one hour on a good night, or two or three hours on a bad night, you begin to doze off. Finally, you are asleep.

But it feels like you've only just closed your eyes and then suddenly you wake up! Without realizing it, you thrust yourself up into a sitting position, eyes wide open. Sweat is pouring down your face. You are drenched. You gasp for breath. Your heart is thumping as though it's going to jump out of your chest. You can feel your blood rushing through your body. You are trembling. 'Who's there?' you cry out! 'Who is it?' You listen intently! Your heart is thumping so much and the adrenaline is rushing through your body that you cannot settle down again. You try to console the young child in you that everything is going to be okay but she/he has trouble trusting and the whole cycle of hyper-vigilance that greeted the night automatically kicks in again. You reach for your mobile to check the time ... six more long and agonizing hours to go until daylight!

As much as we want to put the past behind us, our body reminds us of the terror we lived through and the horrendous things that happened to us. As young children, the timing of our body clock was broken. Night should have been the time when we were sleeping peacefully to awake the next morning feeling refreshed and full of energy. Instead, it was the most anxious time of our day, when our body worked overtime as we lay awake, on guard in an attempt to protect ourselves from our perpetrator. Sleepless nights became a pattern, as did waking the next morning feeling exhausted and nauseous and without a single ounce of energy to lift ourselves from bed.

As adult survivors, one of our constant struggles can be trying to reset our body clocks so that the day is for being awake and the night is for sleeping, but re-synchronization takes time and requires a lot of patience with ourselves. While we wish we could wave a magical wand to make ourselves fall asleep, we can't! But what we can do is to learn how to get through the sleepless nights more peacefully.

In the Old Testament there are many references to sleeplessness and we get a hint of the suffering it caused to those who experienced it. We also find some helpful suggestions to deal with it.

You may like to read the following scripture readings and discover through them some ways that you can also deal with sleeplessness.

The scripture readings

You will not fear the terror of the night, nor the arrow that flies by day, nor the pestilence that roams in darkness, nor the plague that ravages at noon.

Psalm 91:5-6

The terror of the night (sleeplessness)

God invites us not to fear 'the terror of the night' nor 'the pestilence that roams in darkness'. The memories of the abuse are like a pestilence – a fatal disease that becomes active at night. Terrifying as the memories are, we need to hear the voice of God constantly saying to us, 'Do not fear the terror of the night!' We can be peaceful knowing that we are safe with him.

> *On my bed I remember you. I think of you through the night. You indeed are my help, and in the shadow of your wings I shout for joy. My soul clings fast to you; your right hand upholds me.*
> Psalm 63:7-9

God invites us through this psalm to try something different. Instead of lying awake in our bed, remembering the person who abused us or the abuse itself, remember God. Turn our thoughts to God again and again. Think of God's powerful presence with us. Think of God's faithfulness in accompanying us through life up until the present moment. Think of his unconditional, unstoppable, unchangeable love for us. Fill our night with thoughts of God. Cry to God for help so that 'in the shadow of his wings we can shout for joy'. Cling to God's presence through the night instead of clinging to our traumatic memories. Let God's hand uphold us through the night and bring us through safely.

> *Rise up, shrill in the night, at the beginning of every watch;*
> *Pour out your heart like water in the presence of the Lord.*
> Lamentations 2:19a

While not being able to sleep is a big suffering, it is also a unique opportunity to grow in our relationship and closeness to God. Since our body is awake when we can't sleep, so too is our heart! God invites us through this reading to 'pour out our heart like water'. Instead of dwelling on unhelpful thoughts as we lay awake, let us try talking to God instead, pouring out our heart and troubles. We will be surprised how much closer we can become to God while suffering a sleepless week if we try this.

CHILD, ARISE!

I rise before dawn and cry out; I put my hope in your words. My eyes greet the night watches as I meditate your promises.
Psalm 119:147-148

We are invited once again to 'cry out' to God. No matter what time of day or night it is, God is present with us, here for us. Think about all the wonderful promises God makes to you through Scripture – of being free, living life to the full, being saved from all fear, being strong and secure in God, being one with God. The more you ponder all of God's promises, the more peaceful your heart will be.

Praying the scripture readings

1. Try to be still and aware of God's presence with you.
2. Read the scripture readings one at a time and slowly, putting your name at the beginning of each phrase.
3. Is there a particular word or phrase that resonates with you? What do these words evoke in you or how do you react to these words?
4. Try to have a conversation with God around these words, asking questions or sharing your thoughts. For example, if it is the words, 'You will not fear the terror of the night', you may want to express to God what you really experience. For example, 'Lord, I do fear the terror of the night and every night seems so long as I wait for the minutes to pass by until the first light of dawn ... What can I do to not be afraid? How can I end the terror of the night? I am tired of being terrified. I can't keep going on night after night without an inch of sleep.' Try to listen to God's responses in your heart.
5. You may want to ask God, 'How can you help me the next time I have a sleepless night? Is there something you want me to do next time I experience a sleepless night?'
6. Perhaps God will invite you to recall one of the above readings that resonates with you or, perhaps, to recall them all. Allow God's Word to speak you as you lie awake in the night. As you recall

The terror of the night (sleeplessness)

God's Word in your sleeplessness, you will experience God's consolation.

The scripture experienced in my life

Around the time I was considering whether to proceed to prosecution or not, I experienced many sleepless nights.

Falling to sleep seemed impossible. Not only was my heart awake and extremely hyper-vigilant to even the smallest sounds around me, but my mind was active and exhausting me as it raced around all the different possibilities and outcomes that the decision of prosecution might lead to.

As I became aware that my heart and mind were like an unending merry-go-round — I was on it only it wasn't merry — I began to think of God as I recalled the words of the psalm: 'On my bed I remember you. I think of you through the night.'

I began to think of God's presence with me as I lay in the darkness of night. I thought about how God already knew what was in my heart and mind. I thought about how great and almighty God's presence is with me and how God's presence is much more powerful than any human presence. I thought of how God is able to conquer even death, demonstrated to us in the resurrection of Jesus.

As I dwelled on God's presence, I began to feel my heart and mind slowing down. When I became aware of scary or terrifying thoughts, I called out to the almighty God in me for help and I experienced my heart and mind settling and calming again.

It is true, O Lord, 'you indeed are my help.' I can call to you in the 'terror of the night' when 'the pestilence roams in darkness' and 'in the shadow of your wings I shout for joy', for together we defend my enemies and you give me great peace. What a sweet and soothing presence! For, just as a mother soothes a young sleepless baby, so God soothes and consoles us in the night!

This gentle exercise of clinging fast to God is one that keeps us sane in the darkness of the night and restores our sleep. What a gift it is, God, to remember you at night! Thank you, Lord.

The scripture experienced in your life

Were you able to experience the scripture reading in your life today? If so, how did this happen? You may like to write down your own account.

Valuing our contribution

OFTEN, SURVIVORS OF SEXUAL ABUSE struggle to value themselves, let alone the contributions they make to their family, friends, social groups, local communities and life in general. A damaging effect of sexual abuse is that our self-esteem and self-worth suffer a very grievous blow. Survivors are left with feelings of being 'no good' and 'never measuring up to the standard'. For many, it is a consequence of the harmful messages that were instilled in us from the past – 'You're no good for anything!' 'You're hopeless!' 'You're nothing but scum of the earth!' 'You'll never get anywhere in life!'

Even decades after the abuse (as I experienced and saw others experiencing), these feelings can come back to haunt us repeatedly, causing us not to value the contributions we make in life, whatever and wherever they may be.

This is often complicated by comparing our contributions to those who have not had a past of sexual abuse. When we look at their lives, perhaps we feel that what they contribute in life through their gifts, talents and creativity is so much more valuable than what we feel we give and have to offer.

We equate the value of our contribution to its quantity and feel that if we are only making small contributions in life then they are not very valuable contributions at all.

But Jesus does not feel or think the same when it comes to our contribution. For him, the true value of our contribution is not how much we are contributing in life (quantity), but how we are making that contribution and how much of ourselves we are spending to do it (quality).

Praying the story of the Poor Widow's Contribution from the Gospel of Mark communicates a very important message and teaches us to value our contribution no matter how small it may be.

CHILD, ARISE!

The scripture reading

He sat down opposite the treasury and observed how the crowd put money into the treasury. Many rich people put in large sums. A poor widow also came and put in two small coins worth a few cents. Calling his disciples to himself, he said to them. 'Amen, I say to you, this poor widow put in more than all the other contributors to the treasury, for they have all contributed from their surplus wealth, but she from her poverty, has contributed all she had, her whole livelihood.'

Mark 12:41-44

Jesus is people-watching and notices how the crowd is putting money into the Temple treasury. While he is watching, his attention is caught, not by the contribution of the wealthy people, but by the contribution of a poor widow who puts in two small coins which is 'all she had, her whole livelihood'. Jesus sees beyond the contribution and is sensitive to how much of the person is being spent. In Jesus' eyes, the little that this poor widow gave was much more valuable than the big contributions of the wealthy because the poor widow spent her whole self in making the contribution. Even though the wealthy people made bigger monetary contributions, Jesus saw that they could have been much more generous.

Every day, we are all being invited to contribute and to put something in to the treasury of life. If we keep comparing ourselves to people who have not been through the same trauma as we have and say, 'Wow, look at how successful they are and how much they contribute to society', then chances are that we will feel that what we have to contribute has no value at all and is worthless.

This is where Jesus teaches us that what is important is not how much we contribute but rather how much of ourselves we spend in making our contribution.

Jesus sees when our seemingly small contribution comes with a big cost. He notices when we are spending all we have like the poor widow – for

Valuing our contribution

example, all our physical, emotional and mental energy, all our creativity, all our talent, all our enthusiasm, all our courage and hope – until we have nothing left to give. This giving our all is what makes our contribution valuable. Jesus looks at the contributions we make and says, 'Amen, I say to you, this person put in more than all the other contributors to the treasury, for they have all contributed from their surplus wealth, but she/he from her/his poverty, has contributed all she/he had, her/his whole livelihood.'

So let us learn to value our contribution in the same way Jesus does.

Praying the scripture reading

1. Try to be aware of Jesus' presence in you. Try to imagine this scene. A crowd comes to make their contributions to the treasury. You too come to make your contribution. You may feel identified with the poor widow in this reading. If so, try to place yourself in her shoes. Try also to notice who is in the crowd of people around you.
2. As the people in your crowd put in their contributions, be aware of what you are thinking or feeling. You may like to express this to Jesus. (Write it down if it is helpful for you.)
3. The time now comes to make your contribution. What contribution do you want to make today? Is there a task you would like to do or something you are feeling called to do but you are not giving value to it? Talk to Jesus about this. Tell him what inhibits you from making this contribution and why you don't think it's valuable. Try to listen to what he says to you deep in your heart.
4. Try to identify what the particular contribution is costing you. It may be all your physical energy, all your will power, all your emotional energy. Tell Jesus about this.

    Imagine that Jesus is looking at you as you make your contribution. Imagine Jesus praising you for your contribution, saying to you personally, 'Amen, I say to you, [your name], you put in more than all the other contributors, for they have all contributed from their surplus wealth, but you from your poverty, have contributed all you had, your whole livelihood.' As you listen to Jesus saying these words to you, what do you experience in your heart? You may like to express this to Jesus. (If you like, write it down.)

5. What do Jesus' words make you realize about valuing your contributions?
6. How can you remember this as you make your contribution to everyday life experiences?
7. Every time you find yourself undervaluing your contribution, try to come back and pray this scripture reading.

The scripture experienced in my life

I woke up today feeling like I was coming down with influenza or the beginnings of a flare up of my auto-immune illness. I had become familiar with the manifestation of the symptoms: fibromyalgia, fatigue, migraine and a general feeling of not being well. I thought 'Yes, it's going to be one of those days!'

Early that morning my friend called me and was quite anxious about seeking work. She asked me if she could come over to use my computer and internet and if I could help her with a job application. I explained to her that I wasn't feeling 100 per cent, but I'd give it my best shot and if I felt it was too much for me I would withdraw.

She came over and we began to tackle the application. What we thought was going to be a simple task turned out to be quite tedious and detailed. It involved all my mind and concentration which was quite challenging for me on that particular day. At the same time, it took all my inner strength to persevere with the little technical problems that were arising and needed more mental energy to sort out. In the process of it all, my friend was getting frustrated and more anxious about the possibility of finding work and I tried to offer her some consolation (which also took a bit out of me, emotionally). However, after several hours, we got through the application.

My friend felt a big sense of relief and she was so grateful to me for my help. I did not think that my contribution was a big one but I believed that

Valuing our contribution

it was a valuable one because I knew that in doing it I had spent my whole self — mentally, emotionally and especially physically for I wasn't feeling well that day. I was so spent that I could not do much more for the rest of that day!

Perhaps, in the eyes of others, my contribution seemed only a small one, but in the eyes of Jesus it may have been a much more valuable contribution than one made by someone else who had 100 per cent of their physical and mental capacities.

The scripture experienced in your life

Were you able to experience the scripture reading in your life today? If so, how did this happen? You may like to write down your own account.

Breaking old patterns

BREAKING PATTERNS FROM THE PAST, especially the ones that cause us to feel powerless and vulnerable, is an essential part of the healing journey for survivors of sexual abuse.

These patterns include the way we learnt to behave, respond to situations, think and feel during the abuse. As we develop into adulthood, so too do these patterns as we repeat them over and over. It is usually not until we seek professional support that we become conscious of them. As adult survivors, we can choose to acknowledge these old patterns in our day-to-day life, break with them, and create new patterns that will empower us as survivors.

An unhealthy pattern of mine that I acknowledged on my journey was trying to please people. When someone called for my help and needed my time I wasn't able to say no, even when I knew it was going beyond my physical and emotional limits. The first time I said no to someone's request for help I felt so cruel. Now I can acknowledge that I felt that way not because to say no was the wrong thing, or because I was being selfish at the time, but because saying no was foreign to me.

It felt wrong for me to say no because I was not familiar with it. 'No' was not a word that was part of my vocabulary, yet it was a very important word that I needed to be comfortable saying, especially if I wanted to establish healthy boundaries to keep me safe.

It is not an easy task to break old patterns. It takes time and we need to have patience with ourselves. Perhaps there will be days when we say, 'I just can't do it! It's too hard!' The following scripture reading can help when these feelings dominate us.

Breaking old patterns

The scripture reading

In the same way, the Spirit too comes to the aid of our weakness; for we do not know how to pray as we ought, but the Spirit itself intercedes with inexpressible groanings.
                                                               Romans 8:24-26

God is aware of the desire we have to break old patterns in our life that have robbed us of life and peace. God supports us in this task by giving us a practical source of help – the Holy Spirit, who 'comes to the aid of our weakness'.

Perhaps we can refer to the patterns we are trying break in our life as our 'weaknesses', since they are patterns that caused us to be weak and powerless in the past. Now, however, it can be different!

When we find ourselves about to repeat an old pattern, it's the time to consciously stop and remember that the power of the Spirit can come to our aid in our weakness. If we don't have the strength to break these patterns at the time, or don't even know how to do it, this is when God says to us, 'It's okay! I will help you.' God helps us by giving us the Holy Spirit, who gives us the strength we need. The Holy spirit will intercede for us. What we can't do, the Spirit can do for us. The Spirit is all powerful and will empower us.

It may help us to remember this scripture reading when we are struggling to break old patterns in our life.

Praying the scripture reading

1. Try to become still in God's presence.
2. Allow God to speak the words of Romans 8:26 to you. It may help you to put your name at the beginning of the verse.
3. How do you feel when God tells you that 'the Spirit comes to the aid of your weakness'? (You may like to express your feelings to God and write them down.)

4. Can you identify an old and recurring pattern in your life that you would like to break?
5. Can you identify how you feel every time you repeat this pattern?
6. Now go back and read this scripture reading slowly, being aware that God is saying to you at the present moment, 'The Spirit comes to the aid of your weakness', so that you can break this pattern.
7. Try to open your heart and accept the help of the Spirit. Try to listen to the 'groaning' of the Spirit within your heart indicating how you may be able to break this pattern. (You may like to write this down.)
8. If a situation arises where you are about to repeat an old pattern, try to practise what you have seen in today's prayer. First, let the Spirit come to your aid and ask the Spirit for the strength to put in practice what you saw in this prayer.
9. Repeat the above step as many times as you need to during the day. The more we do so, the more we will experience that the old patterns are being transformed as new life-giving patterns emerge in our life.

The scripture experienced in my life

Today I planned to finish an assessment task for the course I am currently studying. The assessment isn't due for a couple of days but I knew that I wouldn't find the time to work on it in the following days because of other commitments. At breakfast, I received a call from a friend who just took it for granted that I would be able to help her with a task today. She began telling me about her plan and where I fitted in to it. She didn't ask me at all in the conversation if I was free to help her or not.

In the past, because of my pleasing nature, I would have put aside my plans to help her out. Consequently, I would have stayed up and worked late into the night to get my assessment finished, at the cost of being physically and mentally exhausted the next day. But, now, I am aware how this old pattern of pleasing people led me to be vulnerable in the past. I know now that

Breaking old patterns

I can choose to break this pattern by saying no to people, and every time I do I know that new patterns are being forged in me.

I tried not to get upset with my friend. Instead I took a moment to call on the Holy Spirit (in my heart) to give me strength to say no to her. Then I simply said to her, 'I'm sorry, but you should have asked me earlier. I can't help you today. I need to finish my assessment. It is the only time I have to do it.'

She got very upset about it but I tried not to take this on board. On my part, I did what was necessary for my personal healing.

I have been very surprised though! Since I had this interaction with my friend, my relationship with her has changed in a positive way. Creating new patterns for ourselves also creates newness in our relationships.

The scripture experienced in your life

Were you able to experience the scripture reading in your life today? If so, how did this happen? You may like to write down your own account.

A clean touch – healing

PART OF THE HEALING JOURNEY for survivors of child sexual abuse is learning to nurture our inner child. There may be days when we experience that the feelings of our inner child are slowly surfacing and affecting the way we deal with our different contexts of family, work, and social activities.

It may not be difficult to identify when this is happening because we experience the insecurity, lack of confidence, fear, lack of trust and isolation that was all part of the child's past. The child in us is trying to ask the adult, 'Please! attend to me!' Like all children, the child in us needs to be assured, consoled, affirmed, loved, accepted and embraced. As our inner child experiences this, he or she can start to feel peaceful and at home with the adult we now are. By doing this, the adult part of us learns to integrate the child within us and the healing process takes place.

Prayer and our relationship with God is an excellent means to achieve this. God, through Jesus, teaches us as adults how to embrace the child in us.

The scripture reading below can be extremely painful for survivors of clergy abuse because of the language and images that may be associated with our traumatic memories of the abuse, but it can also offer us deep inner healing. This will involve being gentle with ourselves to know when we are prepared enough to go through the painstaking process of learning to read and pray this scripture reading seeing the face of Jesus, who is God's pure love, instead of seeing the face of our perpetrator.

I am aware of the issues that survivors may have with this reading from my own processes of healing and I have tried to address these in my explanation. However, I will leave it up to the discretion of the reader to decide whether they are ready to attempt it or not. If not, you can always return to it in the future when you are further along in your own journey.

A clean touch – healing

The scripture reading[46]

People were bringing children to him that he might touch them, but the disciples rebuked them. When Jesus saw this he became indignant and said to them, 'Let the children come to me, do not prevent them, for the Kingdom of God belongs to such as these. Amen, I say to you, whoever does not accept the Kingdom of God like a child will not enter it.' Then he embraced them and blessed them, placing his hands on them.

Mark 14b-16

I imagine that a survivor of abuse may read this scripture and think, 'Why on earth were people bringing children to Jesus so that he might touch them?' The image of being touched may stir up terrifying memories associated with our perpetrator. Being touched may still be an issue for us. We may cringe or stiffen, depending on who is touching us. There may be times when our loved ones touch us as a way of demonstrating love, reassurance, consolation or solidarity and we get very uncomfortable and perhaps even say. 'Don't touch me!' It may even be that a handshake, a kiss on the cheek or a hug from a friend still sends a shiver up our spine. For survivors of sexual abuse these expressions of touch, that are a normal part of friendship and mateship, have sadly been coloured by our trauma of the past.

While some gestures of touch are clean, dignifying and healing, others are unclean, undignifying and make the receiver feel like an object of another's pleasure. Sadly, the latter is the way that perpetrators touch their victims, so it is normal that, even years after the trauma has taken place, survivors are extremely cautious and sensitive around the issue of touch and can be hyper-reactive in situations where touch is involved.

In this reading, the children were being brought to Jesus for him to touch them. We need to remember that Jesus is the Son of God, and God is Love (we are talking about a pure and clean love). Jesus is not our perpe-

---

[46] For some survivors, this reading may trigger traumatic memories for the reasons mentioned in the introductory paragraphs above.

trator and we must not confuse the two and associate them as we read this scripture. Even if our perpetrator was a member of the clergy and supposed to be a holy reflection of God, Jesus and our perpetrator are very different. Our perpetrator is a human person with human limitations, while Jesus, although being fully human is also fully divine (God) and the perfect image of love. The greatest part of our spiritual struggle, especially if we are trying to pray with Scripture, is learning to separate our perpetrator from Jesus/God. Dissociating the two is an art that we become better at by practising it every time we are aware we are associating the two.

When Jesus touched the children at this moment in the gospels, it was an expression of something clean and pure. It was a gesture that dignified and healed, and one that communicated love, reassurance, acceptance and peace. The people bringing the children to Jesus were aware of this: perhaps they had witnessed other people being healed by Jesus' touch.

The disciples were obviously not happy about this and they rebuked the people for bringing the children to Jesus. Perhaps the reaction of the disciples resonates with us. Perhaps the adult part of us rebukes the thought of our inner child being touched by Jesus for understandable reasons.

Jesus rebukes the disciples and tells them, 'Let the children come to me!' Jesus knows that these children are in need of his nurturing and healing touch and he welcomes them to his presence. In the same way today, Jesus may rebuke the adult in us and tell us, 'Let the child come to me! For the Kingdom belongs to such as this.' Jesus knows how much our inner child has suffered. He understands when our inner child is feeling afraid, lacking trust, insecure, restless, sad and disappointed. He knows that our inner child needs nurturing and healing. For Jesus, touching the children is a means of healing. It is his way of communicating, 'I love you, accept you and welcome you the way you are. I don't want you to feel afraid, sad, or insecure any more. I want you to feel peaceful and at home.' Jesus' touch is quite different to the touch of our perpetrator, the one that our child experienced in the past.

In the measure that we can trust Jesus' touch and feel comfortable enough for him to embrace our inner child, the more we will experience how the adult part of us can come to embrace the child in us. As this hap-

A clean touch – healing

pens, a healthy integration and healing will take place as the adult and the child learn to be at home with each other.

Today let us allow Jesus to place his hands on the child in us and bless us. Let us listen to his call, 'Let the children come to me!'

Praying the scripture reading

1. Try to make yourself aware of Jesus' presence with you.
2. Read the scripture reading slowly. Try to picture the scene.
3. Try to identify who you relate to most, either one of the people who is bringing their child to Jesus to be touched by him or the disciples who were indignant. Then try to acknowledge what you are feeling as you imagine that you are coming towards Jesus. Share those feelings with Jesus. For example, 'Jesus, I am a little apprehensive as I bring my child to you because of what has happened to me in the past but I do believe that your touch can make a difference.' Or 'Jesus, can I trust you as I bring my child to you to be touched?'
4. Let Jesus say to the adult in you, 'Let your inner child come to me!' Try to identify how this makes you feel. You may like to tell Jesus this. For example, if it makes you feel angry then express this to Jesus: 'Why should I, Jesus? You didn't protect me in the past.' Or if you feel ashamed: 'Jesus, I'm afraid that you might reject my child and I'll be ashamed. I don't want my child to get hurt again.' Whatever it is, express it to Jesus.
5. Let Jesus tell you again, 'Let the children come to me!' You may want to ask Jesus, 'Why is it so important for you to touch my child?' or 'Why are you so concerned about my child?' or 'What if I don't let you touch my child?'
6. See if you can summon up the courage to let your child be in Jesus' presence.
7. Let your inner child express himself or herself to Jesus.
8. If you are able to, try to imagine that Jesus is placing his hands on

your head and blessing you (touching you). You may want to ask him, 'What are you praying for as you bless me, Jesus? Why do you want to bless me, Jesus?'

9. If you are comfortable enough with Jesus, try to take your prayer a step further by allowing Jesus to embrace you. If you are uncomfortable tell Jesus. Jesus is very compassionate and he understands where we are coming from and he will always treat us with the deepest respect.

10. As you prepare to go on with your day, try to remember Jesus' invitation, 'Let the children come to me!' During the day when you experience that the child in you is insecure, afraid, lacking trust, anxious, then take a couple of minutes of time out in prayer to try to imagine Jesus touching you, placing his hands on your head and blessing you. He will bless you with the appropriate words that you need at the time: for example, 'I bless you with boldness' or 'I bless you with peace' or 'I bless you with confidence'.

11. In the measure that you practise this, you will experience that Jesus' touch is clean and healing. You can always use this reading and image when you feel it can be helpful.

The scripture experienced in my life

I was out having lunch with one of my brothers. To get the cafe we were going to, we had to pass by an old building that carried significant memories for me going back to the time when the abuse was taking place in my childhood. As I walked past that building with my brother, I felt anxiety surfacing in me. I knew that the anxiety belonged to the child in me who had gone through terrible things. I did not want to allow this anxiety to stop me from being present to my brother and enjoying his company.

During a few moments of walking silently with my brother, I took advantage to recall the words of this scripture reading in my heart and I listened to Jesus saying, 'Let this anxious child in you come to me and I let me

A clean touch – healing

bless her!' I imagined Jesus walking next to me and holding his hands over my head and saying 'Bless her God, give her peace and tranquillity. Let her know that no harm will come to her again for I am with her.'

It was only a short moment of prayer but in that moment of silence and walking, I experienced that Jesus had touched my inner child and some healing had taken place. I experienced my anxiety slowly dissipating and thanks be to Jesus, I was able to enjoy the afternoon in my brother's company.

The scripture experienced in your life

Were you able to experience the scripture reading in your life today? If so, how did this happen? You may like to write down your own account.

Safety comes first

FOR SOME TIME, I HAD BEEN FEELING very unsafe every time I went to visit my doctor who I had been seeing for the last thirteen years. She was an excellent doctor who had taken very good care of me throughout my years of chronic illness. I felt very fortunate to be under her care.

However, in recent times, each time I went to see her I left feeling so nauseous because of a traumatic event I had experienced in a location close by ten months previously. Being in that area triggered terrible memories and I would arrive an emotional and physical mess and my stress and anxiety levels would increase rapidly.

As I took the short walk from where I parked my car to the doctor's practice, I was hyper-vigilant, noticing every single car and person that went by to make sure it was not any of the people involved in my recent trauma. Even inside the surgery, I did not feel safe. I would make sure that I didn't sit in front of the glass entry doors in open view of those entering the surgery. The more hidden I was, the better!

I tried to calm myself by reading a book but I was so anxious I could not focus on what I was reading. I would jump every time someone entered the practice and each time I was ready to bolt off. I kept imagining that the people who caused my trauma were going to walk through the doors. What would I do? I was so afraid that I would freeze as I have on many occasions before. 'Please, Lord, protect me!' I kept looking at my watch. Every second I waited seemed like an hour. Visiting my doctor had become an agony for me. I was in a dilemma.

After months of experiencing this I thought, 'This cannot go on.' I knew I needed to do something but the question was what? The answer came when I was praying the following scripture reading.

Safety comes first

The scripture reading

When the people in the synagogue heard this, they were all filled with fury. They rose up, drove him out of the town, and lead him to the brow of the hill on which their town had been built, to hurl him down headlong. But he passed through the midst of them and went away.

Luke 4:28-30

Before this outburst takes place, Jesus stands up in the synagogue and reads the scripture from the Prophet Isaiah where the ministry of the prophet is outlined. Jesus announces that this scripture passage is fulfilled as they hear it. Some of the crowd however, are infuriated. They challenge Jesus' identity – 'Isn't this the son of Joseph?' And when Jesus responds to them, their fury is even greater.

We can imagine that when Jesus experienced the fury of the crowd he began to feel unsafe and even afraid. Suddenly he was surrounded by this group of fuming people. You can imagine the scene: the group of people rising up in fury, getting hold of Jesus and taking him to the brow of the hill to hurl him down headlong. Jesus is definitely in serious danger.

Perhaps, for some survivors, this will conjure up memories of certain traumas in our lives of being controlled by the fury of our perpetrators. Undoubtedly, some of us may have lived through situations where our life was in extreme danger and we were afraid for our safety. Our lives may have been threatened repeatedly: 'If you say anything, I will kill you!' Like Jesus, we too have felt trapped and controlled by our fuming perpetrator.

However, in this scripture reading, Jesus' actions can speak volumes to us about how to take back control of our life when we experience that our safety is being threatened and that we are in danger.

What does Jesus do? First, he makes a choice between staying in the unsafe situation and walking away from it. Jesus 'passed through the midst of them and walked away'. It can seem like Jesus is caught in an unescapable situation of grave danger and he is bound to get hurt but the miracle is that

Jesus walks away from this danger untouched. It would have taken great courage for Jesus to walk away like that but by him doing so we see the great power of God at work in Jesus.

As adult survivors of abuse, making personal choices is important. Through our choices we can take back control of our lives, something we weren't able to do as young children during the time of our abuse. Usually choices are made for children by adults. But as adults we have the power to choose. Making personal choices empowers us.

When we are dealing with the question of personal safety, we can make choices. It's important that our choice is based on our reality at the time and not on self-deception. Sometimes we believe that we are ready and able to cope with certain situations and that nothing will happen to us when the reality may be that we are not yet ready to face these situations and that they may be detrimental to our well-being. Jesus didn't stand in the midst of his enemies trying to prove that he was tough and that he could handle them. Instead, he courageously chose to put his safety first and walked away!

Walking away when we feel unsafe is not a sign of weakness but a sign of the greater power of God working in us. Making choices to put our safety first empowers us and helps us to truly take back control of our self.

Praying the scripture reading

1. Try to imagine this scene. Imagine the furious crowd at the top of the hill and Jesus there in the middle of them. You may be watching from a distance or you may be coming up behind the furious crowd trying to catch a glimpse of him.
2. Try to imagine how Jesus must be feeling in this situation, particularly in relation to his own safety.
3. Imagine Jesus passing through the midst of the furious crowd and walking away. What do you find admirable in Jesus? How does this inspire you?
4. Is there currently a situation where you feel unsafe and in danger?
5. After seeing how Jesus responded when his safety was threatened,

is there something you can do to guarantee your safety when you feel threatened? (You may like to write it down.)
6. Remember what you have reflected on as you continue your daily routine and if you find yourself in a situation where you feel your safety is threatened. Try to practice what you have seen in today's prayer.
7. Repeat the above step whenever you find yourself in an unsafe situation.

The scripture experienced in my life

After praying this reading, I made an appointment to see my doctor and spoke to her specifically about my issue of not feeling safe when I came to see her because of my recent trauma (which she was aware of). As she was aware of the symptoms of complex post-traumatic stress disorder, she was very understanding. I assured her that, although I was very happy with the medical care that she had been providing for me, I would feel more comfortable and safer seeing another doctor in my local area and that this was a difficult decision for me to make. I mentioned to her some names of doctors that had been recommended to me and I asked her opinion. She supported me in putting my safety and general well-being first. Although I was sad to leave my doctor after thirteen years of being under her care, I felt I was gaining more control over my life as I 'walked away'.

Now I can experience the good that came from this choice. What a difference it is now to go to my doctor without feeling so anxious, stressed and unsafe.

Putting safety first benefits survivors of sexual abuse at all levels: physically, emotionally, mentally and, yes, spiritually!

The scripture experienced in your life

Were you able to experience the scripture reading in your life today? If so, how did this happen? You may like to write down your own account.

Anger: channelling it for good

IT IS NORMAL FOR SURVIVORS of sexual abuse to experience anger for the wrong perpetrated against them. Although anger is a healthy emotion, it is also a powerful emotion that can either be constructive or destructive depending on how we direct it.

While survivors of sexual abuse have the right to be angry, the challenge is learning to channel our anger in healthy ways so that we can experience it as an energy that is creative and constructive.

On my own journey, and while accompanying other survivors, I have seen that often survivors struggle to know how to direct and vent the overwhelming anger that is experienced towards the perpetrator. It is very easy to misdirect our anger by either lashing out at our loved ones or by turning our anger inwards on ourselves through destructive self-harming behaviours and suicidal tendencies. Channelling our anger towards ourselves is not only unhealthy and consuming but it often leads to depression, withdrawal and social isolation.

I have also experienced that survivors can feel guilty for being angry because they feel it is wrong according to their own faith belief. We need to realize that anger is a good and healthy human emotion and, if it is channelled properly, it can bring about a lot of good. It is not bad or wrong to feel angry – after all, God created us with this emotion.

Even Jesus, who was divine in nature, got angry, but what is captivating in the gospel scene below is to see how Jesus channelled his anger to do good.

The scripture reading

The Cleansing of the Temple

When it was almost time for the Jewish Passover, Jesus went up to Jerusalem. In the Temple courts he found people selling cattle, sheep

Anger: channelling it for good

and doves, and others sitting at tables exchanging money. So he made a whip out of cords, and drove all from the Temple courts, both sheep and cattle; he scattered the coins of the money changers and overturned their tables. To those who sold doves he said, 'Get these out of here! Stop turning my Father's house into a market!' His disciples remembered that it is written: 'Zeal for your house will consume me.'

John 2:13-17

In this gospel reading Jesus is very angry and it is for a good and right cause. For Jesus, the Temple in Jerusalem was a sacred place he had grown to respect highly as a holy place of worship (Luke 2:41-49). He is scandalized this day when he walks into the Temple courts and sees the temple being desecrated by people selling cattle, sheep and doves, and others sitting at tables exchanging money. It is clear to him that these people had no intention of worshipping but were out to make a profit for themselves at the cost of abusing the Temple.

This scripture reading can speak volumes to survivors of sexual abuse. The 'temple' that Jesus wants to enter today is you and me. St Paul reminds us of this in his first letter to the Corinthians, 'Don't you know that you yourselves are God's temple and that God's Spirit dwells in you?' (1 Corinthians 3:16). It is a truth that calls for every single person to be treated with the highest respect and dignity, based on the reality that we are the home of God's sacred Holy Spirit. Sadly, this has not been the case for survivors of sexual abuse. Like the Temple in Jerusalem that was abused by people seeking self-profit, we too have been abused and violated by perpetrators who were self-seeking a profit of sexual pleasure.

When Jesus saw the Temple being abused in this way, he became enraged and infuriated. His anger was a very appropriate response to a wrong that was taking place and it angered him so much that he could not pretend to turn a blind eye and carry on as if nothing wrong was happening.

The first lesson we can learn from Jesus is that we do not need to feel guilty or bad for the anger we experience as a consequence of abuse. Jesus understands our anger very well.

While Jesus does not cause any physical harm or hurt to those who have perpetrated the offence, he channels the energy and power of his anger towards the good and purposeful outcome of externally cleansing the temple and restoring its sanctity. In this process, he publicly shows his disgust at the root cause of the desecration of the Temple by turning over the tables of the perpetrators and scattering the money they had profited.

With great authority and energy we see Jesus speaking out strongly and powerfully against the abuse of the Temple, challenging those who have perpetrated the offence (as well as those in authority who were aware of it and allowed it to happen). Jesus courageously and passionately advocates for immediate action to stop the abuse, demanding, 'Get these out of here! Stop making my Father's house a market place.'

Perhaps Jesus' anger woke the consciences of the people around him to see the wrong that they did not want to see, and hear the wrong that they preferred to be kept silent.

Anger can be (and throughout history has proven to be) a powerful stimulus for creating so much positive change – a change that can begin within us and extend to our family system, public and institutional systems, or church and local community groups. Learning to vent our anger in healthy and creative ways is an art, and each person needs to find out what works well for them. For some it may be journaling, creative writing, poetry, playing an instrument, song-writing, singing, art, gardening or building.

Some have improved their own physical well-being by doing physically exerting exercises such as running, swimming, cycling, fast-paced walking or some team sports as a way of positively releasing the energy and stress of anger in their body.

Others have found themselves doing things that they would have never imagined they were capable of doing like speaking out publicly and advocating for a certain cause, or confronting and challenging particular authorities. Thanks to the very hard work of survivors who belong to many groups advocating to stop child sexual abuse, we saw the establishment of the Royal Commission into Institutional Responses to Child Sexual Abuse in November 2012. Hopefully, the work and outcomes of the Royal Commission will

Anger: channelling it for good

lead to some very positive changes, making our institutions much safer places for children in the future and eradicating child sexual abuse.

So, the next time we experience anger, we can turn to this scripture and, as we contemplate Jesus, we can be reminded that it is okay to be angry when a wrong has been done and that our anger is a good emotion if we express it in healthy ways. Let us try to learn the art of channelling our anger to do good as Jesus did and perhaps we will discover new ways of being creative and constructive with it.

We never know, perhaps in the future we will look back on our healing journey and be thankful for the anger we experienced because it may well have been the source of something good arising (a new change, talent, gift, relationship, fulfilling a dream) from a very painful and traumatic experience .

Praying the scripture reading

1. Try to be still and aware of Jesus' presence with you.
2. As you read the reading, try to picture the scene. Imagine that Jesus is coming into the Temple courts and seeing the panorama. Imagine him getting angry and overturning the tables and scattering the money.
3. What is it that calls your attention from the reading? It may be the fact that Jesus got angry and expressed it in public. It may be how he was not afraid of the authorities. It may be how he doesn't physically harm anyone while he is angry. It may be how he challenges the ones who are perpetrators of the abuse. Once you have identified this, you may want to express it to Jesus.
4. Try to identify what emotion this evokes in you – surprise, wonder, fear, dismay, anger… (You may also want to write down.)
5. In this scripture reading, how do you see Jesus constructively and creatively expressing his anger? (You may want to write this down.)
6. How is it different from the way that you vent your anger? (You may want to tell Jesus about this.)

7. What are the things that you could do to constructively and creatively channel your anger (either personally or in society)? What is the good that you would like to achieve from working at channelling your anger? (You may want to talk to Jesus about this and write it down.)
8. If you know the situations or circumstances that normally trigger your anger, try to set yourself some goals on how you would like to channel your anger in that moment. You may want to create a table titled 'Channelling Anger', with two columns – the first, 'Situations that trigger my anger' and the second, 'What I will do to constructively channel my anger'. You may like to add to this table as you discover new things that trigger your anger.
9. Every time you get angry, you may like to come back to this scripture reading to remember how Jesus channelled his anger to do good. It is also important to try to practise your own goals and, in the future, not to be afraid to set yourself new and more challenging ones.
10. Remember to keep asking Jesus to help you to channel your anger for good.

The scripture experienced in my life

On this particular night, I was watching the news on television. There was some coverage about the Royal Commission's questioning of some prominent Catholic Church leaders. The church leaders admitted knowing about certain priests who were perpetrators of sexual abuse and harming children. The more I listened, the more infuriated I became.

At the time, I was not alone. In fact the person I was watching the news with became very defensive of the church leaders which infuriated me even more. I could sense myself about to explode with anger and my temptation was to take it out on the person I was with at the time. Instead I left and went to my room.

I remembered the scripture reading of Jesus in the Temple and how he

Anger: channelling it for good

channelled his anger constructively. I remembered Jesus' words in that reading: 'Get these out!' I felt in that particular moment Jesus was asking me to get my anger out but to do it in a healthy and constructive way.

Over the years I have tried to personalize ways of venting my anger that I find are constructive for me.

Normally, in a situation like this I would go for a walk or do some form of exercise to get some of the stress out of my body but because it was late in the evening I sat down at my piano and began to play. I have discovered that this can be a form of expressing and channelling my anger. There is something about concentrating on a certain rhythm and repeating it that seems to calm me down.

Afterwards, I began to write what I was feeling and why. I was writing for quite some time. It is amazing how much better I felt after that! I guess it is true what they say – 'It is better out than in!' And, at least, getting anger out through writing doesn't harm me or anyone else. On the contrary, writing is what has helped me to learn to articulate what I could not previously put into words. It has also helped me to get to know myself more. Most of all, through writing it has been possible for me to put together this handbook and hopefully much good will come out of it either for survivors or those who are working pastorally and spiritually with survivors.

The scripture experienced in your life

Can you name what was new for you from this scripture reading? How can you practice it in your life? Are you able to write down your own account of how you have practised it in your life?

Discovering power in vulnerability

BEING VULNERABLE IS PART OF OUR human existence. As adults who survived childhood sexual abuse, being vulnerable or feeling exposed to the possibility of being attacked or harmed, either physically emotionally, psychologically or spiritually, is something that terrifies us. As young children, we were extremely vulnerable and those who abused us took advantage of this. For victims and survivors of abuse, it is difficult to imagine that anything positive can come out of the experience of being vulnerable because for us being vulnerable has been tainted with sexual abuse and a deep sense of feeling overwhelmingly powerless.

Yet being vulnerable is an inescapable part of our human existence. Every person, regardless of whether they have been sexually abused or not, will experience being vulnerable on their journey of life. This may be through illness, loss of a loved one, simply by becoming older, or many other circumstances.

As survivors of sexual abuse, learning to embrace our own vulnerability is vital for our life-time journey. To do this we need to be prepared to let go of the belief that being vulnerable means experiencing overwhelming powerlessness. This belief has been conditioned by our past experience. The secret to embracing our own vulnerability is to believe that even though we are vulnerable we have power – a power that helps us surpass suffering so that in the end we triumph and have a deeper sense of life.

We all hold power within us; we only need to discover it. As we do, our whole perception of being vulnerable will change. No longer will we associate being vulnerable with being powerless. On the contrary, being vulnerable will be the means to experience that we have an overwhelming power within us. Experiencing our own vulnerability can also lead us to a more meaningful faith experience.

Discovering power in vulnerability

In the following scripture reading, St Paul communicates his own experience of discovering power in human vulnerability and how he found great meaning in it.

The scripture reading

But we hold this treasure in earthen vessels, that the surpassing power may be of God and not from us. We are afflicted in every way, but not constrained; perplexed, but not driven to despair, persecuted, but not abandoned, struck down, but not destroyed; always carrying about in the body the dying of Jesus, so that the life of Jesus may also be manifested in our body.

1 Corinthians 4:7-11

St Paul is confronting the difficulty of his ministry and he reveals how he is constantly challenged to endure many experiences of suffering and death. These experiences emphasized his fragile and vulnerable human existence. However, St Paul asserts and bears witness to one of the most empowering truths of our faith: life triumphs over suffering and death through the powerful indwelling presence of God.

St Paul has come to know through his faith in Christ that, even though he is a vulnerable 'earthen vessel' and risks being broken through human experiences of affliction, perplexity, persecution, being attacked by enemies, he holds a hidden treasure in his humanity – 'the surpassing power of God'.

Through God's power the suffering and death we carry in our body is transformed by God's very own life and presence dwelling within us. It gave St Paul great meaning and purpose to know that in his own vulnerability he was carrying about in his body the dying of Jesus, so that the life of Jesus may also be manifested in his body.

So, when we next experience our own vulnerability and are plagued by affliction, perplexity, persecution or whatever it may be, let us try to discover that 'in our earthen vessel' (our life) we too hold a treasure – the surpassing power of God. God's powerful presence dwelling within us is able to surpass all the suffering and death we experience when we are afflicted, perplexed or persecuted, and it transforms our vulnerability into life so that, like St Paul, we too can say, 'We are afflicted in every way, but not constrained; perplexed, but not driven to despair, persecuted, but not abandoned, struck down, but not destroyed.'

We too can find great meaning in our human vulnerability as St Paul did because we also 'carry about in our body the dying of Jesus, so that the life of Jesus may also be manifested in our body.' In other words, our experiences of human vulnerability are a means to manifest the surpassing power of God's presence in us.

Let us take advantage of the opportunities to discover the surpassing power of God within us every time we experience our human vulnerability!

Praying the scripture reading

1. Try to be still and aware of God's presence with you.
2. As you read the reading, put your name at the beginning of each sentence (this helps us to be aware that God is speaking to us through his Word).
3. As you read the words, 'But we hold this treasure in earthen vessels that the surpassing power may be of God and not from us', what do they evoke in you? Surprise, wonder, joy? Express this to God. (You may want to write down your conversation.)
4. If you have any thoughts or questions arising around these words, express them to God. For example, 'How long have I been holding this treasure in me? Why haven't I known about it earlier? How come I haven't experienced it earlier during my childhood days? Why have you given me this treasure?' (Your questions may be different.) Try not to rush and allow God to speak to your heart. When you feel ready, you can move on.
5. St Paul experiences being 'afflicted in every way, but not constrained; perplexed, but not driven to despair; persecuted, but not abandoned; struck down, but not destroyed.' You may like to talk to

Discovering power in vulnerability

God about what happens to you when you are afflicted, perplexed, persecuted, struck down. Express your suffering to God.

6. Allow God to make you aware through the reading that you hold a 'treasure' within your earthen vessel, your body, and that this treasure is God's surpassing power.
7. Ponder on God's power and what it can achieve in you by reading his Word slowly and putting your name before it. 'Because of my power, you will be afflicted in every way, but not constrained; perplexed, but not driven to despair; persecuted, but not abandoned; struck down, but not destroyed.' You may like to express to God what this evokes in you. (it could be a desire for this experience, it could be the opening of a new door, or joy.)
8. You may want to ask God; 'How can I experience your power the next time I am feeling vulnerable? What do I need to remember?'
9. Perhaps the next part of the reading is something that you may not have thought much about. When you are vulnerable, you are 'carrying about in your body the dying of Jesus, so that the life of Jesus may also be manifested in your body'. Does this make being vulnerable meaningful for you? (You may want to talk to God about this.)
10. You may want to conclude by resolving how God is inviting you to embrace your vulnerability.
11. Remember to practise this in every situation where you experience your vulnerability. In the measure you do, not only will you experience 'the surpassing power of God in you' but you will learn to embrace your own vulnerability.

The scripture experienced in my life

For some time now, I have avoided confronting an important issue because the person I need to speak to has some association with a recent trauma I suffered. Every time I thought about getting in touch with the person, my anxiety and stress levels peaked. However, I could not delay addressing the issue any longer. I sent an email to arrange a time when we could speak on the phone.

When the day arrived I spent time praying this scripture reading beforehand. Indeed, I was feeling very vulnerable. As the appointment time drew closer, I could feel my stress and anxiety levels rising. I felt that my 'earthen vessel' was about to break under the stress. Jesus kept reminding me not to focus on how I was feeling but on the great treasure that I possess within – the surpassing power of God (through the indwelling presence of the Holy Spirit).

I made the phone call. I was very stirred up and felt particularly vulnerable. All I wanted to do was to get off the phone as quickly as I could. However, it took time to explain the issue. It was impossible for me to do this without getting emotional. I knew before making the call that no matter what I explained, the person at the other end was going to have difficulty understanding what I had been through. This was humbling; it was the last thing that I wanted to do at this particular moment, but necessary. This made me feel very vulnerable.

I felt afflicted throughout the phone call. All I wanted to do was hang up, but I persevered until the end. By the end of it, I felt as though I was dead! As I reflected more on my sense of feeling 'dead', Jesus reminded me of the words from Scripture that I had prayed: 'You are carrying in your body the dying of Jesus so that the life of Jesus may also be manifested in your body.'

By experiencing my own vulnerability, I also experienced the suffering and dying of Jesus in my body. To my surprise, my experience did not end in death but in life and like St Paul I too can say through this experience and others, 'I have been afflicted in every way, but not constrained; perplexed, but not driven to despair; persecuted, but not abandoned; struck down, but not destroyed', because I hold the treasure of God's surpassing power of life in me.

It is a call for me to embrace my vulnerability as a gift!

The scripture experienced in your life

Were you able to experience the scripture reading in your life today? If so, how did this happen? You may like to write down your own account.

Set free from paralysis

THE WORD 'PARALYSIS' MAY BE USED in various contexts. In the physical context paralysis is defined as the inability to move or function, the total stoppage or severe impairment of activity. Paralysis can be temporary or permanent.

When survivors of abuse talk about their traumatic experiences it is not uncommon to hear expressions such as 'I was paralysed with fear' or 'I wanted to run as fast as I could but I just couldn't get my legs to move!' or 'I wanted to shout and tried but no voice came out!' It is shocking to go through this experience and extremely distressing because just at the moment where function and movement is so crucial we experience paralysis.

However, there is also another type of paralysis that is just as devastating for survivors of sexual abuse - spiritual paralysis. The spiritual aspect of our life allows us to find meaning and purpose in life. However, when we are spiritually paralysed it means that this part of our life is not functioning. I like to think of our spiritual being as a deep well from which we can draw strong spiritual resources of faith, hope, trust, courage, new life, enthusiasm, determination, inner strength and energy. Experiencing spiritual paralysis not only means that it is difficult for us to find meaning and purpose in our life experiences but also that we can be devoid of inner spiritual resources.

If we were brought up in a family of faith believers and then became the victim of sexual abuse committed by either a family member or a member of the clergy, it is likely that we stop believing in God altogether and blame God for what happened: 'It is all your fault, God! You let that happen to me! You could have done something to stop it if you wanted but you didn't! How come you didn't protect me? How am I supposed to believe you if those that claim to love you have done this to me? How could you let that happen to me?' Or perhaps over the years we hold on to a sliver of our faith but we have strong doubts because we are trying to make sense of what has happened to us and we ask God constantly, 'Why did you let this bad thing to happen to me?'

Unfortunately, sexual abuse has grave effects on a survivor's faith and, through my ministry and sharing with other survivors, I have found that it is common for survivors who have faith to blame God and transfer their feelings of grief on to God. However, when we don't work through these attitudes we have against God, in the same way that we would work through them in any human friendship, then our relationship with God becomes cold and distant, and eventually it is paralysed and stops developing. Consequently, we lack the vital spiritual resources that come from God and those we crave deep within us.

Another cause of spiritual paralysis in adult survivors is when we place all the responsibility on ourselves and blame ourselves for what has happened – self-blame (even though we know we were only a young child and that the responsibility belonged to the adult who knew he was doing wrong). When we self-blame we don't forgive ourselves because we think 'I should have been able to stop it! I should have just said no! I should have told someone!' But the reality is that we could not because we were overpowered and controlled by an adult who misused their power and authority and took advantage of our trust to abuse us.

An attitude of self-blame can be detrimental to all aspects of our life. By blaming ourselves, we are led to believe that we are unlovable, unworthy, bad, and that we have nothing good to contribute or offer anyone. These beliefs paralyse us spiritually and affect our relationship with God and with others.

God's heart is filled with great love and compassion for us when he sees our spiritual paralysis. He wants to set us free from it so that we can live life to the full and be renewed with a rich supply of spiritual resources.

In the scripture reading below from the Gospel of Matthew, we can grasp God's desire through the person of Jesus. Jesus shows us through this scripture that God's love has the power to set us free from our paralysis.

We are invited to give Jesus permission to work this miracle in our life and to believe that it is possible.

Set free from paralysis

The scripture reading

He entered a boat, made the crossing and came into his own town. And there people brought to him a paralytic lying on a stretcher. When Jesus saw their faith, he said to the paralytic, 'Courage, child, your sins are forgiven.' At that, some of the scribes said to themselves, 'This man is blaspheming.' Jesus knew what they were thinking, and said, 'Why do you harbour evil thoughts? Which is easier, to say, 'Your sins are forgiven,' or to say, 'Rise and walk?' But that you may know the Son of Man has authority on earth to forgive sins' – he then said to the paralytic, 'Rise, pick up your stretcher and go home.' He rose and went home.

Matthew 9:1-9

Praying the scripture reading

1. As you read this reading, try to imagine the scene. You may imagine Jesus getting off the boat and coming into his own town. As he does, a crowd begins to build up around him .... You may like to imagine yourself as the paralytic who is now present before Jesus.

    PAUSE

2. Notice what you are feeling in Jesus' presence.

    PAUSE

3. The paralytic was carried on a stretcher. Do you come before Jesus on a stretcher today? Your stretcher may be a certain emotion that you are presently experiencing, for example: anger, disappointment, grief, sadness ... Try to identify your stretcher.

    PAUSE

4. Try to identify if you experience spiritual paralysis. Do you feel you have strong attitudes towards Jesus? Do you blame Jesus for what happened to you in the past? Perhaps you are angry with him.

    PAUSE

CHILD, ARISE!

At this point try to have a dialogue with Jesus about this. Express honestly what you feel and what you think, even if you are angry. Jesus is ready to listen. After you have expressed yourself to Jesus, try to listen to his response in your heart.

5. It may be helpful to identify if your spiritual paralysis is the result of self-blame and having an unforgiving attitude towards yourself.

PAUSE

Try to have a dialogue with Jesus and once again, being honest about what you feel and think. Allow Jesus to respond.

6. Imagine that Jesus is looking at you with a heart that is full of love and compassion. As he looks at you he says, 'Courage [put your name here], child, your sins are forgiven.'

People often ask, what is sin? Sin is best understood when we talk about it in the context of a loving relationship between two people. In a loving relationship when one person hurts the other by saying or doing something that is heart-breaking, the relationship is strained and broken. Both people experience the brokenness, the one who has been hurt and the one who has hurt, until the relationship is reconciled and made whole again.

So we can think of our relationship with God in the same way. God is a person with emotions and has a heart that feels for us (more than any other person in the world can ever feel for us). God truly loves us. So when we say, think or do something that hurts God, we either consciously or unconsciously break our relationship with God. As a result, God suffers immensely because of this intense love for us, but we also suffer because when we break our relationship with God we also cut ourselves off from One who is the source of all life and love in the universe. When this happens, God longs for our relationship to be reconnected so that we can be made whole again.

Self-blame and not forgiving ourselves for the past are attitudes that hurt God because, although God says to us repeatedly, 'I love

Set free from paralysis

you! I believe you (and 'in you')! You are precious to me!', we are saying to God, 'I don't believe you! I'm unworthy of your love! I'm bad!' When we are stuck in this attitude, even though we may be moving and walking around physically, there is no movement in our spirit and our relationship with God – we are spiritually paralysed and we feel dead from within.

7. Jesus sees our spiritual paralysis and he says to the small child in us, as well as the adult: 'Courage [put your name here], child, your sins are forgiven.'

    Jesus knows when we cannot forgive ourselves, so he forgives us instead. With such tenderness he says to us, 'Child, your sins are forgiven! You are clean! Stop blaming yourself! Stop being hard on yourself! See my mercy and compassion with you.'

    He wants to free us of the heavy burden, the unhealthy guilt, that has paralysed us for so many years. Jesus invites us to have courage in our heart to believe this.

    PAUSE

    You may like to express your thoughts and feelings in dialogue with Jesus.

8. At the end of this scripture passage, Jesus says to the paralytic, 'Rise, pick up your stretcher and go home.'

    Imagine the grandness of this miracle! Not only does Jesus set the man free from his spiritual paralysis by offering him forgiveness through his compassion and mercy but Jesus goes further and then recovers the man to full health by healing his physical paralysis.

    There are two major miracles in one encounter: a physical miracle and a spiritual miracle, restoring the man to complete health. In this miraculous encounter with Jesus, the man's life was suddenly turned around and changed for the best. He was no longer a disabled paralytic but an able and functioning person both physically and spiritually. Jesus had opened up a door of new and unimaginable possibilities for this man's future.

CHILD, ARISE!

Imagine the man's joy as he experienced what it was like to walk again! Imagine the joy of going home a new person!

When Jesus sets us free from our spiritual paralysis, not only do we experience the spiritual fruits of being closer to him and drawing from his well of courage, hope, love and life but we also experience the joy of being empowered to walk again on our journey.

Like the paralytic in this gospel, we too can be restored to complete well-being.

We may also experience that as we encounter Jesus each day in our prayer that he opens up a door of new and unimaginable possibilities for our life.

So let Jesus say to you today, 'Rise [put your name here], pick up your stretcher and go home.'

In other words, 'Get up and walk ... Pick up your stretcher ... Don't lie on it or get carried away on it any more. Don't allow those feelings and emotions to have authority over you any more. Take authority of your own life! I tell you, walk your journey with the new spiritual strength I have given you.'

The man 'rose and went home.' Today let us rise from our prayer and be at home with God. Learning to be at home with God is the key in learning to be at home with ourselves and others. Let us continue our daily activities as the new person who has been set free from spiritual paralysis. As we walk our journey, let us remember to draw our strength from our internal supply of God's abundant life and love.

PAUSE

9. You may like to conclude your prayer by asking Jesus what is he inviting you to 'rise' from? And how is he inviting you to walk your journey (with optimism, enthusiasm, joy, hope)? You may also want to ask him for the spiritual resources that you will need for your journey today.

Set free from paralysis

The scripture experienced in my life

These past days have not been easy for me. I became aware of some issues that are re-surfacing (from the abuse) and my inner child was calling me to attend. My adult self was trying to soldier on, pretending that everything was okay, but there was a tension building up in me and I was becoming more irritable than usual in my relationships. To top it off, the familiar self-blaming attitude from my past began to slowly creep in to my mind and find its way down to my heart where it was trying very hard to make its home.

It was dangerous to feed these thoughts because they would become stronger. 'Why didn't you just tell someone! Why didn't you just say no! Why didn't you run away!' I could sense the lurking lack of forgiveness that lay beneath all these damaging thoughts. My adult self was trying to reason with my inner child telling her that these thoughts are completely senseless and a lie yet she was struggling to believe this.

With this battle going on within me I began to melt down. I was brought to a full halt. My self-blaming attitude was crippling me, not only spiritually but emotionally and even physically.

At this time, I experienced the indwelling Spirit gently prompting me to set myself in Jesus' presence and to become aware of him. I withdraw from all the noises and hustle and bustle around me and found a quiet spot to be alone with him. In this space, I began to listen to the sweet voice of Jesus speaking to my heart, to my inner child who is so self-condemning: 'Courage, child, your sins are forgiven! ... There is nothing that remains to be forgiven in you! You are clean of sin! Be at peace! Believe me! I don't want you to blame yourself any more or to be so unforgiving towards yourself. I know you. I know what's happened to you more than anyone else. This is all that's important. Courage, child!'

My inner child, not instantly convinced of this, continued on with her thoughts, so we brought these thoughts to Jesus: 'Why couldn't I have just rebelled? Why couldn't I have just said no, or just told someone?' The more we talked with Jesus about this and listened to his response, the more I experienced that he was so much more understanding and compassionate of my circumstances and the context at the time than I was myself. The broadness of Jesus' vision and his deeper grasp of what happened to me as a young child, as well as his natural understanding of all my reactions at the time, enabled me to be more forgiving and compassionate with myself. It was a gift to listen to Jesus telling me my story through his eyes of love and compassion.

Through my encounter with Jesus, my spirit was gently released once more! My sin was not anything that I had done or failed to do as a child, my sin as the adult survivor was to allow the self-blaming attitude of my inner child to invade my heart again. I understood how self-blame paralyses my relationship with Jesus and how this stops me from walking my journey of healing. I allowed Jesus to repeat the words, 'Courage, child! Your sins are forgiven!' Each time he did, I experienced a gentle movement from within my spirit. I experienced that there was life within me again!

I continued to converse with Jesus for a long time until he eventually said to me, 'Rise and go home!' I knew a transformation had taken place within me. I was not the same person as when I first came to Jesus that afternoon. I was a new person through my encounter with him in prayer. Like the man in the scripture reading I too had experienced a double miracle. Not only was I healed of my spiritual paralysis but I was also empowered to rise physically and walk on my journey as an abled and functioning person. As I went home that afternoon I felt a huge peace permeating my spirit and others also noticed it. Yes, miracles are possible!

The scripture experienced in your life

Were you able to experience the scripture reading in your life today? If so, how did this happen? You may like to write down your own account.

Stripped but not broken

MEDICAL EXAMINATIONS, INVASIVE SURGICAL procedures, and even physiotherapy sessions have proven to be challenging, especially when I foresee that I will be asked to undress and to put on a hospital gown. Being asked to undress has horrifying associations with being violated in the past. While the request to undress for specific medical procedures is standard and necessary, feelings of immense vulnerability, anxiety, fear, helplessness, humiliation and shame are triggered in me. Being asked to undress for a medical procedure seems to undress the past trauma of the abuse so that I experience a strong sense of also being naked emotionally and psychologically.

Although I have grown to trust my medical specialists who treat me with the highest respect, every time they make this request I find that I am taken back to those devastating events and I find myself trying to deal with the feelings of my panic stricken inner child. For a moment (that can seem eternal at the time) my body seems to be paralysed behind the curtain in the consultation room while my mind is flooded with questions from my inner child who is remembering the trauma of the past: 'Can I trust him? Am I safe? Will I be trapped? Will I be abused again? How will I escape if I don't feel safe?' The rebellious voice of my inner child cries out: 'No, I don't want to undress! Don't do it! Say no!' Then there is the voice of my adult who tries to soothe and calm my inner child, reassuring her: 'It is safe! It's a different situation! He will not hurt me or touch me! I can trust him! I am no longer helpless! I have a voice and if I need to I can say no!' Apart from it taking me perhaps longer than it normally would take someone to change into a hospital gown, I am sure that my doctors and nurses are totally oblivious to the ordeal and chaotic turmoil that I experience by being asked to undress.

Tomorrow I am due to have a medical procedure that requires me to undergo a general anaesthetic, and the fact that I will be lying on an operating table unconscious while my body is exposed to a team of doctors and nurses who will invade and probe me with surgical instruments terrifies me. At least on other occasions I could try to be in control by being vigilant as to when my life might be in danger. But undergoing a general anaesthetic would mean that I would have no control and be unaware of what is going on. That whole sense of not knowing what will be done to my body as I am anaesthetized makes me feel terrified and anxious.

While I know with my rational mind that I will be safe and that nothing will happen to me and that there are strong reasons for having the medical procedure, my body communicates to me the opposite, tempting me to postpone the procedure.

Although this inner conflict is painful, every time I go through it I sense an invitation to reconcile my past and present in a way that is dignified and empowering.

By reflecting on Jesus' passion in the Scriptures, I discovered that Jesus was showing me the way to do this through his own life.

The scripture reading[47]

> *When they came to the place called The Skull, they crucified him there, along with the criminals — one on his right, the other on his left. Jesus said, 'Father, forgive them, for they do not know what they are doing.' And they divided up his clothes by casting lots.'*
>
> Luke 23:33-34

The context is a stark one. The earthly life of Jesus, Son of God, is slowly drawing to a tragic close. This is the brutal ending of a young man who lived his whole life par excellence only ever proclaiming and living the message of God's love, peace, joy, kindness, goodness, truth, gentleness, faith and

---

[47] I am aware that this particular scene of Jesus' crucifixion, as well as other scenes from Jesus' Passion which demonstrate aggression, abuse and violence towards Jesus, may cause survivors to become disturbed or distressed and even trigger certain traumatic memories, particularly if we are at the stage of processing our trauma. In this case, it is appropriate for a survivor to discern if the use of imagination with this particular scripture will provoke unnecessary trauma. Should this be the case, I would suggest entering the guided steps for prayer at a place that you feel is more comfortable for you.

Stripped but not broken

hope with the greatest integrity. But his life is unjustly and catastrophically cut short by a plot, instigated by the religious authorities, to have him condemned to death by crucifixion. It is the conclusion of an innocent life that seems to have gone shockingly wrong.

Although we can never fully grasp what those last dying moments must have been like for Jesus, there are some things we can consider as we reflect upon this scene. Jesus' death was not a dignified and private one but rather a public affair. Instead of being surrounded by those who loved and esteemed him, Jesus was circled by his enemies who taunted and shouted abuse at him (Matthew 27:39-40). It is the kind of death that none of us would desire.

At this stage of the condemnation process, it is imaginable that Jesus was not only trying to deal with the limitations of his beaten and exhausted physical reality as well as his pending death sentence that lay only moments away but also the intense mental and emotional pain that his enemies were causing him. Further along in this gospel, we have the sense that Jesus was also struggling with what appears to be spiritual darkness which urged him to call out to his Father from the cross 'My God, my God, why have you abandoned me? (Matthew 27:46).

As if all this wasn't enough, Jesus is then ruthlessly stripped and publicly exposed before his enemies. His battered body is stretched out on the cross to which he is tortuously nailed. The wooden cross is lifted high, maximizing his public humiliation. From his death bed – the cross – he watches on as his enemies cast lots for his clothes. Not only has Jesus been stripped physically but he has also been stripped of his dignity by this cruel act of humanity.

Yet in this callous revolt his enemies have not been successful in stripping him of the one thing that had always been at the core of his preaching and teaching – his merciful compassion. We can imagine that as Jesus' enemies stood by and watched his final moments they must have been totally intrigued, amazed and even stupefied to see such a response from Jesus, especially considering how viciously he had been treated. We can imagine that the majority of people in Jesus' same situation would more than likely respond with anger, hatred, vengeance, resentment and certainly bitterness.

However, Jesus' final words communicate the very essence of who he is – Son of God – God's love manifested in human flesh.

Only hours before this, Jesus was standing in the presence of Pilate, the Governor of Judea, when this same crowd now beneath his cross roared out, 'Crucify him! Crucify him! (Matthew 27:22-26). It was this cry that led Jesus to be condemned to die a barbarous death like a criminal. In strong contrast, we now see Jesus in his affliction crying out to God, 'Father, forgive them, for they do not know what they are doing.'

Even in his anguish, Jesus still finds it in his heart to pray for those who perpetrated his execution, saying to His Father, 'They do not know what they are doing.' As St Paul later put it in his first letter to the Corinthians, 'For if they would have known, they would have never crucified the Lord of Glory' (2:8). Jesus is aware that there is a disturbing level of unconsciousness involved on the part of the perpetrators.

As we reflect on this scripture, I am sure that we will find it striking and even unbelievable that Jesus responds like this, especially since there is no remorse shown on the part of the perpetrators – on the contrary, they extend his suffering.

It is as if Jesus graciously goes beyond what he is suffering to foresee that if his enemies ever do come to be conscious of the gravity of what they have done and are full of remorse and repentance then they will need to experience God's mercy. So Jesus 'fore-gives', asking his Father to grant to his perpetrators mercy and compassion even while they are causing him suffering. We must not understand this incorrectly. This does not mean that Jesus makes the wrong they are doing right. By no means is Jesus saying to his perpetrators: 'What you are doing to me or have done up until now is right.' A wrong is wrong. What Jesus does in forgiving his perpetrators is to 'fore –give' them the possibility in the future of being put right again with God should they ever come to admit the gravity of the wrong they have done with repentance and remorse.

Jesus' forgiveness has a double effect. While his enemies will experience the fruit of his forgiveness in the future (if they repent), Jesus experiences the personal effects of forgiveness in his present suffering. Through forgiveness,

Stripped but not broken

Jesus becomes free of the intense mental, emotional, psychological and spiritual distress that pertains to such an excruciating death to the point where he finds peace and gracefully surrenders his life to his Father: 'Father, into your hands I commend my Spirit' (Luke 23:34). Jesus has been totally stripped in all human aspects but he is not broken. Jesus maintains his dignity in this undignifying context; Jesus transforms what is disgrace to grace, dishonourable to honourable, hatred to peace, crucifixion to freedom, brokenness to wholeness. In that place called The Skull, which was such a harrowing place for Jesus to be, God was present and working vigorously in Jesus' heart.

While we will never understand completely what Jesus suffered in his Passion and physical death by crucifixion, there may be some aspects in the context of his death that resonate with survivors of sexual abuse. While the sexual abuse for many of us may have taken place decades ago, we continue to suffer the consequences and effects in our being as our body remembers what happened. Throughout this process, we can be thrust into a place of deep inner darkness, and coming to this place within us is like being at that place called The Skull, where Jesus was crucified. Even though our perpetrator is not physically present during these experiences, their voice may become very audible within us as we involuntarily recall their verbal mockery, abuse and taunts. Every time we are brought to this place through memories, we re-experience the humiliation, shame, and dishonour that are attached to it.

However, through God's grace we too can transform this place within us making it the place where, over time and through a gentle process, we are set free and made whole again through forgiveness. Forgiveness does not mean that we are saying to our perpetrator 'What you did is okay! Forget it' or 'It's all right!' Sexual abuse never will be right: it is wrong and will always be wrong. The premise of forgiveness is that a wrong has been done. When Jesus asks the Father to forgive his perpetrators, he admits and accepts that a grave wrong had been done to him and that he will die unjustly as a result. Jesus' gracefulness in forgiving can leave us deeply perplexed. Only moments before his death, we do not detect any display of anger, hatred or retaliation in Jesus towards his enemies.

I am sure that many survivors would agree that the bridge between admitting a wrong has been done to us and accepting it usually involves intense emotions of anger, rage, resentment and fury which are a very normal part of the healing process. However, in the measure that we are graced by God's strength and able to accept the wrong that has been done to us and its lifelong consequences and effects, then we too will find a peaceful place in our heart (but it is a journey).[48] It is from this peaceful spot that over time we can gradually be set free from the mental, emotional and even spiritual torment that can overshadow us at different times on our healing journey.

This process can happen in us every time we are brought to the place in our heart that reminds us of the place called The Skull, where Jesus was crucified. Often coming to this place is involuntary and is triggered by memories, whether through an interaction with someone, something that we heard, a tone of voice, a sound, a gesture, a smell, a certain place, an event. We don't want to be at this place, but I imagine Jesus didn't want to be at the place called The Skull either.

Being at this place, we are invited first to admit to ourselves what is happening to us and why, and second to accept that this is the truth. For example: 'Right now, in this interaction, or hearing this news item, or smelling this fragrance, or seeing this gesture, or hearing this tone of voice, I realize that I am becoming distressed mentally, emotionally, spiritually, physically. I know that this is happening because I have been sexually abused and through the trigger my body is remembering the abuse.'

If we can learn to admit and accept the truth every time we are brought to this place, we will eventually experience a peaceful place within our hearts and gradually experience a greater freedom, for 'the truth will set us free'.[49] While we may never be totally free of the memory of the sexual abuse or the effects of it over our life time, by repeatedly admitting and accepting the truth through our lived experiences we may surprisingly discover that some things that were once powerful triggers in our life begin to lose their

---

[48] Acceptance does not mean to condone the wrong but rather to come to the realization that the wrong done is a part of our personal history that cannot be undone or changed; it makes up who we are.

[49] John 8:32 'Then you will know the truth, and the truth will set you free.'

power and intensity as we slowly but surely take back power and control in these experiences.

However, there is another step in forgiveness that has the effect of freeing us even further. This is the ultimate challenge not only for survivors of abuse but for any Christian – asking God to forgive our perpetrator. This challenge can cause many Christians to struggle or give up or close their heart, because it is 'way too hard' and seems crazy or illogical. Why should we ask God anything for our perpetrator, let alone asking God to forgive him or her? Especially when we continue to suffer the effects of the wrong that has been done to us and will probably do so over our life time! And we are right – for us it is too hard and it certainly goes beyond our human capacities and according to our human logic it is crazy and illogical! This is precisely why this ultimate challenge – asking God to forgive the perpetrator – is only possible through God's love and big doses of mercy and compassion. For this reason, forgiveness to this degree does not happen overnight: it comes with a lot of blood, sweat and tears and, undoubtedly, a lot of prayer.

But, again, why should we ask God to forgive our perpetrator? Forgiveness is the key. It is a means to let go of our anger, rage, resentment and any other bad feelings and emotions stored up in our body. If we keep holding on to a lot of negative emotions and experiences, we often don't realize it but they can slowly eat away at us adding more to the impact on our physical, emotional, mental and spiritual health. Forgiveness is the key to loving ourselves and choosing the best for ourselves, and too often we totally miss this point.

We can think that forgiveness is all about the perpetrator but we are wrong: forgiveness is also about us and is for ourselves. It is about us choosing to be free of all the negativity and emotions that destroy our happiness and our desire to live more fully. It is about letting go of all that holds us back and throwing off all that keeps us bogged down. Forgiveness allows us to welcome and take hold of a new life. Forgiveness is about becoming whole. There is much more to forgiveness for us than we realize!

Yes, forgiveness is also about the perpetrator. Although the perpetrator may be grossly unconscious of the life-long harm and damage that they have caused us through committing the offense, if in the future, by the grace of

God, the perpetrator shows repentance and remorse for the offenses committed and seeks to be put right with God, forgiveness provides the proper climate for this to take place so that peace and reconciliation can be found with God.

Forgiveness is a big call, and it requires a heart beyond our human heart – God's heart – which is why we need to ask God our Father to intercede for us. Yet while we face the challenge to forgive every time we come to the place called The Skull – the place where the layers of our past trauma are stripped back and exposed – let us also remember that this place is our sacred ground because God is present here (even though, like Jesus, we may not feel God's presence) and working in us to transform what is disgraceful to graceful, dishonourable to honourable, hatred to peace, crucifixion to freedom and brokenness to wholeness. If we have sufficient faith in our heart, this place, painful as it is to come to it, is the place where God works a miracle and makes us new so that we are no longer victim but victor through the power of God's love.

Praying the scripture reading[50]

1. Try to be still and aware of Jesus' presence with you.
2. As you read the scripture, try to imagine that you are one of the crowd who has followed Jesus to the place called The Skull.

    As you do, try to notice what is happening around you – the atmosphere (is it loud, hostile, aggressive?), the crowd's attitude towards Jesus, the way the soldiers treat Jesus. What calls your attention the most?

---

[50] May I repeat here footnote 47 from page 204.) I am aware that this particular scene of Jesus' crucifixion, as well as other scenes from Jesus' Passion which demonstrate aggression, abuse and violence towards Jesus, may cause survivors to become disturbed or distressed and even trigger certain traumatic memories, particularly if we are at the stage of processing our trauma. In this case, it is appropriate for a survivor to discern if the use of imagination with this particular scripture passages will provoke unnecessary trauma. Should this be the case, I would suggest entering the guided steps for prayer at a place that you feel is more comfortable for you.

Stripped but not broken

Try now to focus on Jesus and what is happening to him in this scene. What do not notice about Jesus? What is calling your attention the most about him? (If you are able to, you may like to imagine yourself beneath his cross and talk to him there. Tell him personally what do you notice about him (his suffering, his attitude, his acceptance?). Share with him how this makes you feel.

3. Try now to listen to Jesus' words from the cross: 'Father, forgive them, for they do not know what they are doing.'

   What calls your attention about Jesus when he says these words? For example, that he says them to the Father, that he is in excruciating pain when he says them, that they are directed towards his Father in prayer and not directly to his perpetrators, that he is full of compassion ... You may like to continue talking to Jesus about this beneath his cross.

   If you have some burning questions (for example, 'Why did you feel the urge to ask the Father to forgive your enemies before you died? How could you ask that they be forgiven when you are going through immense pain?'), ask Jesus and let him answer you in the depth of your heart.

   Is there something about Jesus that you find inspiring? Can you name it? (You may like to tell Jesus.)

4. In the next part of this prayer, we are going to try to apply this scene to our own life experiences.

   Are you able to identify situations or experiences in your life that resonate with this place called The Skull where Jesus was crucified,[51] that is, where you relive the past trauma of the abuse? (This can be anything that triggers these experiences.)

   Can you identify how you react in these situations. Do you fight or resist them? Avoid the pain with escape? Admit and accept what is happening to you and why it is happening? Find that they are an

---

[51] 'Resonate', not in the sense of the physical crucifixion that Jesus experienced but in what was happening in Jesus' interior – the emotional, mental and psychological pain and torment.

opportunity to forgive and let go? You may like to talk to Jesus about the way you react.

Is there something from Jesus' life in this reading that inspires or encourages you to try and deal with these situations differently? If so, what is it? (You may like to talk to Jesus about this.)

How is this inviting you to change the way you deal with situations that bring you to the place called The Skull? (You may like to write this down in your prayer journal so that you can come back to it as a resolution.)

How do you think that making this change will benefit you? For example, a greater freedom, help to take back power and control in situations, a feeling of empowerment …

5. Go back to the scripture reading again and imagine Jesus asking the Father to forgive his enemies. Perhaps you can ask Jesus, 'How did asking the Father to forgive your enemies make a difference to the way you died?' Take the time to try to listen with your heart for the answer. (You may like to write down what you understand.)

6. You may like to express your difficulties around the theme of forgiving to Jesus. Allow any questions in your heart to arise, for example, 'Why should I Jesus? Isn't this saying to the perpetrator that everything is okay? Shouldn't they have to pay for what they have done? Doesn't forgiving mean they get away with it scot free while I have to suffer the consequences for the rest of my life?' As you do, try to listen to Jesus' response allowing him to bring you back to the reading. Is there something in Jesus' response that surprises you or is new to you? (Talk to him about this)

7. You may like to ask Jesus to help you understand why forgiving is important for you in your process of healing? (If you want, write it down.)

8. Do you believe that by forgiving you will experience inner peace and freedom?

9. Try to determine how you could practise forgiving when you find

that you are at the place called The Skull? (This may involve the process of acknowledging your truth by admitting and accepting what is happening to you and why, trying to be gentle with yourself in the process. If you have anger, resentment, fury or bitterness in your heart, forgiving means learning to let go of these emotions and understanding that as long as you hold on to these emotions they are causing you harm.[52] Or you may be at a stage in your process where you feel ready to ask God for his help to forgive your perpetrator. If you are not, remember, forgiveness is a long and painful process.

10. Try to remember to put the last step into practice when you next find yourself at the place in your heart that resembles The Skull. As painful as it is to be in this place, try to remember that this is the place from which you can be set free and made whole again.

The scripture experienced in my life

Yesterday I had my medical procedure. One of the nurses came to the waiting room where the day surgery patients were seated. She called out my name and as I came towards her she introduced herself briefly and quickly handed me a hospital gown to change into and a plastic bag to put my belongings in. She showed me where the change room was and pointed out where I was to wait after changing.

Immediately I felt the young child in me resisting and crying out to me with loud protests, 'No, I don't want to go in there! Tell her no! Give her the gown back and let's go! Please!' Immediately, I could feel myself getting very hot and clammy. My arms and legs became like jelly and I felt as though I was going to collapse. I wondered if the nurses, doctors and administration staff around me had noticed that something was wrong. The voice of my inner child did not stop. She was terrified, 'How can we trust them? How do you know they won't hurt me? I don't want to go through this again?'

---

[52] In reference to letting go of certain emotions, each person needs to find healthy ways that enable them to let go of emotions that are consuming them.

CHILD, ARISE!

Fortunately, I felt more prepared than usual for what I was going through because the day before I had prayed this scripture. I recognized that being asked to undress brought me to that place in me called The Skull. In the physical sense it was nowhere near as severe and excruciating as the physical crucifixion that Jesus would have experienced, but in relation to the mental and emotional torment I was experiencing it helped me to understand (even if only to a small degree) some of what Jesus may have gone through.

I finally got myself to enter the change room. I sat down for a moment and remembered the resolutions from my prayer of the previous day. My adult self tried to reason with my inner child and calm her down. I took time to talk to her as a mother would talk to her young child. I explained what was happening and why she was in anguish, 'In the past, when you were asked to undress, the next thing was that you were abused. Every time you are asked to undress in the present, you think that the abuse is going to happen again. But it is not going to happen again. This is a completely different situation. You are safe. The perpetrator is not around and we are never going to let him near us again. These people are nurses and doctors and they are here to take care of us. It is important to have this procedure to find out if something is wrong.'

My inner child was not yet fully convinced. I felt that, out of respect for her, I could not start changing until she understood and was pacified. I continued to talk to her with compassion and mercy. As I did, I experienced Jesus' presence with me (the adult and young child). I listened to all my inner child's fears, despair, anxiety. I allowed her to let go of all these intense emotions. I imagined myself holding my inner child and then Jesus embracing the both of us. As he did, I asked him to help me forgive the perpetrator who would never know how much harm he has done to us and the long-term suffering he has caused. This place called The Skull was an opportunity to reconcile past with present, child with adult, survivor with God. Being at that place is definitely a bitter-sweet experience.

I must have been in the change room for at least half an hour and I had not yet begun to change. What must have the nurses been thinking! It didn't really matter what they were thinking... My struggle warranted extra time and space. Slowly, I managed to change into a gown and I was able to walk out of that change room but, to my pleasant surprise, I did not come out as the broken little girl who had been stripped and abused in the past.

As I walked out I was able to recognize that something new had happened in me. Instead of the memory of the abuse having power and control over me, I was able to take back power and control, which left me feeling empowered. I walked out of that change room freer than when I had entered. Who would have thought that something as small as being asked to change for a medical procedure could offer so much!

The scripture experienced in your life

You may like to write down your own account of how you experienced this scripture reading in your life.

Suffering for a purpose

I KNEW THAT TAKING MATTERS to the police and pursuing prosecution was never going to be easy and that much personal suffering would be involved and it is has proven to be so. Undergoing the initial interviews with the police and providing a statement that required me to recall and retell my story in detail not only demanded my physical energy and time but also all my emotional, mental and psychological resources. These resources were not only claimed during the face-to-face time spent with the police but also in what I experienced after those sessions – re-traumatization.

I have been blessed to have the ongoing support of many people who have accompanied me and encouraged me during this part of my journey: family members, my psychologist, my spiritual director, my medical specialists and other support networks like ASCA. They have witnessed the suffering that this course of action inflicts on survivors of sexual abuse.

However, there is a support in my life that has been absolutely crucial and I would even go to the extent of saying that without this support I would not have been able to go through this heart-wrenching part of the journey. I am talking about the spiritual support I have received in the past and continue to receive from God the Father, Jesus, and the Spirit in my daily prayer and reflection on Scripture. What they have injected into my journey up until now has been vital because they give me strong reasons and a purpose to pass through suffering, making it meaningful, and they promise me that in the end this suffering will be a life-giving one and not useless. How existential their support has been for me! Suffering with or for a purpose and having meaning in the midst suffering and agony is what spurs us on our journey.

All of us need a reason to go through suffering in our life. If we don't have strong reasons, we tend to avoid suffering altogether and whenever it comes our way we run away from it desperately attempting to escape the pain. Sometimes we struggle to find a reason or a purpose that is strong enough to move us through suffering.

Suffering for a purpose

In the scriptures, particularly in Jesus' own suffering, we can discover a reason to suffer that will give us meaning, particularly in the most agonizing part of our healing journey.

The scripture reading

The agony in the garden

Then Jesus went with them to a place called Gethsemane; and he said to his disciples, 'Sit here while I go over there and pray.' He took with him Peter and the two sons of Zebedee, and began to be grieved and agitated. Then he said to them, 'I am deeply grieved, even to death; remain here, and stay awake with me.' And going a little farther, he threw himself on the ground and prayed, 'My Father, if it is possible, let this cup pass from me; yet not what I want but what you want.' Then he came to the disciples and found them sleeping; and he said to Peter, 'So, could you not stay awake with me one hour? Stay awake and pray that you may not come into the time of trial: the spirit indeed is willing, but the flesh is weak.' Again he went away for the second time and prayed, 'My Father, if this cannot pass unless I drink it, your will be done.' Again he came and found them sleeping, for their eyes were heavy. So, leaving them again, he went away and prayed for the third time, saying the same words.

Matthew 26:36-44

Jesus has just finished celebrating the Jewish Passover feast with his disciples. This was to be his last supper with them before his death. At this time, he is very aware that his death is pending. He goes with his disciples to a quiet place called Gethsemane to gather himself in prayer. Here he reveals his suffering humanity to those who intimately support him, saying that he is 'deeply grieved, even to death'. We get a sense of the overwhelming, immense and intense sorrow and suffering that Jesus is confronting and struggling to hold in his body. The weight of it nearly crushes him to death. Jesus looks for support from those who are closest to him by asking them to stay awake and to remain with him in his sadness and pain. He knows how challenging it is going to be for his disciples to watch him suffering.

Although we would like to, we cannot pass through the process of healing from sexual abuse without suffering. There are many times along our journey where we too come to 'the place called Gethsemane'. Gethsemane represents the place where, like Jesus, we feel the crushing weight of our sorrow, even at times to the point where we think our body cannot possibly contain it and we are going to die. These are desperate times when we are afraid to be alone and we yearn for others to accompany and support us. Yet even though we have support we can still search for something more within ourselves to move us through this suffering – a personal reason or purpose. Without this it is extremely difficult to pass through suffering.

Gethsemane is the place where we see Jesus suffer, desperately clinging to his personal purpose – accomplishing his Father's will. Yet, even with this purpose, Jesus struggles to accept the suffering his journey involves. He prays, 'If it is possible, let this cup' – meaning the cross he would shortly endure entailing his physical death – 'pass from me.' Jesus could have escaped his suffering but instead chose to wrestle with it by facing and processing what he experienced in repeated and prayerful conversations with his Father. While these conversations reveal the humanity of Jesus in his suffering[53], they also reveal how he was empowered by his purpose until he could eventually embrace his suffering: 'Father, if this cannot pass without me drinking it, your will be done.'

This purpose gave Jesus a very strong conviction to say yes to what he could perceive was going to be the greatest suffering of his life on earth. Jesus' purpose was to do God's will, and we need to understand this correctly. God is not some tyrant who wanted to see Jesus suffer: on the contrary,

---

[53] See Luke's parallel account of the Agony in the Garden (Luke 22:39-46). At one point (verse 44), Jesus is described as being in 'such agony and praying so fervently that his sweat became like drops of blood falling to the ground'. See also Hebrews 6:7: 'In the days when he was in the flesh, he offered prayers with loud cries and tears to the one who was able to save him from death.'

Suffering for a purpose

the Father would have suffered greatly to see the Son he loved suffering so much. However, after conversing with the Father in prayer, Jesus understood that suffering is an inevitable part of the human condition and journey that needs to be accepted and embraced. From his own prayer, Jesus came to understand that his suffering, although painful, would be fruitful not only for himself but for many. This came to be true when he overcame death and triumphed in his Resurrection.

Being with God and prayerfully conversing with him in Gethsemane (the quiet place in our heart where we struggle with suffering) is a gift, and God leaves us free to accept this gift or reject it. Like Jesus, even though we have the support of those closest to us, and psychologists, counsellors, spiritual directors and support and advocacy groups, there may still be times when we find that we lack a meaning and purpose to suffer. Through this scripture, Jesus invites us to find our purpose by conversing with God in prayer. When we spend prayerful time with God, especially when we experience the weight of sorrow and despair, and honestly share our feelings (even if we are tempted to escape or avoid the suffering), God will help us to accept our suffering as part of our life journey and the human experience.

It needs to be clearly said again that God does not enjoy seeing us suffer, nor wants to see us suffer: on the contrary, God suffers immensely when we suffer. But God tries to help us understand that suffering is an inevitable part of the human experience that we are invited to embrace in our own humanity, just as Jesus learnt to embrace it.[54] Part of the secret to becoming fully human is learning to embrace suffering in our lives. Through Jesus' suffering in Gethsemane, we are invited to understand that while God may not take away our suffering or wave a magic wand and make it disappear, God empowers us as we pass through it by supplying us with the strength and grace we need to accept it.[55]

St Paul reminds us of God's strength in suffering through his own experience when he begs the Lord three times in prayer to take away his suffering

---

[54] Hebrews 6:8: 'Son though he was, he learned obedience from what he suffered …'
[55] Luke's parallel of the Agony in the Garden, verse 43: 'And to strengthen him an angel from heaven appeared to him.'

(which he describes as 'a thorn in the flesh'). God responds to him in prayer: 'My grace is sufficient for you, for my power is made perfect in weakness' (2 Corinthians 12:7-9). Through this empowerment God promises us that like Jesus we will also triumph over suffering.[56]

So, while the story of Gethsemane is full of meaning, what may call the attention of survivors of sexual abuse is the importance of having a personal purpose that enables us to accept our suffering as part and parcel of our own healing journey. By accepting our suffering, we will pass from sorrow to glory as Jesus did. However, as we suffer, may we hold on to the hope of our Resurrection with Christ and the fruit of a journey that is beneficial and freeing not only for us but one that is also light for other survivors of sexual abuse.

Praying the scripture reading

1. Try to be still and aware of Jesus' presence with you.
2. As you read the reading, try to picture the scene. You may like to imagine that you are Peter or one of the sons of Zebedee. Imagine that Jesus says to you, 'I am deeply grieved, even to death. Remain here, and stay awake with me.' Watch him as he throws himself on the ground and prays to the Father. Listen to Jesus as he pours out his sorrow to the Father and begs him 'My Father, if it is possible, let this cup pass from me; yet not what I want but what you want.'
3. What is it that calls your attention about Jesus in his suffering? Is it that he is honest about communicating his grief to those who are intimate to him; he does not want to be alone as he suffers; he turns to God his Father to pray in his suffering and faces it; he asks the Father to let the cup pass, or something else? Once you have identified this, you may want to express it to Jesus.
4. Try to identify what emotion this evokes in you. Surprise, wonder, uneasiness, fear, dismay, resistance ... or perhaps you feel challenged. (You may also want to write this down.)

---

[56] John 16:33: 'In the world you will have trouble, but take courage, I have conquered the world.'

Suffering for a purpose

5. When you listen to Jesus praying to God in his suffering, saying, 'My Father, if it is possible, let this cup pass from me, yet not what I want but what you want', what calls your attention? (You may want to converse with Jesus about this.)
6. What is different about the way that Jesus faces suffering and the way that you face suffering? (You may want to converse with Jesus about this in prayer and write it down.)
7. What do you find challenging about Jesus in his agony? (You may want to converse with Jesus about this.)
8. Reflecting on this reading, what would you say is Jesus' purpose to suffer? Can you identify how this purpose helps Jesus face his suffering? (You may want to converse more with Jesus about this.)
9. Do you have a purpose to move you through your suffering? If so, what or who is it? (You may want to converse with Jesus about this.)
10. Have you ever thought that God can be a powerful support in suffering or that God could give you strong reasons that empower you to pass through suffering? (Try to converse with Jesus about this.)
11. It could be that you are presently wrestling with suffering in your life and experiencing deep sorrow. You may like to take the time to express what you are feeling to God in prayer.
12. Do you also find yourself saying to God, 'Let this cup (whatever suffering this may be) pass from me', as Jesus did? Are you able to say to God, 'Yet not what I want but what you want'? If not, what prevents you from saying this? (You may want to converse with Jesus about this.)
13. In our struggle with suffering we can ask God for his strength and grace. Spend time asking God to strengthen you in your suffering. Let God remind you, as with St Paul, that 'My grace is sufficient for you.' Try to let these words resound in your heart, giving you consolation, peace, reassurance and strength. Try to believe that God is filling you with grace as you pray.

14. Is it possible that Jesus is inviting you through this scripture to discover in God a purpose for suffering? If so, what would you like to do differently in the future or change about the way you suffer? (Try to be as concrete as possible and converse with Jesus about this. It could be not to escape or avoid the pain of suffering but instead to spend time praying, opening your heart to Jesus and finding reasons in him to pass through your suffering, or you may have another light).
15. Before you finish prayer, ask Jesus to help you to be faithful to your purpose and to practise what you have understood from today's prayer.
16. Always try to be hopeful in suffering. Remember, while suffering was a part of Jesus' journey, it was not the end. Jesus triumphed over it and was raised from the dead. So too, while we suffer, we can also look forward to being raised up from what we now suffer.

The scripture experienced in my life

The past several days have been very sorrowful for me. A person I deeply respect and who knows that I have been sexually abused brought the topic up with me. Although they wanted to be a support to me, they obviously had no understanding of the way that victims are 'groomed' by their perpetrators and how they are silenced and left feeling helpless, powerless and hopeless. This person was insinuating that I should have spoken up and told someone what was happening and even that I could have avoided the perpetrator. I'm sure it was not their intention but they were implying that I had some responsibility and was to blame for what happened. Unfortunately, this person was saying all the wrong things to the point that I became extremely distressed, agitated and grieved.

In previous years, I punished myself for not having said something to someone earlier and condemned myself, 'Why didn't I just run away from my perpetrator? Or tell him to get away or leave me alone?' I blamed myself for so long because my perpetrator made me feel that I was the bad one. It

Suffering for a purpose

took years for me to rectify all these distorted thoughts in my mind and to put the responsibility back on the perpetrator. Even though I know in my mind that I cannot blame myself for my past it still brought me to a place in my heart of deep sorrow – Gethsemane.

Following this conversation, I struggled for several days feeling that no one or nothing could console me. However, in this place in my heart – Gethsemane – I found myself alone and praying repeatedly to God. I have been writing and pouring out my sorrow and despair to him and I have tried to be honest with him about my feelings and the exhaustion of carrying the weight of ongoing suffering. Like Jesus, I found myself asking God to 'let the suffering pass.' I confess that it has been so hard for me to say, 'Not what I want but what you want.' I kept telling God, 'I don't want to suffer any more. I've had enough!' But then I dared to ask, 'But what do you want, God? Do you want me to go through this suffering? Why do you want me to go through it? Is it because you like to see me suffering? Or is it for something else?'

I understood in prayer that God was inviting me to embrace this suffering as part of human experience. He made me see that even Jesus who is God had to pass through suffering during his earthly life, but he reminded me that beyond suffering Jesus showed us that there is the glory of the Resurrection awaiting us all. God reminded me that by passing through my suffering I will come to experience the glory of the Resurrection and be a sign of hope to other survivors. Through many conversations with God over several days I eventually found myself in a place of peace and acceptance where I could say to God, 'This suffering is very painful God but your will be done!' Having surrendered to God, not only did I have fresh reasons to pass through this suffering but I felt empowered with God's grace and strength. My heart felt ready to continue on my journey.

The scripture experienced in your life

You may like to write down your own account of how you experienced this scripture reading in your life.

It is finished

ISN'T IT SATISFYING TO REACH THE END of a task and to be able to say 'It is finished! I've done it!' especially if the task has used up all of our physical, emotional, mental and spiritual resources.

From the time we are small children we are challenged to finish tasks and this challenge stays with us throughout our life time. One of our big challenges as a teenager may have been whether to finish high school or not, for some others it may have been whether to complete tertiary studies or not, whether to finish an apprenticeship or not, whether to complete any sort of course they may take on.

Once working life begins, we are constantly challenged to finish tasks and to meet deadlines by the end of each day, requiring responsibility and commitment. Perhaps some people have been chosen for a certain role, either at work or in some other organization, that demands they give more of themselves and they will feel challenged to complete their role to the end. These challenges grow even more in marriage and family life. Finishing off payments on the family car or home can be very challenging. Parents will be challenged and feel committed to seeing their children finish school and grow to be independent.

In society, we often mark an achievement or completing something with some sort of ceremony or celebration. Finishing high school is marked with a graduation ceremony; likewise, finishing a degree at university. We celebrate finishing a big project at work, as we celebrate the completion of building a first home. We even celebrate finishing each year with a New Year's Eve celebration. Throughout our life we learn to celebrate the joy of having completed a task and being able to proclaim, 'It is finished!'

However, while we are finishing these external tasks, we may be procrastinating finishing some very personal business that we have to do in our own life which involves emotional work, such as facing painful and bitter past experiences that remain unresolved – a falling out with someone we

It is finished

love, an infidelity in a marriage, a betrayal of trust in a partnership, a divorce settlement, a prosecution outcome, taking care of someone who is chronically or gravely ill or had an accident, or saying goodbye to a loved one who has died. At times, we can find it very difficult to confront these experiences when they happen to us because we lack the strength and courage to do so. We may try to bury them deep inside us and hope that they will just disappear only to find that they resurface or revisit us at times in our life when we least expect it. We may see these occasions as gentle reminders that we have some unfinished business to take care of.

Choosing to face these situations and doing what we have to do to finish our unfinished business requires bravery. Even when we attempt to finish this business, sadly, the outcome may not always be a desirable one but instead a very bitter one. Often we struggle against, resist and reject bitter endings. Wanting them to be different, we can work hard to turn them around and make them otherwise. It is difficult for us to accept to accept bitter endings, and, although the outcome is not what we would like it to be, or how we thought it would turn out, this is what it is – 'It is finished!' There is a sweetness if we manage to accept even the most bitter ending – it is the peace of knowing in our heart that we have done all that we could to say, 'It is finished!'

For survivors of abuse, just the thought of ever being able to say 'It is finished!' is a challenge because, even when we are trying to do what we have to do in our healing process, it can seem like the end is never in sight as new issues surface throughout our life time. Just as we are beginning to get on top of one issue, another one arises. It can feel like the well of the deep effects of abuse within us is never ending.

Survivors of sexual abuse may be very well acquainted with such bitter experiences! The issue alone of telling our loved ones what happened to us and to experience their denial or disbelief or dismissal (if this is our case) can be a very bitter experience. As is the experience of confronting our perpetrator who denies it, or reporting it to the appropriate institution who should be held accountable and take responsibility only to experience that our claim has been silenced and dismissed and that no action is being or has been taken. These are all very bitter experiences that cause us to feel grief. These experiences crush us and leave us feeling that we have spent the whole of ourselves (physically, emotionally, mentally, psychologically, and spiritually) in facing these issues and we are at a stage when we have nothing left to spend. It is so hard to accept such bitter outcomes. We want to be able to say, 'It is finished!' I've done all that I can possibly do and all I can do now is to accept it and surrender it to God.'

Jesus knew the pain of a bitter ending but he also knew the sweetness of being able to say, 'It is finished!' He can teach us how to conclude our unfinished business in life, even when the ending is so bitter.

The scripture reading

The death of Jesus

Near the cross of Jesus stood his mother, his mother's sister, Mary the wife of Clopas, and Mary Magdalene. When Jesus saw his mother there, and the disciple whom he loved standing nearby, he said to her, 'Woman, here is your son', and to the disciple, 'Here is your mother.' From that time on, this disciple took her into his home. Later, knowing that everything had now been finished, and so that Scripture would be fulfilled, Jesus said, 'I am thirsty.' A jar of wine vinegar was there, so they soaked a sponge in it, put the sponge on a stalk of the hyssop plant, and lifted it to Jesus' lips. When he had received the drink, Jesus said, 'It is finished.' With that, he bowed his head and gave up his spirit.

John 19:25-30

Jesus has reached the end of his earthly life and the circumstances surrounding him are bitter – circumstances that none of us would ever wish for. Jesus – an innocent man – is condemned to the tortuous death of a criminal. His death bed is a wooden cross from which he hangs as his enemies surround him.

Jesus knows what it is like to experience that justice on earth has not

It is finished

prevailed and to feel let down by the religious and civil law systems. He knows because he passed through the process of these systems right to the end.[57] He knows what it's like to come through these systems and to face a death sentence while the real perpetrators walk away scot-free, gloating over their apparent triumph!

What they do not seem to understand is that this apparent triumph will be short-lived because in the not too distant future they too, like all of us, will need to pass through an even greater justice system than the human-made justice systems on earth – the justice of God's Kingdom. In this system, everyone will stand before God, our final judge, and give a full account of our life on earth and in God's presence everything that has been concealed during our earthly life will be made known and brought out into the light (Luke 8:17). In the end, God's justice will prevail for all and will not disappoint us!

Although Jesus' life is ending in bitter circumstances, he is extraordinarily graceful – graceful enough to let go and accept his death. As Jesus exhales his last breath, we see him gently letting go as he surrenders his life to God the Father. He lets go of the two people who stood beneath his cross supporting him: his mother and his beloved disciple... He lets go of the things he cannot change: dying at a young age and as a criminal, the failure of the justice systems on earth, the unjust religious leaders (who proclaimed to believe and love God) who instigated his death, that there was so much more he would have liked to teach his disciples for their mission, that he would have like to reach out to so many more people with God's compassion and kindness.

Letting go is not only part of the process of dying physically but it is also part of the process of dying spiritually. We may have experienced or be presently experiencing circumstances in our life where we are being invited

---

[57] For Jesus before the Sandhedrin, see Matthew 26:57-69, John 18:19-24, Mark 14:55-64, Luke 22:66-71. 'Sanhedrin' is a Hebraized form of a Greek word meaning council, and refers to the elders, chief priests and scribes who met under the High Priest's leadership to decide religious and legal questions that did not pertain to Rome's interest (from *The New American Bible*). For Jesus before Pilate (the Roman Governor of Judea 26-36 CE) see John 18:28- 19:16, Matthew 27:1-2;11-26, Mark 15:1-15, Luke 23:1-5.

to let go; whether it is past events we cannot change, grievances, dreams we could not realize, circumstances we are not in control of, people we must say goodbye to. As we walk through these experiences and learn to let go, we feel that part of us is dying within. It is a spiritual experience in which we are invited to share in Jesus' death which gives us great hope because, as St Paul says, 'Christ has been raised from the dead ... so too in Christ shall all be brought to life' (1 Corinthians 15:20-22). We too will be raised from the experience of death to a new life in Christ! As we learn to let go, this process takes place within us.

At times we resist letting go and we make our spiritual death agonizing because while we are holding on to the issue we are also storing all the emotions associated with it in our body. Letting go is an art we are invited to practise throughout our life time. The secret to learning to live well is learning to die (in the spiritual sense of the word) well. Jesus knew the art of dying well because he had practised it throughout his life time.

By contemplating Jesus' last moments on the cross, we can learn how to bring closure to the painful and bitter events that take place in our life by learning to say with Jesus 'It is finished!' Only moments before Jesus dies, he utters the words 'I thirst!' While there is no doubt that Jesus was physically thirsty it is not difficult to imagine that there was an even deeper thirst in his heart that he would have liked to be quenched – a thirst for justice, compassion, mercy, peace, love.

This final plea is Jesus' last to humanity and through it we are able to see the miraculous power of God's grace gently breaking into the heart of humanity, for it is not a friend who responds to Jesus' plea with kindness but an enemy – a Roman soldier. The best he can offer Jesus is bitter wine which he soaks on a sponge and raises to Jesus' mouth on a sprig of hyssop. Jesus doesn't reject the wine, bitter as it is, but accepts it and after drinking it speaks his last words, 'It is finished'. Finally, he bows his head and surrenders his spirit. Jesus gracefully brings this bitter ending to a closure.

Don't you find that, even though Jesus' death is surrounded by brutality and cruelty, he reveals a deep peace that is magnetic – peace with himself, peace with God and peace with humanity – a peace that comes from

It is finished

knowing that he has finished the will of the Father to the best of his ability. Although I'm sure that Jesus would have welcomed a more positive final outcome, Jesus accepts and embraces the bitter ending that his life has come to and he dies with a sense of fulfilment and satisfaction, despite such a tragedy.

There is something profound calling to us in Jesus' last moments of life. To experience a sense of fulfilment and satisfaction as events are brought to a conclusion does not depend on how the final outcome appears to be. Just because the result may not seem to be a positive one or a successful and just one does not mean that we have failed and that our efforts have been in vain. Even though situations and circumstances in our life can prove to be tragic at times, a deep peace in our hearts can still prevail. This peace comes from knowing that we have finished the mission and purpose we have been called to, and that we have done all that we can possibly do to be faithful to our purpose.

We will have many opportunities over our life time to put this into practice – opportunities where we know in our hearts that we too need to say with Jesus, 'It is finished. I have done all that I can possibly do and there is no more that I can do. It is time to surrender to accept whatever the situation is and to surrender myself to God.' For each survivor, the experience of arriving at this conclusion will be different since each survivor is unique in their capacity to bear suffering.

As it was with Jesus, we will know as we listen to our heart and our body, when it is time to say, 'It is finished'. It may be letting go of a long-term relationship or a family member who has caused us grief by disbelieving our story or not supporting us in our healing journey. For some it will be accepting that, because of trauma, there may be many things from the past we do not remember and which don't allow us to join all the dots in our mind, so we need to move forward with the sufficient yet incomplete knowledge of what happened to us and why we are the person we are today. There may be some who have reported this crime to the institution concerned and who are persevering to seek justice. For some it may be arriving at the end of a course of prosecution. Each of these survivors will need to know when to say, 'It is finished! I have done everything I can do.'

The outcome of each of these circumstances may be undesirably bitter and perhaps all our resources will have been consumed in the process, but we can still come to the end of these processes with a deep inner peace and the satisfaction of knowing in our heart that we have completed our mission or purpose. We can say with Jesus that this particular part of our journey is complete, and experience closure, even though the outcome may look like a failure according to human logic.

What we cannot assess at the time and often fail to recognize is the powerful after-effect that our life has on those who are silently witnessing us during our ordeal, be it closely or from a distance.

Even as Jesus was hanging on the cross, his life was positively influencing some of those who were witness to his anguish. We see it in the criminal who defends Jesus before the taunts of the second criminal and then asks Jesus 'Remember me, when you come into your Kingdom' (Luke 23:39-43). We see it in the Roman soldier who offers Jesus a final gesture of kindness by giving him bitter wine to quench his thirst. It is evident in the group of women who do not lose courage and stand firm beneath the cross supporting Jesus as he passes through this final trauma. Most of all, we see it after Jesus' resurrection as more and more people are baptised and begin to follow the Way of Jesus.

From the perspective of these truths, we can say that the end of Jesus' life, bitter as it was, was not a failure. There was much more success than the human mind would be ever able to recognize.

And so it is with our life too, although often we are very hard judges when it comes to our own situation. It could be that we have come to the end of a particular part of our healing journey and had some closure but, according to our own assessment, it was a disaster and we've written failure all over it! This is where we need to turn on our eyes of faith and believe that our investment has not been in vain and that there have been some successes we may only discover years after passing through these stages of the journey.

Perhaps telling your story to a family member or to someone you trust (even though it may have been dismissed) changed some patterns in the family culture and ways of behaving, or saved someone in the next generation from being abused, or encouraged someone to break the silence and admit their own history of abuse so that they could begin their healing. Perhaps some

It is finished

healing as a family has taken place. Perhaps other survivors witnessing your journey have been given hope to not despair and to persevere along the journey, others may be encouraged to prevent abuse in the future by working as an advocate. Perhaps those who have been walking and supporting you on your journey have become better people in the process, more compassionate, more sensitive and caring.

So, let us always remember this as we continue to finish our unfinished business, and may we never allow the apparent outcome of anything that we attempt to bring to a closure on our journey, ever to steal away the peace that comes from knowing that we have 'finished' what we knew in our heart we needed to do.

Praying the scripture reading[58]

1. Try to be still and aware of Jesus' presence with you.
2. As you read the scripture, try to imagine that you are beneath Jesus' cross. You may like to take the place of one of the women, the crowd, or even one of the Roman soldiers.

    As you do, try to focus on Jesus and what is happening in this scene. What do you notice about Jesus? What is calling your attention the most? (Jesus' last words to his beloved disciple, his last words to his mother, the gesture of kindness of the Roman soldier, that Jesus accepts the bitter wine …) If you are able to, tell Jesus why you are moved by these things.

    Now focus on Jesus. What calls your attention about him? (His ability to let go, his ability to accept the bitter circumstances surrounding his death, knowing that he has done everything he needs to do) Share this with Jesus and let him know how this makes you feel.

---

[58] I am aware, again, that this particular scene of Jesus' crucifixion, as well as other scenes from Jesus' Passion which demonstrate aggression, abuse and violence towards Jesus, may cause survivors to become disturbed or distressed and even trigger certain traumatic memories, particularly if we are at the stage of processing our trauma. In this case, it is appropriate for a survivor to discern if the use of imagination with this particular scripture will provoke unnecessary trauma. Should this be the case, I would suggest entering the guided steps for prayer at a place you feel is more comfortable for you.

3. Next, listen to Jesus' words, 'It is finished.'

    You may want to talk to Jesus about these last words he spoke on the cross. Perhaps you are thinking: What was 'it' for you Jesus? How were you sure that you finished it? Why was it important for you to finish it? How did finishing it make a difference for you at your death? As you ask Jesus your questions, give him time to answer them in the depth of your heart.

4. In the next part of prayer, we are going to try and apply this scene to our own life experiences.

    Are you able to identify the bitter situations or experiences that are part of your healing journey where God may be inviting you to have closure by letting go and accepting them for what they are?

    When you recall these 'bitter' experiences and the thought of being able to say 'It is finished. I have dealt with this situation and done all that I can possibly do to the best of my ability and there is nothing else that I can possibly do apart from accepting it is what it is and letting go.' How does this make you feel? (Happy, peaceful, satisfied, empowered, hopeful, afraid, resistant, rebellious …) You may like to talk to Jesus about these feelings.

    Is there something that is preventing you from being able to say in these bitter situations 'It is finished'? (A lack of justice, a lack of acceptance, a fear to speak out …) You may like to express your difficulties around the theme of letting go and seeking closure. For example, 'How can I let go or say it is finished? My offender has not yet been brought to justice. How can I let go when those closest to me still don't believe me? How can I say it is finished if the offender is still offending?' You may want to tell Jesus about this and listen to his response in your heart.

    Is there something that you could do to overcome these obstacles that prevent you from saying 'It is finished'? If so, what? (You may like to write this down in your prayer journal so that you can come back to it as a resolution.)

It is finished

It could be that you feel in this bitter situation that you have done everything that you can possibly do. Perhaps you feel you do not have the physical, emotional, mental, psychological and spiritual resources. If this is the case, you may want to share this with Jesus.

Are there some steps you could take that would lead you to a deeper acceptance and help you to have some closure? You may like to talk to Jesus about when and how you could practise these steps.

5. You may want to ask Jesus to help you understand why letting go, accepting and having closure is important for you in your process of healing. (If you want, write it down.)
6. Do you believe that as you pass through bitter experiences on your healing journey that your inner peace will come from being able to accept the circumstances, let go, and say as Jesus did: 'It is finished'?
7. Next time you find yourself going through a bitter situation or experience, try to come back to this scene in the gospel and listen to Jesus' words, 'It is finished'. Try to remember your resolutions from this prayer reflection and try to put them into practice.

The scripture experienced in my life

One of the most painful and bitter experiences for survivors is when we reveal our story to those closest to us or those we trust and they fail to believe us or believe that we could have done something to prevent the abuse from happening, therefore burdening us with guilt and blame.

I have gone through the anguish of such an experience. After my private hearing session for the Royal Commission I revealed my story to someone I trusted and who I believed would support me 100 per cent. I had the biggest shock of my life when I was told, 'If only you had said something to someone ... Why didn't you just tell your offender to leave you alone?' I became so distressed with the 'If only you ...' and the 'Why didn't you ...'

CHILD, ARISE!

No matter how many times I tried to explain how I was groomed by the perpetrator, emotionally manipulated and overpowered, threatened, and forced into silence by violence, the person questioning me could not understand or grasp the gravity of what I was describing and it became evident to me from what they were saying that they may never come to understand.

I would have stopped conversing about my story with this person much sooner and not attempted to talk to them about it again, had it not been that the person was someone close to me, whose support would have been helpful. I do not believe that they were aware of how distressing their responses were and the impact they had on me.

After several sincere attempts of trying to talk about my story with this person, and finding that these conversations were leaving me in a negative head and heart space, I felt a call from within to let go.

On this particular day, I went to my room and attempted to quieten my mind and heart from all the negativity that the conversation had left me with. I remembered the scripture reading mentioned here and the bitter circumstances that surrounded Jesus when he uttered the words, 'It is finished.'

There was something in this reading that resonated with me. It was not that I was dying physically, but, yes, this was an occasion when I was being invited to die spiritually. I would have delighted in a more positive outcome of my conversations with this person: some empathy, understanding, compassion, sensitivity, deep listening, encouragement. Instead, I came away feeling more burdened, guilty, shameful, desperate, anxious and deeply saddened by the lack of support. After each conversation, I felt as though I was thrown into grieving the loss of this person's support in my heart. I knew deep down that they were not going to change and perhaps didn't have the capacity to understand my story.

It became clear to me that it was time to accept that, although I wanted this person to understand my story, at this point in time they could not and it might be that they never would in the future. I felt Jesus was not asking me to persevere in trying to explain myself but was inviting me to die spiritually by letting go of the outcomes that I would have liked from my conversations with this person and accept that they did not and could understand.

It is finished

Deep within my heart I knew that there was nothing else that I could do that would change the situation. The person was not open to reading literature on the topic or to going to a group of supporters for survivors. I knew in my heart that I had done all I could possibly do and that I did not have more inner resources to keep confronting the topic since each conversation was so consuming and re-traumatizing. I knew that Jesus was inviting me to say with him, 'It is finished.'

I spent a long time conversing with Jesus and sharing my pain and tears with him. Jesus encouraged me, painful as it was, to accept this bitter outcome and the fact that I could not do anything else to change the situation. I knew in my heart this was true. With all my being and a deep surrender of my heart I cried to Jesus, 'It is finished. I know that I cannot do anything else and I believe it would not be helpful for me to attempt to do more at this moment in time.' Jesus supported me in my decision and I made a promise that I would not pursue the topic any more.

Jesus invited me to hand this bitter situation to him. I imagined myself doing this. As I surrendered it, I felt the huge burden in my heart had been lifted. The guilt, shame, despair, sorrow, anxiety had all been replaced with a deep peace. This was unexpected but I welcomed the change I experienced through the grace of Jesus Christ.

This experience drove home the power of the words 'It is finished.' Letting go, accepting our circumstances as bitter as they may be, and seeking closure to them through the grace of Jesus is the key to our own inner peace on our healing journey.

The scripture experienced in your life

Were you able to experience the scripture reading in your life today? If so, how did this happen? You may like to write down your own account.

Plans to prosper

EVERY PERSON YEARNS TO PROSPER IN LIFE and be successful at whatever they set out to do. None of us ever begins something with the desire to fail. Initially, we may need to combat some negative thinking but once we proceed with our plan, we hope to succeed and to grow and flourish as a person in the process.

Adult survivors of abuse also desire to flourish, thrive and live life fully, despite the experience of personal tragedy. However, the difference is that when we make plans to prosper, the negativity we experience is not something that we can easily hurdle. Our negativity is like climbing Mount Everest – a huge and challenging mountain – and the task requires physical, mental, emotional, psychological and spiritual stamina. Climbing beyond this negativity seems to cost us more than a person who may not have been sexually abused.

For adult survivors, prosperity can seem too far out of our reach as it was for us when we were children. Normally, in childhood, the tiny seeds of talents and gifts planted within us begin to develop. As children grow, so too do these talents and gifts if they are nurtured properly. Already from a young age, children can start to architect their own plans, dreams and desires that are expressions of their wish to prosper and flourish in life.

Survivors of sexual abuse may experience that these dreams and plans have been stolen at the hands of our perpetrator. I experienced this throughout my childhood. Initially, I enjoyed primary school and the early experiences of learning and achieving. This made me happy with myself as a young child. I was a good student and I became quite competitive and wanted to excel at school. At the same time, I was very athletic and on many occasions I was chosen to represent my school in the combined school carnivals for athletics. I began piano lessons and, again, enjoyed learning to play the piano. I continued to have lessons through primary and high school. As I transitioned to high school I developed a love for netball and played in competitions. These were all things I enjoyed doing and planned to continue doing

Plans to prosper

in the future because they helped me thrive as a person. However, during the years I was sexually abused, these plans began to disintegrate in a world of destruction.

In high school, even though I was good at athletics and my teachers encouraged me to continue, I slowly lost interest and stopped competitive athletics altogether. I did the same with competition netball. I lost my drive for everything. I was often sick and missed a lot of school during Years 8, 9 and 10 and my grades starting falling. I managed to keep up my piano until Year 11 but demanding hours of practice combined with the stress and anxiety of performing for the Higher School Certificate was too great. I stopped playing altogether. (I did not touch a piano for another twenty years.) Up to this day, I still do not know how I managed to get through my Higher School Certificate with a good enough mark to enter a Science and Mathematics degree at university. However, after only one semester at university, I chose to defer my course because of my inner chaos.

Not only did my perpetrators harm me physically, emotionally and psychologically, they also harmed me spiritually by destroying the parts of my life that provided meaning and purpose and a sense of prosperity. For some time I did think I could be a doctor or a professional athlete or continue a career in music or be a biochemist and excel in medical research, but each time my plans to succeed in these areas were shattered by the damaging effects of being abused and trying to deal with this as a child and young adult.

I am sure most survivors can tell a similar story. So it is understandable that as adult survivors we can make plans to prosper but find that we are standing in front of Mount Everest. All the negativity from the past stares us in the face, making us ask, 'Is this going to end in destruction again just like …?' Every time we attempted to thrive in the past it didn't come to fruition. As adult survivors, we can prosper and go forward in life, even achieving great things by making marvellous contributions to our world. It is possible – we just need to believe it!

God not only believes that we can do it but God has plans for us to prosper and to be fruitful. This is confirmed and reaffirmed through the beautiful scripture reading below from the Prophet Jeremiah.

The scripture reading

'I know the plans I have for you', declares the Lord, 'Plans to prosper you and not to harm you! Plans to give you a future full of hope.'
Jeremiah 29:11

The Prophet Jeremiah is speaking here to a nation who at the time is exiled and in crisis and yet another national disaster awaits them (the fall of Jerusalem). When the prophet spoke these words, the circumstances surrounding God's people were bleak but, in the thick of negativity, discouragement and hopelessness, the prophet communicates God's plans for his people not to be harmed but to prosper and experience a future 'full of hope'.

I imagine that as God's people listened to the words of the prophet they would have found them extremely difficult to believe because of the dark circumstances surrounding them. What was so tangible for them up until now was destruction, yet the prophet invited them to believe against all the odds in God's plan for their life which would make them prosperous.

I have no doubt that the experience of this nation in crisis to some degree resonates with all survivors of abuse. What has been so tangible for us also, both in the past and present, has been the destructive and damaging effects of sexual abuse, yet God invites us to believe against all odds that his only plan for us is that we prosper and have a future full of hope.

Our God is a God of Love. Destruction and harm go against God's being. God cannot and would never desire destruction or harm for us. All God has ever wanted for us is a prosperous and hope-filled life. Although we have been unfortunate to experience the opposite, at the hands of human beings, God invites us to believe that the future can be new and different. While we cannot turn back time to change our past and the harm that has been done, it is not too late to make decisions and plans with God now and move us towards a very different future, one that is more prosperous and hopeful. God, more than anyone else, knows our past, for God has suffered every minute of it with us. God knows how devastated we were as children to experience that our prosperity was always being quashed through the harm done to us.

Plans to prosper

Today, God invites us to not give up on believing that we can still prosper and have a future full of hope. God wants to remind us of this through this scripture: 'I know the plans I have for you, plans to prosper you and not to harm you! Plans to give you a future full of hope.'

So when we are trying to make plans for the future, but experience the strong forces of negativity from our past telling us it is not possible, let us turn to God in prayer and be reminded that it is possible because God has planned it for us from long ago.

Praying the scripture reading

1. Try to be still and aware of God's presence in you.
2. Read the scripture reading slowly, putting your name at the beginning of the verse.
3. Go back to any particular words that have called your attention. Try to be aware of what the words evoke in you. For example, surprise, fear, curiosity, anxiety, peace ... You may then like to express this to God. (You may want to write this down.) For example, 'God, the possibility of a 'future full of hope' makes me excited and feel hopeful that there are still good things to come in my life!' After you express yourself, allow God to respond to you in your prayer. It may simply be an affirmation: 'Yes! That is true!'
4. Try to deepen these particular words by having a dialogue with God, asking questions, sharing your thoughts and reactions honestly. For example, if the word 'prosper' calls your attention, you may want to ask God, 'What does prosper mean for you, God? Am I prospering the way you planned for me to prosper? What stops me from being prosperous now, God? What would help me to prosper?' Try to have a dialogue with God until you feel you cannot go any deeper.
5. Before you finish this prayer, you may have some plans in your life you would like to talk to God about. Perhaps you may want to ask, 'Lord, are these plans going to lead me to have the prosperous and

hopeful life you planned for me? Is there something that I should do differently?' Listen to God's response in your heart.

6. Before you conclude your prayer, it may be helpful to make some resolutions in dialogue with God. 'Is there something I can begin to do that would lead me to have the future of hope that you planned for me?'

7. As you continue with your daily activities, try to see ways you can put these resolutions into practice. Prosperity and a future of hope are not instantaneous: they are the result of taking many small steps that lead to the final goal.

The scripture experienced in my life

As I write this today, I acknowledge that it is a significant day for me. It marks one year since I have been living away from my local missionary community for health reasons. At the time, it was a very painful decision to come to terms with. For twenty-two years, my religious vocation, my sisters in community and my ministry had been my life. Coming away from all that, I felt devastated. For some time, I experienced an emptiness within me and a sense of loss.

One year ago, I recall praying the scripture reading above. At that time, I could identify with the people of Israel who were passing through a crisis. After having reached a point in my life where I felt content and prosperous, I was again experiencing the familiar gloom of my past and I felt its sombre weight upon me. My circumstances were dark and although I did not see any tangible evidence of a hope-filled future I do recall that this scripture reading gave me great comfort and consolation. As hopeless as my circumstances seemed to me at the time, God assured me that God had a plan for me. God invited me to believe in these plans for my life. I tried to hold on to these words with all my heart and I practised recalling them on many occasions, particularly when I was feeling hopeless and fruitless and struggling with the forces of negativity. Each time, God's Word had great power in my life.

So today, a year down the track, I can certainly say that God's plan for me to prosper and to have a future full of hope is in process, although it is not all clear yet. God is slowly opening up new doors and presenting me with new possibilities. Not only that, but God is putting some amazingly gifted and skilled people in my path to inspire me on my journey and to help me reach this goal.

One year ago, I would have never imagined that I would be putting together a spiritual handbook for survivors of sexual abuse, but here I am doing it. I did not think to pursue further studies, but I am now studying for a Master of Arts degree. One year ago I would not have imagined myself carrying out a different ministry from the one I had known for the past twenty-two years. However, I have been offered the new possibility to do this. One year ago, I had not played a piece of music for more than twenty-four years and here I am today playing piano again. Most of all, one year ago, I would have never thought of coming forward to have a private hearing with the Royal Commission into Institutional Responses for Child Sexual Abuse and I never ever imagined that I would pursue the matter further but this too is happening. Thanks be to God's grace and the support of so many extraordinary people God has placed in my life.

When I look back over the past year, I am in awe as I see how God's plan is gradually unfolding in my life – and how far it is from being harmful in any way! Who would have ever thought that it would be possible to prosper and experience a future of hope while being in the midst of darkness! While it is true that the past year has contained periods of sadness, loss, disappointment, frustration, and even despair at times, God has opened up new doors that are leading me to a future of prosperity and hope and I am forever grateful for this.

'I know the plans I have for you: plans to prosper you and not to harm you! Plans to give you a future full of hope.' Let us believe this against all the odds in our life!

The scripture experienced in your life

Were you able to experience the scripture reading in your life today? If so, how did this happen? You may like to write down your own account.

*See – I am making
all things new.*
>   Revelations 21:5

Appendix 1

A blueprint for praying with the Bible
(The Word of God / The Scriptures)

Prayer is a dialogue with God

| **We speak to God** | Awareness and acknowledgement of God's presence with us (as if you were meeting a friend – *'Hello, God! It's good to be here with you. How are you?'*) |

| **God speaks to us** | We listen to God through a specific reading from the Bible. *How?* See 'Listening to God through a specific reading' (see page 244). |

| **We speak to God** | Always conclude your prayer with a *resolution*. Remember, God invites us not only to listen to the Word but to translate it into our life and practise it.

Is there something God is inviting me to do differently or change in my life so that it is more fruitful?

Through our Baptism, Christ invites us all to participate in his Mission by sharing the Good News with others. Who is God inviting me to share this prayer with? How will I share it (through a word, an action, a different attitude)? |

Listening to God through a specific reading

1. Before you take up the scripture reading, try to be aware that it is God who is about to speak to you through these words.
2. Read the scripture reading very slowly aware of each word, and, as you do, try to make the reading as personal as possible by substituting your name where 'you' is mentioned or where a character comes into play (for example if it talks about the 'blind man', the 'Samaritan woman', or 'Zacchaeus', substitute your name). If you are able to, try to imagine the scene.
3. Once you have read it slowly, following the steps above, go back to the words or phrases that have called your attention in some way. It may be that they evoked a feeling in you: joy, wonder, surprise, sadness, fear, hope, encouragement … This is important because God wants to speak to you personally through these words.
4. Try to begin a dialogue with God around these words, expressing to God whatever thoughts may come to mind, or feelings that are aroused, or questions that arise from them. For example, Why do you say that God? Or, Why did you do that? Or, Those words caused me to feel afraid– are they meant to God? Try to listen to God's response in your heart.
5. Try to have a deeper dialogue with God around the topic of the specific scripture passage you are reading. For example, it may be around God's compassion, forgiveness, unconditional love … Remember, once you have expressed yourself to God, keep trying to listen to God's response through his Word. Do not be rushed to move on but try to savour God's words through Scripture as much as you can.
6. When you feel that nothing more is happening, move on to the next part of the scripture reading that calls your attention, repeating the steps above.
7. When you have finished listening to God through the scripture reading, conclude your session of prayer by making a resolution.

Appendix 2
Support Services

This is a listing of suggested support services around Australia, though by no means an exhaustive one. Many of the services listed here give more detailed suggestions for further support.

Adults Surviving Child Abuse
National professional phone counselling, information and support for adult survivors of child abuse with referral database of experienced professionals and agencies. Workshops for survivors, workshops for family members, partners and friends.
website www.asca.org.au   *phone* 1300 657 380   *email* counsellors@asca.org.au

Australian Childhood Trauma Group
Professional support.
website www.theactgroup.com.au   *phone* 03 9415 6066

Bravehearts
Specialist case management, counselling and telephone counselling for child and adult survivors, non-offending family members and friends.
website www.bravehearts.org.au   *phone* 1800 272 831
email rc@bravehearts.org.au

Care Leavers Australia Network
Support and advocacy for people who grew up in Australian orphanages, children's homes or foster care, and their families. Counselling and case management available.
website www.clan.org.au   *phone* 1800 008 774   *email* support@clan.org.au

Child Migrants Trust
Social work services including counselling and support for family reunions.
website www.childmigrantstrust.com   *phone* 1800 040 509

Child Wise
Telephone and online counselling for childhood abuse. Training and organisation building for prevention of child abuse
website www.childwise.net   *phone* 1800 99 10 99

Children with Disability Australia
Provides information, referrals and education to people with disabilities.
website www.cda.org.au   *phone* 1800 222 660

CHILD, ARISE!

CREATE Foundation
Information, support and advocacy for young people up to 25 years of age.
website www.create.org.au   *phone* 1800 655 105

Drummond Street Services (Victoria)
Provides a wide range of support and recovery for individuals, families, couples, young people and children.
website www.ds.org.au   *phone* 03 9663 6733

Find and Connect
Support and counselling for Forgotten Australians and former Child Migrants. Family tracing and access to care records.
website www.findandconnect.gov.au   *phone* 1800 161 109

Headspace
Counselling and referral service for young people aged 12- 25 years. Also supports parents.
website www.headspace.org.au   *phone* 1800 650 890
online counselling www.eheadspace.org.au

Healing Foundation
Service to help build the capacity of Indigenous organisations and support the development of the Link Up network.
website healingfoundation.org.au   *phone* 02 6124 4400 (NSW)

Heartfelt House, Alstonville, Northern Rivers region
Support to adult survivors of childhood sexual abuse and their family and friends by qualified counsellors.
website www.heartfelthouse.org.au   *phone* 02 6628 8940
email heartfelthouse@westnet.com.au

In Good Faith Foundation
Provides counselling and support services to people who have experienced religious/clergy abuse.
website www.igfa.com.au   *phone* 03 9326 5991

Interrelate
Building family relationships. Counselling and support for those affected by institutional child sexual abuse or by the Royal Commission. Locations: Caringbah, Bella Vista, Central NSW Coast, Coffs Harbour, Dubbo, Lismore, Newcastle, Orange, Port Macquarie, Sutherland.
website www.interrelate.org.au   *phone* 1300 736 966 02 8882 7800 (head office)
email RCCBSS@interrelate.org.au

Support Services

Laurel House North and North West
Therapeutic services and support for men, women and children impacted by sexual violence.
website www.laurelhouse.org.au *phone* 03 6334 2740
24/7 phone counselling 03 6431 9711 *email* counsellors@laurelhouse.org.au

Lifeline
24-hour crisis support and suicide prevention.
website www.lifeline.org.au *phone* 13 11 14

Lighthouse Foundation
Specialist attachment and trauma informed training.
website www.lighthousefoundation.org.au *phone* 03 9093 7500

Link Up – NSW Aboriginal Corporation
Provides counselling, healing and culturally appropriate support for indigenous Australians.
website www.linkupnsw.org.au *phone* 1800 624 332

MensLine Australia
A national telephone and online support, information and referral service for men with family and relationship concerns.
website www.mensline.org.au *phone* 1300 78 99 78 (available 24/7)
online counselling – www.mensline.org.au

Mental Health Professionals Network
Provides mental health practitioners with networking and online professional development opportunities across Australia
website www.mhpn.org.au *phone* 1800 209 031

NSW Rape Crisis Centre
Crisis counselling service for anyone in Australia who has experienced or is at risk of sexual assault. Staffed by qualified trauma counsellors.
website www.nswrapecrisis.com.au *phone* 1800 424 017

People with Disability Australia
Operates a national telephone line for advice, information, referrals and advocacy support. Provides training and individual advocacy support to people with disability.
website www.pwd.org.au *phone* 1800 422 015 *TTY number* 1800 422 016
email pwd@pwd.org.au

CHILD, ARISE!

Rape and Domestic Violence Services Australia
24/7 telephone and online crisis counselling, information and referral for anyone in NSW who has experienced or is at risk of sexual assault. Staffed by trauma specialist counsellors.
websites www.rape-dvservices.org.au www.nswrapecrisis.com.au
phone 1800 424 017 (24/7)

Relationships Australia
Individual and family counselling. Intake and referral to additional specialist support services for people effected by the Royal Commission.
website www.nsw.relationships.com.au
phone 1800 025 441 *email* royalcommissioncommunitybasedsupport@ransw.org.au

Relationships Australia (Tasmania)
Family and relationship counselling and specialist support services for individuals engaged with or affected by the Royal Commission. Offices located at Devonport, Launceston and Hobart.
website www.tas.relationships.org.au *phone* 1300 364 277

Sexual Assault Counselling Australia
Trauma specialist counselling for anyone in far west NSW, New England, north-west NSW and Albury regions who has been affected by the Royal Commission into Institutional Responses to Child Sexual Abuse. Contact the service via telephone to make an appointment to discuss face to face counselling options.
website www.sexualassaultcounselling.org.au *phone* 1800 211 028

Sexual Assault Services – NSW Health
Information, counselling, court support for anyone who has been sexually assaulted in NSW.
website www.health.gov.au/sexualassault *phone* 1800 424 017
online counselling www.sexualassault.nsw.gov.au

Sexual Assault Support Services Inc
Counselling and support for men or women affected by sexual assault, survivors of sexual abuse, family members and support people.
website www.sass.org.au *phone* 03 6231 1817 *email* admin@sass.org.au

Survivors Network of those Abused by Priests (SNAP) Australia
Information and support for those who have been abused by clergy.
website www.snapaustralia.org

Support Services

Suicide Call Back Service
24/7 counselling for people 18 years and over who are suicidal, caring for someone who is suicidal or people bereaved by suicide.
website www.suicidecallbackservice.org.au *phone* 1300 659 467

Survivors and Mates Support Network (SAMSN)
Facilitated groups and workshops for male survivors of childhood sexual abuse and their families.
website www.samsn.com.au *phone* 0439 838 787 *email* support@samsn.com.au

Tzedek
Provides advocacy, referrals and support services to people who have experienced religious/clergy abuse, with a focus on the Jewish community.
website www.tzedek.org.au *phone* 1300 893 335 *email* info@tzedek.org.au

Victims Access Line
Single entry point for Victims of Crime in NSW to assist them in accessing services, including counselling and support.
website www.lawlink.nsw.gov.au/vs *phone* 1800 633 063 *email* vs@agd.nsw.gov.au
Aboriginal contact line 1800 019 123

Victim Support Services
Personal support, counselling, information and referral services to help people deal with the impact of crime. Website gives contact details for all states and territories.
website wwwvictimsupport.org.au *24-hour counselling* 1300 300 238

Victorian Centres Against Sexual Assault
Provide free ongoing specialist counselling and support for victim/survivors and family members of those who have experienced sexual assault, including those affected by institutionalised abuse.
website www.casa.org.au *phone* 1800 806 292 (24/7)

The Women's Cottage, Hawkesbury
Community based support and resource centre run by women, for women and children.
phone 02 4578 4190

1800 Respect
24/7 telephone and online crisis counselling, information and referral for anyone in Australia who has experienced or been impacted by sexual assault, domestic or family violence. Staffed by trauma specialist counsellors.
website www.1800respect.org.au *phone* 1800 737 732
online counselling www.1800respect.org.au

www.ingramcontent.com/pod-product-compliance
Lightning Source LLC
Chambersburg PA
CBHW071336080526
44587CB00017B/2861